MENTAL MANIPULATION:

2 BOOKS IN 1:

Discover Manipulation Techniques And Discover Dark Psychology

By

Jake Bishops

© Copyright 2020 by Jake Bishops - All rights reserved.

DISCOVER MANIPULATION TECHNIQUES

How to Analyze People and Influence Them to Do Whatever You Want Using Manipulation Techniques and NLP

By

Jake Bishops

Table of Contents

Introduction 17
- The Mental Health Effects of Manipulation 19
- Manipulation When It Shows Up in Relationships 21
- Examples of Manipulative Behavior 22

Chapter 1: How to Influence People 25
- Win People in Your Mind 25
- The 6 Standards of Influence 26
  - *Preferring* *28*
  - *Authority* *29*
  - *Social Confirmation* *29*
- Weapons of Influence 31
  - *Reciprocation* *31*
  - *Commitment and Consistency* *32*
  - *Social Proof* *32*
  - *Liking* *33*
  - *Authority* *33*
  - *Scarcity* *34*

Chapter 2: What Is Persuasion and NLP and How to Use It 36

Models of Neuro-Linguistic Programming 36
   Strategies 36
   Memory 36
   Belief 37
   Motivation 37
   Decision 37
   Learning 38
   Submodalities 38
   Anchoring 39
   Visual Anchors 41
   Auditory Anchors 41
   Kinesthetic Anchors 42
   Trans-derivational Search 42
   Leading Statements 43

Chapter 3: What Subliminal Messages Are the Best Persuasion and Manipulation Techniques 45

   Common Techniques to Use in Manipulation 47
      The Advantage of Home Court 48
      The Target Is Always the First One to Speak 48
      The Facts Are Always Changing 49
      They Show Their Negative Emotions with Loud Voices 49

Not Giving the Target Enough Time to Make Decisions 50

Criticism and Judgment against the Target 51

Using Guilt All of the Time 52

Chapter 4: How to Analyze People 53

Why Analyze People 54

How to Analyze People 56

When to Analyze People 57

In Parenting 58

In Relationships 58

In the Workplace 59

In Public 59

In Arguments 60

In Self-reflection 60

In Self-regulation 61

Chapter 5: The Logic behind Psychological Manipulation 62

Gaslighting 64

Projection 69

Chapter 6: What Is Dark Psychology and by Whom Is Used 70

Chapter 7: The Psychology of Body Language 78

Cultural Differences 79

Study Other People's Movements 79

    Eye Contact 81

    Mouth Movements 82

    Nodding 83

    Hands and Arms 84

Chapter 8: How to Learn Speed Reading People 86

What Is Speed Reading? 86

    1. Train Your Eyes to Make Bigger Jumps 87

    2. Go Straight Ahead 87

    3. Stop Speaking the Words 88

    4. Use Skimming Technique 89

    5. Use the Scanning Technique 89

    6. Monitor Your Performance 90

    7. Train Your Focusing Ability 91

    8. Find a Quiet Place to Do Your Reading 92

    9. Do Not Insist When You Are Tired 93

    10. Read Whenever You Can 93

Chapter 9: Understanding Deception and Deceptive Tactics 95

The Media 95

Food 95

Religion 95

Personal Relationships.. 96

The Psychology of Deception... 98

Top Ways to Effectively Deceive 101

Reasoning Is Everything.. 101

Have Your Story All Laid Out......................................102

Create a Lie That Is Not Completely a Lie 102

Chapter 10: Narcissism in a Relationship 104

Signs of Narcissism in a Relationship..........................105

They Often Make One Feel Guilty................................105

They Are Manipulative 106

Entitlement 106

They Seem to Defy Some Rules That Apply to Everyone...106

Frequent Threats 107

Externally Impressive 107

They Believe They're Very Special................................107

Hot and Cold 108

Narcissistic Abuse 108

Workplace 108

Parent-Child 109

Love Relationships *110*

Narcissism and Healthy Relationship *111*

Respect for Each Other *112*

Chapter 11: Setting Boundary Not to Be Manipulated 113

Misconception #1: I May Look Self-Centered If I Set Boundaries 113

Misconception #2: Boundaries Are Symptoms of Disobedience and Un-Submissiveness 114

Misconception # 3: Setting Limits Indicates I Am Always Upset 115

Misconception #4: When I Begin Creating Borders, I Might Be Injured by Others 116

Misconception #5: When I Set Limits I Might Injure Others 117

Misconception #6: Boundaries Might Become Difficult to Accept 118

Misconception #7: Boundaries May Result in Feelings of Guilt 120

Chapter 12: NLP for success 122

NLP Techniques 122

Meta Model *123*

Mirroring *123*

Framing *124*

Pattern Interruption *124*

Manipulation through NLP Techniques 125

    The Eye Cues *125*

    Anchoring *128*

    Setting the NLP Anchor *130*

Chapter 13: When the Opponent Is a Manipulator 131

Golden Key 131

Become a Mythical Person 132

Arouse Emotions 132

The State of the Interlocutor 133

Pain Points, Weaknesses, Fears, Doubts 134

    Play on Weaknesses *134*

We Are Not Robots; Robots Are Not We 136

Territory Development 136

The Best Alternative to Negotiations 137

    Let the Walls Help You *138*

    Who Is Around? *139*

    Leeway *139*

    Where Is the World Heading? *140*

Chapter 14: Creating Strategies for Manipulation 141

Steps 1 - Define Your Goal(s) 141

Step 2 - Chart the Paths to Success 142

Step 3 - Collect enough Information 143

Step 4 - Identify Opportunities and Threats 145

   Opportunities 145

   Influence 146

   Persuasion 146

   Deception 147

   Threats 148

Step 5 - Take Action 148

Chapter 15: Self-Confidence and Self-Love 150

Why Do We Need Confidence? 150

   1. *Self-confidence Shows True Acceptance and Self-love* 151

   2. *Self-confidence and Positivism* 152

   3. *Self-confidence Shows Maturity* 152

Actions That Help Develop Self-Confidence 153

   High Self-Confidence 154

   Low Self-Confidence 156

The Effects of Low Self-Confidence 157

Chapter 16: Victims of the Narcissist 159

Conscientious people 161

People with Empathy 162

People with Integrity 163

People with Resilience 164

Extremely Sentimental People 165

People Who Were Raised in Dysfunctional Environments 166

People with a Frantic Need to Be Loved and Are Lonely 166

People Who Accept Blame Willingly 166

Chapter 17: What Is Covert Emotional Manipulation 168

How Will a Manipulator Target? 168

Polishing and Improving Your Manipulation Strategies 168

Applying Various Methods of Manipulation 169

Using Manipulation Techniques on Your Friends and Acquaintances 169

Theories on Successful Manipulation 169

Practice Regularly 170

Take Your Time Expanding Your Skill 171

Start Small 171

Be Choosy about Who You Brainwash 172

Be Selective about Phrasing and Actions 172

Manipulative Looks and Stares 173

Shouting Down on Someone or Yelling 174

Manipulations by Avoiding you at All Means 174

Preferential or Silent Treatment 175

Playing on the Emotions 175

Chapter 18: Victims of Manipulation 177

Three Ways of Becoming the Victim of a Controlling Manipulator 177

1. Sales Tactics 177

2. Working Environment 180

3. Personal Relationships 184

Chapter 19: Attraction and Manipulation - Put This in Correlation 186

Facial Expressions, Features, and Head Movement 188

Playing with Hair and Moving the Head 188

Eye Movement 189

Eyebrow Movement 190

Lips 190

Body and Limb Movements 192

Body Positions 192

Standing Positions 192

Arm Positions 193

Leg and Foot Positions 194

Sitting Positions 194

Chapter 20: Brainwashing 196

The Cultish Brain...198

Brainwash, Abuse, and Stockholm Syndrome 199

A Recipe for Brainwashing 200

Depersonalization 201

Acclimation 201

Conditioning 202

Hypnosis 203

Chapter 21: Being Proactive 205

Leading by Example 205

Reflecting and Growing 207

Motivating Your Team 208

Increasing Listening Skills..210

Chapter 22: Identifying Manipulator Types 213

Illustration 214

Harassment and Concealed Manipulation 216

Internal Symptoms of Concealed Manipulation.................219

Chapter 23: Seduction of Dark Psychology 221

Why Use Dark Seduction? 221

Dark Seduction Techniques..223

The Friendly Opener..223

Show Off (A Little Bit) *224*

Be Mean (But Again, Just a Little Bit) *225*

Send Mixed Signals *225*

Give the Ego a Nice, Long Stroke *226*

Be a Little Bit Taboo *226*

Chapter 24: The Dark Core of Personality **229**

A Major Fact Box of Dark Psychology 236

Chapter 25: Understanding Emotions **239**

Conclusion **249**

© Copyright 2020 by Jake Bishops - All rights reserved.

This Book is provided with the sole purpose of providing relevant information on a specific topic for which every reasonable effort has been made to ensure that it is both accurate and reasonable. Nevertheless, by purchasing this Book, you consent to the fact that the author, as well as the publisher, are in no way experts on the topics contained herein, regardless of any claims as such that may be made within. As such, any suggestions or recommendations that are made within are done so purely for entertainment value. It is recommended that you always consult a professional prior to undertaking any of the advice or techniques discussed within.

This is a legally binding declaration that is considered both valid and fair by both the Committee of Publishers Association and the American Bar Association and should be considered as legally binding within the United States.

The reproduction, transmission, and duplication of any of the content found herein, including any specific or extended information, will be done as an illegal act regardless of the end form the information ultimately takes. This includes copied versions of the work, physical, digital, and audio unless express consent of the Publisher is provided beforehand. Any additional rights reserved.

Furthermore, the information that can be found within the pages described forthwith shall be considered both accurate and truthful when it comes to the recounting of facts. As such, any use, correct or incorrect, of the provided information will render the Publisher free of responsibility as to the actions taken outside of their direct purview. Regardless, there are zero scenarios where the original author or the Publisher can be deemed liable in any fashion for any damages or hardships that may result from any of the information discussed herein.

Additionally, the information in the following pages is intended only for informational purposes and should thus be thought of as universal. As befitting its nature, it is presented without assurance regarding its prolonged validity or interim quality. Trademarks that are mentioned are done without written consent and can in no way be considered an endorsement from the trademark holder.

Introduction

Manipulation is a topic that most people are going to turn their noses up at. They do not like the idea that comes with it, and they assume that they are above and beyond using these kinds of techniques. Each of us uses manipulation in some form or another to get what we want, even though most of us are not going to do it at the expense of someone else in the process.

To help us out with this, we need first to take a look at manipulation and what it is all about. Manipulation is going to be the practice of using some indirect tactics to control the relationships, emotions, decisions, and even behavior over the target and how they react to things. This is often going to use a lot of different options that you are allowed to use including persuasion, mind control, deception, and more to get what they want.

Most people are going to use some form of manipulation at some point or another in their lives. For example, if you have ever had a day that wasn't going well or you weren't feeling that good, but you told someone who asked that you were doing "fine" then this is a form of manipulation. This is considered manipulation because it is going to control the perceptions and the reactions that the other person has concerning you. Even if you did it to avoid a confrontation, to avoid having someone pity you, or some other reason, it still changed these perceptions of you.

Manipulation, at least the way that we often think about it, and the manipulation that is used in dark psychology, is going to have consequences that are often more insidious. This can sometimes include some form of emotional abuse, especially if the manipulator is in an intimate relationship with the other person. This is why a lot of us assume that all forms of manipulation are bad, but we will hold this opinion, even more, when we see that it harms the mental health, emotional health, and physical health of the other person who is the target.

While people who are the manipulators are going to do this to their target because they want to have some control over their surroundings and environment, the urge to do the manipulation is indeed going to stem from some anxiety and fear that is deep down. In any case, it is not going to be seen as a behavior that is all that healthy for either party.

Engaging in manipulation is going to seem like a great idea to the one who is manipulating. It allows them to gain the control that they want, and they get to receive whatever they wanted in the process. However, when they use this tactic, it is not only going to cause some harm to the other person, the target, it is going to make it hard for the manipulator to connect with their authentic self and get the benefits that come with that.

The Mental Health Effects of Manipulation

If manipulation is not addressed in the manner that it should be, there are going to be a lot of mental health concerns that the target is going to have to deal with. While we all may be manipulated at one point or another, most of the time it is seen as harmless and we don't need to worry about it. But when the target is manipulated on a chronic and consistent basis in close relationship to the manipulator, it could be a sign that some kind of emotional abuse is going on at the same time. Depending on theindividual, this is going to show up similar to a form of trauma as well.

There are a lot of different signs and symptoms that can show up when someone has been manipulated for a longer period. Some of the signs of a victim of chronic manipulation can include:

- They will always put the needs of someone else before their own, no matter how bad it may hurt them or how much the other person is asking of them.
- They are used to lying and covering up for the feelings that they have.
- They are always working to make the person who is manipulative as happy as possible, but it always seems like they are failing.
- Their coping patterns are not as healthy as they should be.

- Many targets of manipulation are going to develop deep anxiety.
- Those who are the targets of manipulation are often going to have some level of depression to work through as well.
- Those who have gone through this kind of manipulation for a longer period may find that it is really difficult for them to put their trust in anyone else.

There are some cases when the manipulation is going to become so pervasive that it will cause a victim to start questioning the perception that they have when it comes to reality. A good example of this is the movie "Gaslight." This story shows us how her husband subtly manipulated one woman for a long time. This was so persistent that the wife started to no longer trust what she saw or her perceptions of things. For example, the husband was able to turn down the gaslights and then convinced his wife that the dimming light she was seeing was just something in her head, not a part of reality.

While most of us are not immune to using manipulation at some point or another, a chronic pattern of manipulation can indicate that there could be a sign that there is a health concern mentally to work with.

Studies have shown that manipulation is going to be common when it comes to personality disorder diagnoses, including narcissistic personality and borderline personality. For many people who are dealing with BPD, manipulation is going to be the means that the patient can meet some of their needs emotionally or that they can obtain the validation that they need. And the manipulation in these cases is more often to occur when the person with BPD feels like they are abandoned or insecure. This doesn't excuse the behavior or makes it any better, but it does explain the kind of person who is most likely to use this kind of technique.

Now there are also going to be patients who are dealing with narcissistic personality disorder going to have many different reasons why they will want to use manipulation. When we encounter someone who has NPD, it is easy to see that they run into issues forming close relationships, they may end up turning themselves into the victim to help make sure that their partner is going to stay in the relationship. They are also likely to use a few of the other techniques that come with manipulation, including gaslighting, controlling, playing the victim, blaming, and shaming.

Manipulation When It Shows Up in Relationships

When it comes to manipulation that stays around for the long term, we will quickly find that it can have a big effect on the relationships that we have. This can include the relationship that we have between our romantic partners, family members, and even friends. When it is used for too long and too often, manipulation is going to run the health of any kind of relationship.

And for the target, it is going to result in poor mental health. Over time, the target is going to catch on to what is happening or get sick of the way that the relationship makes them feel, and they willleave.

Let's look at how manipulation is used in a marriage or another partnership. Manipulation is going to cause one of the partners; this one is the target to feel like they are worthless, isolated, and bullied. Parents who decide to manipulate their children and this can set the child up for a lot of problems in the future as well. This has been shown to result in many mental health conditions, eating issues, anxiety, depression, and guilt in these children.

Examples of Manipulative Behavior

There are a wide variety of behaviors that can be considered manipulative, especially when they end up causing some kind of harm to the other person in the process. Sometimes, someone can manipulate another one without really realizing what they are doing. But then some are going to do this kind of manipulation to help them get better at it in the future or to help them get what they want out of life. Some of the signs that we can see when it comes to manipulative behavior will include:

- They will isolate the target from loved ones and friends to help change up the perception of that target.

- They will keep out some of the most important information that they have in the hopes of convincing the target to act in a certain way.
- They are dishonest and lie from the very beginning.
- They will imply a threat to keep the target where they are.
- There will be a lot of passive-aggressive behavior from the manipulator towards their target.
- Use of sex to help the manipulator to achieve their own goals.
- Verbal abuse.

As the motives behind this kind of manipulation are going to vary and can be something that is done without much thinking, or it can be done with the intent to harm the target to give the manipulator what they want. But no matter what method is goingon here, it is so important for the target and others to identify the circumstances that come with manipulation and how they can dealwith it. While breaking things off with the manipulator as soon aspossible may be so critical when it comes to situations of abuse, a therapist can help others learn how to deal with or confront the manipulative kind of behavior that they are getting from others.

While we are focusing more on the dark psychology that comes with manipulation, you will find that there are examples of using manipulation that can occur in our daily lives. Often we don't think that we are doing it at all. We think of manipulation as the way that we can get what we want from other people, but sometimes we do it to save the feelings of the other person. For example, how many times have you lied to someone to let them know they looked good in something, even though you didn't think so. You did this to spare their feelings, whether they are a family member or a close friend!

Even though the point of doing this was good, you still were looking to save yourself. You didn't want to be the one who said something means about the other person and how they looked this kind of manipulation may be seen as a good thing though because it was done to spare the feelings of the other person in the process.

Chapter 1: How to Influence People

At the point when you talk about affecting or manipulating people, our ears liven up at Buffer. The exhortation from Christine Comaford above has that commonplace ring of Carnegie to it. Expel your personality. Default to joy and inspiration. Be inviting to other people.

Win People in Your Mind

- The best way to outwit a contention is to maintain a strategic distance from it.
- Show regard for the other individual's assessments. Never state, "You're off-base."
- If you are incorrect, let it be known rapidly and vehemently.
- Begin agreeably.
- Get the other individual saying, "indeed, yes," right away.
- Let the other individual do a lot of the talking.
- Let the other individual feel that the thought is his or hers.
- Try sincerely to see things from the other individual's perspective.
- Be thoughtful with the other individual's thoughts and wants.
- Appeal to the nobler thought processes.
- Dramatize your thoughts.

- Throwdown a test.

We intend to incorporate the same number of Carnegie standards as we can in the manner that we impart in messages, in remarks, and obviously via web-based networking media. Here are a few models of how our Happiness Heroes practice benevolence, compassion, and seeing things from another person's viewpoint.

Here is my top choice:

Abstain from deceiving features. A staple of Carnegie's strategies includes perceiving the significance of others. Time after time, we overlook this and treat online crowds as effectively controlled rubes. Rather than composing misleading content features that mean to pressure, it's smarter to rehearse interactive features that work for progressively righteous reasons.

The 6 Standards of Influence

Manipulation is frequently described as a type of influence that is neither compulsion nor discerning influence. In any case, this portrayal quickly brings up the issue: Is each type of neither influence that is neither pressure nor balanced influence a type of manipulation? If manipulation doesn't consume the whole intelligent space of influences that are neither sane influence nor intimidation, at that point, what recognizes it from different types of influence that are neither compulsion nor objective influence?

The expression "manipulation" is ordinarily thought to incorporate a component of good disapprobation.

Types of influence like those recorded above are typical of common life. This recognizes them from types of influence depicted as "manipulation" in the unrestrained choice writing. There, the expression "manipulation" normally alludes to radical programming or reinventing of all or a large portion of an operator's convictions, wants, and other mental states. Such worldwide manipulation (as we may call it) is additionally ordinarily envisioned as happening using strongly extra-standard strategies, for example, extraordinary intercession, direct neurological designing, or radical projects of teaching and mental molding. Worldwide manipulation is normally thought to deny its casualty of through and through freedom. This regular instinct drives the "manipulation contention," which tries to guard in compatibilism by asserting that living in a deterministic universe is practically equivalent to having been the casualty of worldwide manipulation.

In any case, this rundown ought to give a sensibly decent feeling of what we mean by "manipulation" in the present setting. It oughtto serve to outline the wide assortment of strategies generally portrayed as manipulation.

Do any of those sound commonplaces? Put another way, Cialdini's rundown could resemble this:

- Reciprocation, for example, Correspondence Norm
- Consistency, for example, Intensification Hypothesis.
- Social confirmation, for example, Social Influence
- Liking, for example, Social Influence (once more)
- Authority, for example, Yale Attitude Change Approach.
- Scarcity, for example, Shortage Principle.

One of the repeating themes from Cialdini's rundown is that of society. The standards of enjoying, authority, and social confirmation all arrange with associations with others: We are convinced by those we like, by those whom we esteem to be authority figures, and by the all-inclusive community. Here are a couple of novel utilizations:

Preferring

One-way people misuse this is to discover approaches to make themselves like you. Do you like golf? Me as well. Do you like football? Me as well. Albeit frequently these are certified, some of the time, they're not.

Enjoying is comparable enough to a consistency that it bears, calling attention to the distinction here. Somebody may state, "Do you like having more guests to your blog?" They aren't searching for an association with you (as in Liking), but instead, they're looking for Consistency. You'll state truly, and in theory, you'll make some harder memories easing off that explanation when you are pitched an item or administration later.

Authority

Something as basic as advising your crowd regarding your certifications before you talk, for instance, expands the chances you will convince the crowd.

Noah Kagan does this for every visitor post he distributes at OK Dork. He composes a fast introduction on how he made the association with the visitor essayist and all the stunning certifications the visitor author has.

Social Confirmation

People will almost certainly say yes when they see others doing it as well. Social proof isn't all terrible. It's one of the fundamental ways we learn throughout everyday life.

Basecamp has an incredible case of social confirmation on their site, demonstrating the wide assortment of regarded customers that utilization the item—and doing as such in an enjoyable, congenial way.

Two others that merit calling attention to are consistency and shortage.

Consistency is simply the one I generally find defenseless to. I recognize a ton with how Parrish depicts the impact: "On the off chance that you request that people express their needs and objectives and, at that point adjust your proposition to that in mind, you make it difficult for people to state no." truly hit the nail on the head for me. Parrish interfaces this to the Ikea impact, how you love your IKEA furniture since you're put resources into it from building it yourself.

Weapons of Influence

The Motivation behind Why – Attaching motivation to a solicitation expands the achievement rate: "I have 5 pages, would I be able to utilize the Xerox machine before you since I'm in a surge" had a triumph pace of 94% vs.60% achievement rate when no 'motivation behind why' was given.

Indicating potential clients, the costliest thing first at that point, working downwards in cost prompts an expansion in the sum spent (as the following items appear to be less expensive in correlation).

Reciprocation

Social Commitments – Humans inalienably disdain being obliged to somebody, to such an extent that frequently a little blessing or favor will prompt a bigger equal reaction. This reality is misused around the world, for example, Rabbit Krishna's who offer an 'endowment' of blossom while requesting gifts (which they will not reclaim). As the beneficiary can't unburden themselves from the subliminal obligation, the social strain to giveprompts a higher gift rate than only requesting alone. An Indian general store sold £1000 of cheddar in a couple of hours by welcoming clients to cut their free samples.

Reject and Retreat – This strategy comprises first requesting a significant expense (or an enormous kindness), at that point hanging tight for it to be dismissed, just to line this interest up with a little one, (that you truly needed from the beginning). Statement from a youngster: 'On the off chance that you need a little cat, first request a horse' (Ed).

Commitment and Consistency

We will, in general, stay reliable to our duties, when we have made them (consistency is a socially alluring quality). Concentrates found that when people are inquired whether they would cast a ballot prompted an improved probability to finish. This is the reason it is prescribed to record/verbally express our objectives, as we at that point stand a lot more prominent possibility of adhering to them.

Social Proof

People are influenced by what others do. On a new occasion or circumstance, we look to others in the right manner. This is misused, for instance, in bars or at chapel assortments. The tips/gifts are now and again 'salted' by having cash previously put there or having a sap offer cash to invigorate others to tip. This impact is intensified by how comparable the individual whose activities we are viewing are to ourselves.

Liking

When in doubt, we like to express yes to the solicitation of those we like over those we don't. There are a few key properties that decide our perspective on people: Attractiveness, closeness, praises, contact and co-activity, molding, and affiliation. Concentrates discovered us consequently property qualities, for example, ability, benevolence, trustworthiness, and knowledge to appealing people. It is not co-frequency that 'alluring' political applicants got over multiple times the votes of ugly adversaries.

We like people who behave like us, who are like us, with similar perspectives, interests, convictions, and qualities. We, in this manner, need to discover territories of shared enthusiasm to build affinity and association.

Authority

The more prominent the apparent authority of an individual, the more probable people are to go along (cf the Stanley Milgram tests).

Medical clinics have a 12% day by day mistake rate. This is because medical caretakers and junior specialists will once in a while challenge the choice made by a definitive figure, notwithstanding getting conceivably deadly or odd solicitations.

Scarcity

We are progressively roused to act as if we think we will lose something, then if we are to pick up something. 'Spare £50 per month on...' 'Would not be as successful as you are losing £50 every month on...' A rare thing is more alluring than one that is uninhibitedly accessible.

One situation where you may want to exercise your brainwashing abilities is to make a sale in your business. With the modern world being taken over by entrepreneurs, it can be easy to feel like you might be one of the few who struggle with sales. You can certainly change the face of this experience by learning how to use brainwashing to get people to purchase products from you.

Chapter 2: What Is Persuasion and NLP and How to Use It

Models of Neuro-Linguistic Programming

Strategies

The neuro-linguistic programming theory states that every aspect of the world that we live in is one or a blend of five key strategies. However, over the past decade, psychologists have added two more.

Memory

We have talked about how we use our senses to gather data from the external world. Well, our memories come into play when we are processing these inputs. Notice how you tend to access certain experiences when you are trying to determine whether or not an act is good, neutral, or evil. Moreover, this is the same process utilized when you are learning from a mistake or relishing in the memory of your past achievements. You may be unconscious toward this process, but each and every one of us is always retrieving information from our memory so that we can use it in our decision-making and critical thinking.

Belief

As soon as you process these memories, you establish your own set of interpretations and beliefs. By looking at your experiences, you begin to allow yourself to believe in a higher state that is achievable. With this, you try to aim for something higher. Moreover, you also allow yourself to believe in concepts that will aid your journey in achieving something higher than your current state.

Motivation

The strategical concept of motivation is a combination of memory, belief, and decision. You see, memory is accessed by the individual so that reality is set. Then, you start to compare this set reality to a higher state. You decide which of the options available to you can lead you to this higher state. With all of these combined, you feel motivated to achieve your goals. Motivation is typically different for each individual, as it would depend on one's belief and experience.

Decision

As soon as you realize that there is a higher state that can be achieved, you start to notice the options that are available to you, and you begin to evaluate which of these can help you achieve your goals. You undergo an assessment of what you have experienced in the past, your current situation, and your possible future. After which, you identify how each option can lead you to success. These will serve as your guide on the road to achieving your ideal future. Keep in mind that this strategy is about Test-Operation-Test-Exit (TOTE), which is the strategical model that is traditionally used by psychologists.

Learning

Finally, the strategy of learning incorporates memory, decision, and motivation so that you are much more efficient in achieving your goals. Memory is accessed so that you are much more knowledgeable as to how you can handle the current tasks. Moreover, your past decisions allow you to assess all of your successes and failures. As a result, you'll be inclined to make wiser decisions in the future. Motivation, on the other hand, will prevent you from making the same mistakes. With these strategies, you'll be forced to acquire information on what you already know, what you have experienced in the past, and what you plan on doing.

Submodalities

We have already established that an individual will use their five basic senses, which are gustatory or the sense of taste, visual or the sense of sight, olfactory or the sense of smell, auditory or the sense of hearing, and of course, kinesthetic or the sense of touch; these are referred to as modalities in neuro-linguistic programming. Do note that these modalities are systems of representations that are transmitted and sorted out by the brain. These are the things that affect how we see the world. Furthermore, these modalities can be broken down into submodalities or subjective divisions.

One fair example would be to look at a particular experience and determine whether it is considered a good or bad experience. Depending on what you have experienced in the past, you would say that it is a good experience or a bad one. One person as unimportant can view it, while another would see it as life-changing. Thus, these submodalities play a crucial role in your development as an individual. It affects you on a larger scale, and it transforms your personality based on how you transform past experiences.

Moreover, there are certain techniques you can use to establish an entirely different perspective on unpleasant experiences. This idea does not necessarily mean you have to alter reality or completely ignore it. You are only providing submodalities to subjective experiences so that you are better able to alter your attitude into a more useful one for success and learning.

Anchoring

When it comes to anchoring, you are connecting memories to a stimulus. This stimulus, which is referred to by some as an anchor, becomes a set off to the initial reaction. Do note that a particular anchor does not necessarily have any rational connection to the initial reaction. However, the utilization of these anchors willallow you to stimulate reactions that can change your behavioral patterns toward a condition. The stimuli of sound, sight, smell, taste, and touch are used in neuro-linguistic programming to bring about a particular mindset. This situation can be a memory that you wish to access so that you can change your perspective inlife into something more positive. As soon as the stimulus is initialized, it elicits a certain mindset with specific emotions and thoughts. This is why hearing an old song makes you feel nostalgic about your childhood.

In NLP, anchoring becomes useful because you are given a chance to associate certain triggers that you wish to achieve. You are given the power to establish an anchor, as well as create a stimulus and induce a state of mind that is essential for you to achieve success. For example: when someone you love gives you a memento, such as a locket, then this locket becomes the trigger. Moreover, your memories with that person become a state of mind. These two are closely tied together that at times when you look at the particular object, you immediately think about the individual who handed it to you, a resourceful state. These anchors can be visual, kinesthetic, or auditory. You can utilize these as tools to create a mental image that is easily retrievable from your memory so that you are better able to facilitate a response. This tactic improves an individual's critical and subjective point of view of the environment.

You may ask how all of these are essential to dark psychology and the power of manipulation. You need to be able to read them first. If you want to read people, then you would need to have a keen eye as to what their anchors are. Aside from paying attention to how their body reacts to certain things, knowledge of these anchors can facilitate the gathering of information on the one being manipulated.

Visual Anchors

One common misconception about visual anchors is that these are only external. However, visual anchors can be both external and internal. When talking about external visual anchors, we are pertaining to what is seen by the naked eye. An internal visual anchor, on the other hand, pertains to the use of our imagination. Going back to our example of the locket, the external anchor is the locket itself, whereas the internal anchor could be a mental image of the person who gave you the locket. Visual anchors can be objects, people, places, or shapes. This is why some things in our life possess sentimental value.

Auditory Anchors

Similar to visual anchors, auditory anchors can also be internal or external. The exact tune or sound that you hear is an auditory anchor that is external, whereas, when you hear the voice in your head, this is more of an internal auditory anchor. Listening to a particular song to help soothe you is an excellent example of an external auditory anchor. Moreover, you can also recall the voice of your big sister calming you and relate it with a fond memory in your childhood so that you are better able to relax.

Kinesthetic Anchors

When talking about internal kinesthetic anchors, we are about imagined actions or gestures received because you did something great. It could be a memory of a hug, handshake, or a pat on the back. Do note that these are all imagined. These are usually associated with a feeling of success or achievement. As for external kinesthetic anchors, these are the actual hugs felt, handshakes made, and the literal pat on the back.

Trans-derivational Search

This kind of search, which is also known as TDS, is a phrase utilized at times when an individual attempts to search for the meaning of ambiguous statements. It is a fundamental human tendency to look for the missing pieces of data from our experiences and memory to provide significance to these incomplete statements. There is a present state of confusion experienced by the individual when the search is being executed; this allows you to experience a trance-like feeling. Neuro-linguistic programming experts can easily put their patients into a trance- like condition or state of hypnosis because of this. You have a better chance of manipulating another person by taking advantage of the window at which they are experiencing TDS. This is made possible by mentioning ambiguous and incomplete statements.

Leading Statements

If you want to utilize the concepts under TDS, then you should master how to create leading statements. These statements must elicit the feeling of uncertainty from the other person. It must be ambiguous enough to trigger the imagination to try to complete the statement. Furthermore, your leading statement should initiate a mood without providing its full explanation. As a result, the brain will be tempted to process the information provided andto find its missing pieces. Here are some great examples of what your leading statements should be.

"What you said yesterday." This particularly vague statement will allow the mind to wander and retrace everything that has happened within the set parameters of the statement, which is yesterday. The individual that you are trying to manipulate will then consider everything relevant to the discussion. They will consider the period and the words you have said, and then they will search internally for the idea that will make your initial statement complete. Their mind will start to go through a certain process of elimination until they can narrow down to the actual meaning of the statement.

"The different shades of paint." If you utter this statement to an individual, that person's mind will start to explore all the possible shades of paint. Your leading statement was able to set the parameters and scope, which are the shades of paint, without fully divulging the exact answer as to which shade. This will lead the other person to wonder which shade you are referring to.

Chapter 3: What Subliminal Messages Are the Best Persuasion and Manipulation Techniques

One thing that we need to take a few minutes to note when it comes to manipulation is that there is positive manipulation and negative manipulation. These are going to utilize the same kinds of techniques along the way, but the intention behind them is going to be slightly different, and this is how we get each kind.

We have spent some time looking at the negative manipulation and how it is going to try and harm the person who is the target. As long as the manipulator can get what they want and can use thetarget as a tool, they are going to do so—and it doesn't matter to them whether the target gets harmed in the process or not. As longas the manipulator sees themselves as the winner, or as the one incontrol, they will be happy.

Now, there is also a type of manipulation that is seen as more positive. This is going to use the same kinds of techniques that we can see with negative manipulation, but it is going to work with better intentions. The manipulator in this kind is still going to work to get what they want from the target, but they have aconscience here, and they don't want to harm the other person. Often, this kind is going to be beneficial to both parties or will be more beneficial to the target than the manipulator.

For example, if a family tries to use manipulation to get their child to go to addiction recovery from alcohol or another substance, this is still seen as a form of manipulation. Still, it is done for the good of the target, rather than to cause them harm. If you go into a car lot to purchase a car, the salesperson is likely going to use some of the techniques of manipulation and even persuasion to make the sale.

Sometimes, the manipulation is not going to be such a bad thing. Yes, we are using techniques that may be considered bad or unethical, but it is done with the health and safety, and even the benefit, of the target in mind the whole time. This is a manipulator because the person is doing the techniques to get something that they want in life—but in the positive manipulation, the point is not just to help out the manipulator but also to help out the target in the process.

Keep in mind that with manipulation, whether it is positive or negative, we are dealing with the same techniques. But you can use the same techniques to help out if you plan to work with positive manipulation instead.

So, the basic difference that we are going to see when it comes to positive and negative manipulation is how the target is treated in the process. The manipulator is going to win in either scenario. But in positive manipulation, the target is allowed to win and benefit as well. Then, when we are looking at negative manipulation, we are going to see that the manipulator is the only one who wins. The target is going to be used and often harmed in the process as the manipulator gets what they want.

Common Techniques to Use in Manipulation

In reality, there are so many different techniques that a manipulator is going to try and use against you, that it can be hard to know how to defend against them all. Pretty much any technique that the manipulator can use to get you to act in the manner that they want to benefit themselves, whether it is with you doing it willingly or by force, is going to be fair game when we meet with a manipulator. With that in mind, there are a few examples of the techniques that a lot of manipulators like to work with to see the results that they need with their target—and some of these common techniques of manipulation are going to include:

The Advantage of Home Court

When someone is trying to manipulate a new target, they will try to use any method possible to gain the upper hand in that situation. This is why the manipulator may decide it is a good idea to do the meeting at their home, in their office, or somewhere else the manipulator is familiar with, and that the target has no idea about.

On the other hand, the victim is going to be really out of their element. They are happy that the manipulator wants to meet with them, and may think that it is very friendly that the manipulator is willing to pick the place, seeing this as a hospitable thing to do. But in reality, it is all to the advantage of the manipulator, just like anything else they do. It helps them to get the upper hand against the target from the very beginning.

The Target Is Always the First One to Speak

This is something that you will see with sales quite a bit. From here, they can get a good idea of your weaknesses and strengths. This type of questioning will have a hidden agenda, and we may beable to find it in other places of our lives, such as in personal relationships and the workplace.

The Facts Are Always Changing

Whenever you are talking to a manipulator, you will find that the facts are never going to be the same each time you bring them up. And if the manipulator thinks that changing up the facts will make their target look bad and make themselves look good, then they are going to be even more eager to do this. They will deny that plans were made. They will just show a bias towards the side that works for them. They may blame the target for messing things up and not getting things right. They will make up their excuses, lie, and deform and twist the truth as much as they want to confuse the target and get what they want in the process.

They Show Their Negative Emotions with Loud Voices

Another tactic that the manipulator may try to use is to raise their voice to help show off some of their negative emotions. This is going to happen many times during a discussion to show a form of aggressive manipulation and to make the target worry about whether they have upset the manipulator or not. The assumption here with the manipulator is that if they are then able to project the voice and make sure that it comes across loud enough. They can add some negative emotions to this, then the victim is going tobe tense and fearful, and will give the manipulator exactly what they want in the process.

To go along with the aggressive emotions and voice, it is common for the manipulator to make sure that every part of their body language is used to get the message across to the target as much as they can. They will have strong body language that is meant to intimidate as much as possible, show anger, and move the hands around to showcase that the target needs to back off and do what the manipulator wants.

Not Giving the Target Enough Time to Make Decisions

This is one that manipulators of all kinds, even those who are salespeople, are going to use to get what they want. They will present some options to their target and then will limit how much time the target is going to get to make that decision. The hope here is that the target is going to jump right on what the manipulator is suggesting to them, without worrying about doing research or thinking it through. Of course, the position that the manipulator is trying to push is going to be something that benefits the manipulator, and will maybe cause harm to the target.

The idea of giving just a little bit of time to the victim to let them decide on things has been used in many forms of manipulation. We can see this as a tactic that is used in sales and negotiations. When you start to apply this kind of tension and control how long the target gets to make decisions, the hope here is that the target will give in to whatever the aggressor is demanding.

Criticism and Judgment against the Target

This is a type of behavior that can be distinct in several methods from some of the other tactics that we have talked about so far for manipulation. In this one, we are going to see that the manipulator spends a lot of time joking and picking on their target, in the hopes of lowering the confidence and self-esteem of the target as much as possible. By constantly dismissing, marginalizing, and ridiculing the victim, the manipulator is going to be successful at keeping their victim off-balance, while helping the manipulator to stay superior along the way.

Often, the aggressor is going to like this tactic because it is going to deliberately foster the idea that something is going wrong with the victim, and that no matter how hard the victim works, they are never good enough to meet those impossibly high standards that the manipulator is going to set up from the start.

Of course, the thing here is that the manipulator hyper focuses on the bad and ignores all the good things that come with the target. They do this because, if the target realizes there are some good factors about them, then they would ignore the manipulator. With this tactic, the manipulator will learn how to focus just on the negative things about their target (and we all have some negative traits), and then never offer constructive help on how to make it better. This shows that they are doing this just to make the target feel bad.

We think that we are making them suffer some when we don't give them our attention all the time and that by making them sweat it out for a bit; we are more likely to get what we would like.

The silent game is a head game, where the manipulator can use silence as a form of leverage against the victim.

Using Guilt All of the Time

The manipulator can then make you feel bad for something, even if that situation is not your fault, and finds it easier to coerce the target to give in and agree to the demands they give, even when these demands are unreasonable, to make the guilt go away.

Chapter 4: How to Analyze People

Take a moment to imagine a time when the sight of someone sent a chill down your spine. You may not have known why, but you were simply uncomfortable around the person that you were facing. Despite your best attempts to identify the reasoning behind your problem, you found that there was no particular reason that you could discern. The only thing you knew was that you were the only thing afraid of the person in front of you and had no idea how to overcome them.

There was a very good reason for this guttural reaction—your instincts were telling you that something about the other person was not right. You didn't need to know specifics, and all that mattered to you was that your reactions were accurate. This is because all these guttural reactions must do keep you alive. So long as that is managed, your instincts did their job.

There are limitless reasons that being able to rationally understand what is going on in someone else's mind is critical, even if you already have a decent gut reaction. Ultimately, when you can analyze someone calmly and consciously be aware of whyyou are uncomfortable or what is putting you on-edge, you are better prepared to cope with the problem at hand. This is becauseyou can act rationally. You can strategize on how to better react in the most conducive manner that will allow you to succeed in the situation.

This means that in the modern world, when things are very rarely life or death situations, making an effort to switch to responding rationally and consciously is almost always the best bet. You will be able to tell when someone is setting off your alarm bells because they seem threatening, or because they seem deceptive. You will be able to find out what the problem is to respond appropriately.

Why Analyze People

Analyzing people is something that is utilized by several people in different capacities. The most basic reason you may decide that you wish to analyze someone is to understand them simply. When you have an in-built technique of understanding others, you will discover that having a cognitive instead of an emotional connection is critical to establishing a true connection with someone else's mind.

Consider for a moment that you are trying to land a deal with a very important client. You know that the deal is critical if you hope to keep your job and possibly even get a promotion, but you also know that it is going to be a difficult task to manage. If you can read someone else, you can effectively allow yourself the ability to know what is going on in their mind truly.

Think about it—you will be able to tell if the client is uncomfortable and respond accordingly. You will be able to tell if the client is being deceptive or withholding something—and respond accordingly. You can tell if the client is uninterested, feeling threatened, or even just annoyed with your attempts to sway him or her, and you can then find out how to reply.

When you can understand the mindset of someone else, you can self-regulate. You can fine-tune your behaviors to guarantee that you will be persuasive. You can make sure that your client feels comfortable by being able to adjust your behavior to find out what was causing the discomfort in the first place.

Beyond just being able to self-regulate, being able to read other people is critical in several other situations as well. If you can read someone else, you can protect yourself from any threats that may arise. If you can read someone else, you can simply understand their position better. You can find out how to persuade or manipulate the other person. You can get people to do things that they would otherwise avoid.

Ultimately, being able to analyze other people has so many critical benefits that it is worthwhile to be able to do so. Developing this skill set means that you will be more in touch with the feelings of those around you, allowing you to assert that you have a higher emotional intelligence simply because you come to understand what emotions look like. You will be able to identify your own emotions through self-reflection and to learn to pay attention to your body movements. The ability to analyze people can be invaluable in almost any setting.

How to Analyze People

Though it may sound intimidating, learning to analyze other people is not nearly as difficult as it may initially seem. There are no complicated rules that you need to memorize or any skills that you need to learn—all you have to do is learn the pattern of behaviors and what they mean. This is because once you know the behaviors; you can usually start to piece together the intent behind the behaviors.

You can begin to find out exactly what it is that someone's eyes narrowing means and then begin to identify it with the context of several other actions or behaviors as well. You can find out what is intended when someone's speech and their body language do not match up. Body language rarely lies when people are unaware of how it works, so you can often turn to it for crucial information if you are interacting with other people.

The reason this works to understand people is because it is commonly accepted that there is a cycle between thoughts, feelings, and behaviors. Your thoughts create feelings, and the feelings you have automatically influence your behaviors, as you can see through body language.

Effectively, you will be looking at behaviors that people display and then tracing them back to the feelings behind them. This is why body language is so important to understand. When you can understand what is going on with someone's behavior, you can understand their feelings. When you understand their feelings, you can begin to find out the underlying thoughts that they have. This is about the closest thing to mind reading that you can ever truly attain.

To analyze other people, you have a simple process to get through—you must first find out the neutral baseline of behavior. This is the default behavior of the person. You must then begin to look for deviations in that neutral behavior. From there, you try to put together clusters of behaviors to find out what is going on in the mind of someone else, and then you analyze. This process is not difficult, and if you can learn how to do so, while also learning how to interpret the various types of body language, you will find that understanding other people could never be easier.

When to Analyze People

Analyzing people is one of those skills that can be used in almost any context. You can use it at work, in personal relationships, in politics, religion, and even just in day-to-day life. Because of this versatility, you may find that you are constantly analyzing people, and that is okay. Remember, your unconscious mind already makes snapshot judgments about other people and their intentions, so you were already analyzing people, to begin with. Now, you are simply making an effort to ensure that those analyses are made in your conscious mind so you can be aware of them.

Now, let's take a look at several different compelling situations in which being able to analyze someone is a critical skill to know consciously:

In Parenting

When you can analyze other people, you can begin to use those skills toward your children. Now, you may be thinking that a child's mind is not sophisticated enough to get a reliable read on, but remember, the child's feelings are usually entirely genuine. In essence, they have their feelings that they have, and though the reason behind those feelings may be less than compelling to you as a parent, that does not in any way dismiss the feelings. By beingable to recognize the child's emotions, you can begin to understand what is going on in your child's mind, and that will allow you to parent calmly and more effectively.

In Relationships

When you live with someone else, it can be incredibly easy to step on someone else's toes without realizing it. Of course, constantly stepping on the toes of someone else is likely to lead to some degree of resentment if it is never addressed.

Yet, some people have a hard time discussing when they are uncomfortable or miserable. This is where being able to analyze someone else comes in—you will be able to tell what your partner's base emotions are when you interact, allowing you to play the role of support.

In the Workplace

Especially if you interact with other people, you need to be able to analyze other people. You will be able to see how your coworkers view you, allowing you to change your behaviors to get the company image that you desire. Beyond just that, you may also work in a field that requires you to be able to get good reads on someone in the first place.

In Public

When you are interacting with people in public, you need to be able to protect yourself. When you can read other people, you can find out whether you are safe or whether someone is threatening or suspicious. This means that you can prepare yourself no matter what the situation is to ensure that you are always ready to respond.

In an interview, you may find that read an interviewer's body language can give you a clue on when to change tactics or move on to something else. You will be able to tell how you are being taken simply by watching for body language and other non-verbal cues.

In other words, you deem the person speaking authority and therefore deem them to be trustworthy. Instead, make an effort to see the other party as what they truly are by learning to read their body language. You can tell if the politician on television is uncomfortable or lying simply by learning to analyze their behaviors.

In Arguments

When you are arguing with someone else, usually emotions are running high on both ends. No one is thinking clearly, and things that were not meant can be said. However, when you can analyze people, you can start to find out when someone else is getting emotional to disengage altogether.

In Self-reflection

When you can analyze other people, you can start to analyze yourself as well. This means that you can stop and look at your body language to sort of check-in with yourself and find out what is going on in your mind. Sometimes, it can be difficult to identify exactly how you are feeling, but this is the perfect way to do so in a pinch. If you can stop and self-reflect, you can identify your emotions.

In Self-regulation

Identifying your emotions then lends itself to the ability to self-regulate. When you are, for example, in a heated argument and feel yourself tensing up and getting annoyed, you may be able to key into the fact that you are getting annoyed and respond accordingly.

Chapter 5: The Logic behind Psychological Manipulation

Psychological manipulation is defined as a form of social influence that seeks to alter the behavior and the perceptions of others, by the use of tactics that are indirect, deceptive, and underhanded. In other words, it's about using certain tricks to get people to act in a certain way or to think certain things, usually to the advantage of whoever is perpetrating the manipulation.

This way, the interests of the manipulator are advanced, usually at the expense of the other person in that equation. Psychological manipulation employs methods that are both devious and exploitative, and they are often used by people who have one or more of the dark personality traits.

Now, from the very start, we need to make sure you understand that not all psychological manipulation and social influence is negative. It's possible to manipulate someone for their own good. For instance, parents may manipulate their children into eating vegetables. In as much as that is manipulation, it ends up benefiting the child because his or her health is improved. Similarly, friends, family members, and healthcare professionals may try to influence you using certain manipulation techniques to get you to make the right choices in certain situations.

Social influence is a normal and important part of social discourse. In healthy social influence, there is no aspect of coercion. In other words, when a well-meaning person tries to influence you, and you resist that influence, they are not going to strong-arm you into doing what they want. However, in unhealthy psychological manipulation, the manipulator often resorts to coercive techniques if they sense that you are resistant to the softer techniques that they have been trying to use on you.

When malicious people deploy psychological manipulation techniques against you, they usually try to conceal the aggressive nature of their intentions, so you have to understand that most of their techniques are designed to be subtle. Most of them will also take some time to get to know you and understand your psychological vulnerabilities before they can decide which manipulation techniques will work on you. This means that just because you have known someone for a while, and you haven't seen them try to harm you in any way, it doesn't guarantee the factthat their intentions are pure, which means that you shouldn't start disregarding your instincts about them. The best manipulators are those who reveal their intentions long after you have decided to trust them.

Remember that manipulators generally tend ruthlessness, so even if they are treating you well at the beginning of your association with them, pay close attention to the way they act towards others. If you see them using manipulation techniques against other people, you should know that it's just a matter of time before they get around to using the same techniques against you.

We discuss the most common psychological manipulation techniques that are used by people who mean to harm you or to take advantage of you. It's important to understand these techniques and how they work so that you can be able to spot them when they are being used against you or someone close to you, and so that you can know how to defend against them.

Gaslighting

Gaslighting is one of the most lethal psychological manipulation techniques out there. It's where a manipulator tries to get their target to start questioning their own reality. It involves getting someone to doubt their own memories and perceptions, and instead, to start believing what the manipulator wants them to believe.

The manipulator will sow seeds of doubt in the person so that they start thinking that either they remember things wrong, or they are losing their sanity. Gaslighting involves the persistent denial of things that obvious facts. It also involves a lot of misdirection, contradictions, and blatant lying. When a person is subjected to gaslighting for a long time, they start to become unstable, and they start feeling as though their own beliefs are illegitimate.

One common example of gaslighting is where an abuser convinces the victim that the abusive incident she recalls did not even occur. This phenomenon is more common than you might imagine, and it happens in all sorts of relationships. An abusive spouse might deny ever abusing you when confronted later, by either blatantly denying that the abuse occurred, or claiming that it didn't happen as you remember and that your version of the events is greatly exaggerated.

A manipulative boss or colleague might prey on a subordinate and later deny that it happened that way. Someone who groped you might later claim that they "accidentally brushed against you," and they may insist on it so much, to the point that you start thinking that maybe you were mistaken.

You may wonder; "How does it even work? I mean, I have a firm grasp of my own reality, and I doubt someone could be able to convince me that my perceptions are wrong!"

It's easy to assume that gaslighting won't work on you because you are smart or because you are strong-willed, but the truth is that when a manipulator is good at what he is doing, you might not even see it coming. The way it works is that it often starts with small lies on the manipulator's part and small concessions on your part.

Say, for example, your boyfriend shows up a few minutes late to an appointment when you had agreed to meet at a specific time, and he insists that he is on time and that it's you who came in a bit earlier and is mistaken about the timing that you agreed upon. At that moment, you might think, "Well, a 10-minute difference isn't such a big deal, and maybe we just got our lines crossed." You could dismiss this small discrepancy because it seems inconsequently, but that will just be the beginning. The next time, the lie will get a little bigger, and you will feel obligated to excuse it as well, because you already let something else slide, so it would seem inconsistent if you made a big fuss at this point.

After that initial seed is sown, the lies will start to escalate, and you will continue making concessions and agreeing with things that you know are lies, until one day, you realize that you are so far gone. You might not even notice when the small lies graduate into bigger lies. In every step of the way, you will be letting go of your reality and accepting the other person's version of things, and you will find yourself trusting their judgment over your own.

In a nutshell, gaslighting involves desensitizing you to your own reality, until the truth becomes what the other person says it is.

Gaslighting is more likely to work in situations where there is a power dynamic between two people, or between a person and a group of people. In a relationship where the victim is financially or emotionally dependent on the manipulator, the victim may accept to let go of her reality because it's more comfortable to do so than to stand up to the manipulator, only to end up losing the relationship. In the workplace, a subordinate may go along with the boss's lies because he is afraid of losing his job. In a situation where a leader gaslight his followers, it often works because deep within, the followers want to believe whatever lies the leader is telling them.

There are several techniques that gaslighters use to get a stranglehold on their victims. One such technique is withholding. This is where the manipulator refuses to listen to what the victim says or pretends not to understand what they are saying. You might bring up something important, but the response you get is, "I don't even remember this thing you keep talking about."

Another gaslighting technique is called countering. This is where the manipulator questions the victim's memory of the events in question. They say things like "Were you even sober? Because that is not how that happened." The manipulator would then go on to offer an entirely different version of the story where he casts himself as the hero or even the "real victim."

Gaslighters also use blocking and diverting as a manipulation technique. This is where they change the story or question the way the victim is thinking to avoid addressing whatever issue the victim is raising.

Trivializing is also a common gaslighting technique. This is where the manipulator makes the victim feel that her feelings or needs aren't that important, or that she is just being unnecessarily dramatic. Manipulators in such cases may say things like "don't blow things out of proportion."

You may be able to tell if someone is gaslighting you if you find that you are frequently second-guessing yourself, or that your convictions fade away when you interact with a certain person. If a person makes you ruminate about certain character flaws, they are most likely gaslighting you. Someone who tells you that you are too emotional might really be trying to get you to stop trusting your emotions. If you feel confused about the nature of your relationship, or you feel like the person is driving you crazy, or that you are losing control when you are with them, they might be gaslighting you.

If you walk into a room to discuss something specific, but a few moments later, you find yourself arguing with your partner about a whole other topic, it means that the person is deliberately frustrating your genuine efforts to communicate, and it could be a sign of gaslighting.

If you feel fuzzy about your own beliefs, thoughts, and feelings whenever you are with someone, that is a clear red flag. When you are being gaslighted, you might also find that you are constantly apologizing for "being mistaken" or that you are frequently making excuses to yourself and to others for your partner's behavior.

Projection

Projection is a psychological manipulation technique where someone transfers their emotions and mistakes onto you. Projection is a defense mechanism that almost everyone uses to some extent. We all have a natural tendency to project our negative emotions and undesirable feelings onto the people around us, and this often happens when we feel like we have been put on the spot. However, in as much as we all do it, narcissists and people with other dark personality traits tend to do it excessively and to absurd extents.

Toxic people find it very difficult to admit even to them that the nasty things around them could be a result of their own doing, and they always find people to blame for every little thing that happens. Such people often go out of their way to avoid taking responsibility for their own actions. As a result, they may assign their negative behavior and traits to you. For example, if you havea boss who is always late to work, you might be surprised to find him accusing you of tardiness, even if you are consistently punctual. A kleptomaniac is more likely to accuse you of stealing his/her personal items.

Chapter 6: What Is Dark Psychology and by Whom Is Used

In general terms, psychology involves understanding and studying human behavior with a major concentration on how they think, how they act, and how they interact. This is the aspect that deals with the study of the human mind. The science of manipulation and mind control is referred to as dark psychology. No one would love to fall victim to manipulation, but this happens most of the time.

Most people that use dark psychology are people who have an inflated sense of their worth as individuals, and they always need other people to help put validation into what they believe about them being superior. In doing this, they use manipulation and unethical persuasion. Another set of people are those who are emotionally unable to handle the fact of them being impulsive. In the same vein, politicians, salespeople, public speakers, and even leaders use these dark tactics.

However, in dark psychology, we study human issues relating to the psychological nature of them to be able to feed upon other people using instincts and social sciences theory. Dark psychology, being a universal part of the human condition, assumes that any behavior portrayed by someone is purposeful and hereby is motivated to achieve a goal. For example, everybody always has their mind focused on who a criminal is because they are seen as people that should be rejected in society because of their flawed background and maybe upbringing. But in society today, the number of harms done to the public is usually from a corporate system such as government officials and major CEO. There are crimes that most times are not detected and are hard to bring justice to. Dark psychology explains that the dark behavior of people is often developmental such that it is related to how they are being brought up so anyone that acts wicked will be assumed not to have been brought up in a loving and caring way.

Dark psychology will always explain any form of behavior, whether normal or abnormal in a positive way. The major triad of dark psychology is associated with the three words, which are very important to live adaptively. These include sorry, regret, and remorse. The word 'sorry' is an adjective with different types of meaning defining different kinds of communications interactions and expressions in relationships. Sometimes the term stands as a form of apology or an expression of regret. And sometimes, it is an expression of being remorseful. The feeling of being remorseful and communicating regret is necessary for the survival of all humans generally.

You can simply achieve this. Firstly, expect others to offend you, and whether you are innocent or guilty, always initiate an apology with a look of empathy. You need to plan not to want to offend people in the future and, most importantly, always forgive but never forget because this fosters respect.

While interacting whether, with an individual or a group, you will notice that the person that displays the strongest emotion will be the one that will lead the interaction and influence other people's emotions, the same with the dark psychology of all the other people involved.

Same way, when you are in a two-person interaction, if you are displaying a deep sadness and the other person is just a bit happy and joyful. You will notice that you will have a greater influence on the conversation as you have the probability to draw the other person towards being sad.

We humans can be so irrational and emotional at times. You can learn the latest emotional IQ tools in bulk, and yet when you're emotional or triggered by something you are asked messily. There's usually an element of deception in dark psychology. However, it is important to note that deception is necessary to some extent, depending on the kind of result you want to obtain. Deception is not generally an evil concept even though some people use it in extremely evil things, but most times the intentions behind the use of deception are good. It can be said that the use of deception can bring good things sometimes. The major thing is to understand the approach to it. In deceiving people, don't paint the complete picture in lies.

Most times, persuasion is often used by people you love and trust wholly. This tactic involves making compliments of showing affection to someone to make a request, exaggeration or telling partial true stories, holding back affection and attention thereby denying someone of love, and telling a person to do something to motivate them to do the opposite in which is what you really want.

Dark Psychology involves the use of mind tricks, which is in between deception and persuasion. The psychological mind tricks might sound outrageous, but it works well. They are being used to mislead people to think that what they know to be right is wrong, and what they believe to be wrong is right.

In a simple term, dark psychology allows humans to be willing and deliberate to harm others through their decisions and actions, sometimes this might not be physical. However, some emotions are groomed from a very early stage of an individual's life. For example, a child grows to learn how to cry in such a way that the adults around will make themselves available for their bidding. We can call this crying a manipulative tool for the child to be enabled to control people around. As a child grows up, if such a child is not being cautioned on what he's doing, the so-called innocent childish behavior would now become a dark way of controlling people to do what he/she wants.

Dark psychology is a means of studying how a person thinks and also sees a need to understand the intent behind actions and words. In general, it illuminates the dark side of human nature. In dark psychology, the effect is experienced by both the victim and the perpetrator. The personality traits which are considered dark include narcissism, psychopathy, and Machiavellianism.

In a simple term, an excessive admiration of oneself in an obsessive manner towards appearance is referred to as narcissism. Narcissists usually feel superior. They do not subscribe to the rule of giving and take in a normal relationship. They are good at blaming others whenever there is an issue. A common feature is to be an extremely self-centered individual. Narcissists have an unrestricted appetite for control and power. They control people by making them think that they are looking out for them. They are also very smart such that they get involved in your day-to-day activities in life without being noticed. Above all, they are Keen liars and master is the lie skills.

Psychopathy is a trait that is associated with not being sensitive to other people. A psychopath will almost not have empathy for other people. Psychopaths are usually bold, confident, and fearless. They are risk-takers and extremely charming.

On the other hand, the third personality trait is known as Machiavellianism, the term is used to describe someone who lacks emotions and desire to achieve something at the expense of other people's feelings. This can be done through deceit, manipulation, or going against some moral rules. An individual who scores highly in the Machiavellianism test is usually referred to as a "High Mach" These people are always around us, sometimes in our workplace or as a neighbor. They are hard-working people who are smart and are unapologetic about stepping on other people's toes. These sets of people are opportunists and can detach themselves from situations they are in emotionally. Due to this ability, they are capable of involving themselves in several sexual several encounters. They can stand a chance of being good teammates, but certainly not a good friend.

This knowledge of dark psychology is to protect yourself from those personalities when you come across them. Dark psychology cuts across all human conditions, which are universal in nature. It studies how the condition of humans relates to their thoughts, feelings, and perception. The general assumption here is that every human has the potential to be violent. Learning this concept is of two-folded benefits. First, it helps individuals to accept that they tend to become evil, so the knowledge of this will prevent it from erupting. And secondly, it gives everyone a reason to struggle to survive.

This is a technique used in restructuring people's minds on how to get rid of bad habits, how to become productive, and how to make them effective in general. You can use this technique to connect sense, mind, behavior, and language. The technique is designed in such a way that you tend to control people without them even being aware of what you are doing to them.

Neuro refers to the nervous system, which is made up of the mind and all other senses. Your nervous system function when you interact with your environment or people generally that's why when you listen more to people, you get to understand what is being said, also when you pay more attention to what happens around you, you know and see more things about people around.

However linguistic refers to the language, it doesn't necessarily mean the language you speak may be English or Spanish, but it depends more on your usage of words, the underlying tone of your voice, and even the rate at which you communicate with people.

And programming in NLP refers to the act of forming the habit. NLP teaches you how to make sure that the habit you pick is useful to you as a person in your life, and even in your interaction with others. It has been said that it takes approximately 21 days should leave or break and habits formed and 66 days to form a new one. NLP allows you to choose the reality you want for yourself. Also, it helps you to influence other people's reality without them knowing, and this programming relies on other various techniques in which mirroring is one of them.

As the name suggests, mirroring deals with mimicking the behavior of the person you are interacting with in a very subtle way. It is done subtly because the person must not understand what you are doing or else you will not achieve a good result.

In this technique, you must pay attention to the person's body language, tone and tempo of voice, choice of words, vocabulary, and even pattern of thought. The essence of mirroring is to be in oneness with the person you are communicating with.

This technique has also been employed by people to keep a long-term relationship. Psychology explains that when you like someone, you will subconsciously behave like them by mirroring their actions. When you even mirror your potential partner, he/she will be glad to think that you understand them. And, when people have a feeling that you understand them, they become more open to you.

Chapter 7: The Psychology of Body Language

One of the clearest ways to examine others is to look at their body language. How a person conducts themselves, walks and even talks will give you many clues about them. Each individual has a lot of differences in their body language, and there is no perfect way to understand what it reveals about that person. There are however many common signs within groups of individuals that can begin to give you a profound understanding of how they function. It is not a simple process, because it begins with becoming conscious of your own body language.

To comprehend and seek to resolve the enigma of body language, you need to be hyper-conscious. We have taken you through the journey of becoming conscious of your feelings and where they might emerge from. It is time to focus on being conscious of your body. To understand what makes an individual distinct from others based on their body language, you must first look at yourself and examine how you handle your body. Many people may be more conscious of their actions than they are of their feelings. Women are more inclined to be conscious of their bodies and the space they occupy, mainly because of the male-dominated society in which we grew up. Anyone may find it difficult to scrutinize the way they carry their body. You may lose focus when trying to maintain hyper-consciousness, becoming too insecure with your own body and gestures. Once you get to know someone else's body language better, you can also recognize what makes them special.

Cultural Differences

There are many reasons a person's body language varies, so it is essential to note that not everything about a body expression is 100% accurate for every individual. This is particularly important to keep in mind while talking to people of diverse cultural backgrounds. Some societies exercise modesty, therefore contact may be inappropriate. On the other hand, some cultures may be more receptive to communicating their emotions through their bodies. Consequently, the culture is crucial to consider when talking about how an individual might use their body.

Study Other People's Movements

Once you become more conscious of body movements and what they might mean, you may continue to explore them as you communicate with other individuals. Everyone you come into contact with uses their body to reflect various things. Many individuals are fairly shut down, and others may be more accessible. These are some slight variations that you might notice just by watching someone's body language.

While examining other people's and your own body language, it is important to try to behave naturally. It may be possible to become super-aware of your movements, but remember that you don't have to keep your body in a particular way. Not everyone is as mindful of body movements as you may be, so at the end of the day, don't look too much at your movements.

However, once you start learning the body movements of others, you can begin to understand more about them. When meeting some people you know, some things about them might begin to make sense. You might think one of your friends is pretty arrogant in the way they are carrying themselves or interacting. Some friends could demonstrate how nervous they are with themselves, even though you had always thought they were extremely confident.

Reading the body language of a person and having intuition as to why they may be behaving a certain way will help you to fully understand them at their core, which gives you more influence in persuading them. You may want to match your boss's confidence in making an offer for a boost. Maybe you have found that you need to be calmer around some friends who seem to be reserved or anxious. It can be frightening at first to become conscious of your body language, but soon you will be confident with the way you walk.

Always have a mirror around you to start the process of being comfortable with your own body. When you are eating, watching TV, or even lying in bed, put up a mirror so you can see how you are holding yourself. Once you get an outsider's point of view on how you are moving, you will be able to notice how other people are moving as well.

Eye Contact

Keeping eye contact is one of the most important clues to evaluate who someone is. It is necessary to be cautious of your eye contact use, as it provides other hints about your temperament and true nature. Nevertheless, it is important to keep eye contact to let a person know you are listening to what they are talking about and that they have your maximum attention.

However, it can also be misconstrued and make people think you are trying hard to convince them you are paying attention when you are actually distracted. Sometimes too much eye contact will disturb others as well, so if you observe a person becoming uncomfortable because of the extent of eye contact you have with them, switch it up occasionally. Research has shown that dilation of pupils can be a clear indicator of an individual being attentive to what you are saying. You know that you have their undivided attention and that they are genuinely engaged in the interaction. The reverse—shifty eyes—could imply dishonesty. Someone whose gaze is constantly moving could be trying to persuade you that they are listening. They know they need to attempt to maintain eye contact, but they are completely out of touch with what you are saying. Those with shifting eyes may also be pretending to you or trying to trick you in some manner. They may have trouble keeping eye contact with you because they know they are deceptive.

Mouth Movements

What a person does with their mouth is also very important to know their personality. Someone with closed or pursed lips may be trying to focus, or they may even be trying hard to conceal a sour face. You can also examine the smile of an individual. If the corners of their eyes are not wrinkled, they might be faking a smile. Anyone who fakes a smile is not inherently bad; they might just be worrying about something else too distracted to pay keen attention to what you are saying.

Smiles are sometimes responses to unpleasant circumstances, too. When monkeys grin, it is not because they are pleased, but usually because they expose their teeth as a means to taunt those around them. They can open their mouths widely if they become afraid and anxious, revealing that they have teeth they can use to harm. The same is true for pit bulls. They only display their teeth when they feel endangered. This can often also be the case for humans but on a subconscious level. Nervous laughter and grinning may be a way to relieve a person's anxiety. Some people are only genuinely smiling when they have wrinkles in their eye corners. An individual who continually covers their mouth is also typically anxious. They could bite their lips or their fingers or place a hand over their mouth. Often understanding that a person is anxious or upset can be useful when attempting to influence them. We will explore how and when to use that knowledge to influence others.

Nodding

How an individual turns and tilts their head can be a discreet movement. Some people are not as conscious of when they move their heads most of the time. The movements of the neck and head of the individual you are examining can give you a better glimpse into what they might be thinking on a deeper level. Someone who nods their head very frequently when speaking to you may just be nervous or trying to terminate the conversation as soon as possible. They are trying to set up a tempo so you can speak faster. They want you to know they are listening to you, but you are not talking fast enough. If somebody is doing this to you, start speeding up your words to keep their concentration.

If someone tilts their head to the side, they may have a genuine interest in what you are saying. They are trying to turn an ear towards you, so they can understand you properly, whether or not they are conscious of their motions. They also show that they are listening to you and that they need you to continue talking. It is a way for them to come closer to you in the discussion without any digressions or interruptions being required. If somebody nods too dramatically, they might just be trying to convince you they are concerned about what you say.

They might realize they ought to pay attention, but they may have lost interest or not comprehend what you are saying, so they nod to make you believe they are keeping up with the conversation. If you see someone around you shaking their head unnaturally, it may be worth either diverting the conversation to get their attention back or explaining yourself better as they might just be lost. Mimicking the movement of someone's head can be very effective in convincing people. A slight turn of the head when listening to them can show you understand what they are saying. It can also demonstrate that you are sympathetic to them, particularly if they are talking about something that seems difficult for them.

Hands and Arms

How someone utilizes their hands and arms is another way that body language can be used to gain a deeper knowledge of the individuals you communicate with. Our hands give away so much about us. They are a way to express tales, putting specific focus on different parts. If somebody is telling a story, they use hand movements to hold their listeners' attention. Think of someone involved in a dialogue as one who is directing an orchestra; they are going to lift their hands to keep up the rhythm and intensity for the listeners around them. The hands and arms of somebody can also convey just how outgoing or withdrawn they are; they could be like a gateway through the body. If someone has their arms closely crossed in front of their chest, that person may be somewhat more closed off, not wanting to participate too much in conversation.

However, having their arms crossed does not automatically indicate that someone is uncommunicative. They may also just want to relax their arms, and if they are hanging loosely in front of them, they are possibly only listening to you passively. Someone who has their arms spread wide, perhaps over their head, would generally be very accessible and maybe even seek to exert control over a situation. Someone might try to assert their dominance with their hands on their waist.

Chapter 8: How to Learn Speed Reading People

Speed reading is a technique to increase reading without compromising understanding and retention of information. There are several different methods of speed reading, but they all aim to read clearly, but faster.

For those who work as a freelancer, especially the producers of web content, digital marketing, etc., reading is a prime activity. And speed reading lets you take even more of the time you have available for this activity. It is through reading that you deepen your knowledge to argue more strongly and keep your repertoire of subjects relevant and up to date.

Unfortunately, it is not always possible to devote the time needed to complete reading an article or a book. In this situation, speed reading helps you extract the most important information in less time.

What Is Speed Reading?

Speed reading is a technique that seeks to increase the reading speed without compromising understanding and retention of information. There are several different speed-reading methods for both books and online texts and they all aim to read clearly as well as faster.

Check out this step by step guide and learn how to enhance your speed-reading skills!

1. Train Your Eyes to Make Bigger Jumps

Do you know how the movement of your eyes works while reading? Basically, it's a jumping move. Your eyes pin one point on the line and then jump to the next.

The higher this leap, the more proficient is your reading. Beginner readers, like children, skip only one word at a time and therefore take longer to finish each line. Therefore, the first step of speed reading is to train the eye movement so that it is wider.

2. Go Straight Ahead

The second step is to control that anxiety, that sense of obligation to understand 100% of the text. We are going to take this up further, but know that 80% understanding is an excellent goal.

In other words, you do not have to return to the beginning of the page every time you do not understand a line. After all, re-reading can take a long time—and that is precisely what we are trying to avoid.

Besides, you can fully understand the general idea of a text, even though some excerpts are more confusing. Then, after finishing the text, resume only the parts where you have doubts. But if you stop and go back constantly, you will never finish reading.

Another important tip is not to interrupt the reading to check the dictionary. If you are very curious about the meaning of a word, write it down to check later. However, do not abandon the text to browse the dictionary because when you return, it will take you even longer to resume reading.

In the meantime, try to understand the term by context—you may not absorb the exact meaning of the word, but it will be enough to understand the message the author wanted to convey.

3. Stop Speaking the Words

The third step is to eliminate a negative practice that is a habit of many people: to pronounce the words as they read, either loudly or mentally.

This habit prevents the development of speed reading because it means that you will literally read word for word.

The speed slows down and as incredible as it may seem, the capacity for understanding as well. Because your brain will be busy with pronunciation, you will not be able to concentrate on interpreting what you are reading. The result is that you will have to reread the same stretch several times.

If you are too accustomed to pronounce as you read, losing this habit can be a difficult and time-consuming process. An interesting tip is to put a pencil in your mouth as you read. With a little practice, you will lose this "craze" and see how it improves your reading time.

4. Use Skimming Technique

The fourth step is "skimming." This is a well-known technique for Instrumental English, but it is also useful for speed reading in any language.

Skimming consists basically of looking quickly through a text in order to extract basic information—index, title, and author, date of publication, main subject, subtopics developed, graphics, and images.

This technique is useful for you to quickly evaluate any text and then set whether to devote more time to a full reading.

If you are researching a specific subject, for example, skimming will allow you to identify whether a particular article or book has relevant information about the subject. Besides, you will find the excerpts that interest you more easily.

5. Use the Scanning Technique

The fifth step, "scanning," is another technique used in English Instrumental. It consists basically of looking at the text to identify keywords, which in this case are relevant terms, related to the information you want to extract from that content.

Suppose you are reading a twenty-page article on People Management, but the subject that really matters to you is Productivity. In that case, you do not have to read all twenty pages, which will certainly tell you about various other issues that are not important to you right now.

Instead, just look through the article for terms directly related to productivity, such as "time," "organization," "concentration," and so on. When you find one of these terms, you just need to read that passage. Thus, you quickly get information that is of interest to you and "skip" the rest.

6. Monitor Your Performance

Once you incorporate what you have learned in the first five steps, the evolution of your speed reading will depend on practice. But to see if it's working, you need to keep track of your progress.

So, the sixth step is picking up a timer and monitoring how many words you read per minute. As a reference, keep in mind that a typical reader reads, on average, 150 words per minute. Meanwhile, a good speed-reading practitioner can read up to 800 words per minute.

But do not just monitor speed. Take into account, also, the use of reading, that is, how much you can understand the text without having to return to it a second time. Your goal should be an average of 80% utilization.

Remember that there is no point in speeding up reading, and thereby lessening the understanding of what has been read, as the re-reading also represents a waste of time.

7. Train Your Focusing Ability

Now that we've covered the best strategies for speed reading itself, let's take a few tips that will enhance your reading experience as a whole and as a result, help you absorb more information in less time.

The ability to stay focused while reading is critical to being productive and not wasting time. The deeper you "plunge" into the text, the better you understand what the author wrote.

What happens, then, if you go to every two paragraphs to check the notifications on your cell phone? The experience will be interrupted and continually resumed, which diminishes your ability to comprehend and thus takes you to take more time to understand what is read.

In this way, you waste twice as much time: the extra time it takes to understand what you read and the precious minutes wasted with distractions (Smartphone, computer, social networks, etc.).

If you often suffer from it, the key is to turn productivity into a habit. To do so, when you read, keep the distractions away. This means not leaving the phone nearby, not keeping the computer by your side, and, if possible, turning off the internet or at least placing your devices in airplane mode.

This time is for you to dedicate to the text and nothing else! The more you can focus on reading, the better your ability to practice speed reading.

8. Find a Quiet Place to Do Your Reading

The place you choose to do your readings also greatly influences the speed and dynamism of the activity—something very connected to the danger represented by the distractions, as we just mentioned.

Noise from traffic, from work, from an establishment (such as a bar, for example), and even from music can disturb your ability to concentrate, making you frequently "quit" reading. Also, if you are reading in an environment with other people, you will also be directly interrupted if they speak to you, even if it is a quick dialogue.

Besides being silent, it is also important that the chosen corner for reading is comfortable. When you are comfortable reading, it is much easier to indulge in the text and devote your full attention to it. And if you have a special space where you like to read, another advantage is that this will make it easier to establish reading as an integral part of your routine.

9. Do Not Insist When You Are Tired

You may have heard that it is not very productive for a student to spend the night studying for a test that will be given the next day. At that point, the desperation of a few extra hours of study is no longer as important as the rest, which will allow more focus and better memory for the student during the test.

The same principle can be applied to speed reading. When we are tired, regardless of whether the exhaustion reaches our site and/or head, our ability to concentrate decreases dramatically. You will find yourself having to read and reread the same passage several times, and of course, it takes much longer to read each line.

And the worst part is that the next day you can pick up the text and realize you cannot remember much of anything you read the night before. This is because a tired brain also decreases its ability to retain information.

So, an important point of speed reading is to know the time to stop.

10. Read Whenever You Can

What the reader does not like to sit in their favorite armchair and deliver hours and hours to a book or even a relevant and high-quality text? However, as you well know, this is not always (or rather, almost never!) possible.

Does this mean, then, that you are bound to a routine? Of course not! It turns out you do not have to self-punch yourself for not being able to devote several hours of each day to reading.

Start enjoying every free minute, especially with regards to idle time spent in queues, waiting rooms, or on public transportation, for example. And how about going a little early to bed, every night, and reading before bed?

A block of fifteen or twenty minutes in which you would do nothing when dedicated to reading becomes time well spent. With this, you advance much faster in your readings, although you cannot read much each day. Another advantage is that this will help you build the daily habit of reading—and, who knows, it will even encourage you to separate a few hours of your day into the activity.

Do you already practice speed reading? What is your speed reading achievement? If you have not yet reached the goals proposed here, do not worry. Reading is a habit you cannot be afraid to develop, and the benefits are gigantic.

Chapter 9: Understanding Deception and Deceptive Tactics

Deception is a hot topic in today's society. At the root, deception is making claims that are false in nature, which leads people to believe an idea or concept that isn't true. Deception comes in many forms, from propaganda to simple conversation, from the aggressor to the victim convincing them of something false. In today's society, we are faced with deception at all angles. Some of the ways we are regularly deceived include:

The Media

Often times in the media we are given half-truths instead of the full picture. These half-truths lead us to complete the idea on our own. This is often used when it concerns public offices, racial inequality, world events, and even your local weather.

Food

With labels reading everything from no hormones added to healthy and fat-free, we are unable to fully discern what we are eating and what the real regulations are.

Religion

For some, religion is a huge contention of deception. Whether it's the belief as a whole or the misinterpretation of religious text.

Personal Relationships

When we are deceived by the ones we love, it is hard to believe anything anyone says anymore.

The Interpersonal Deception Theory was developed by David B. Buller, and Judee K. Burgoon, both communication professors. At the time of its inception, deceit was not considered an actual form of communication. The IDT is an attempt to relate how people handle deception at both a conscious and an unconscious level. In order to fully understand deception, you have to know some of the forms in which it is presented.

- Misinterpretations of the Truth
- Downplaying of the Truth
- Stretching the Truth
- Holding Back All the Information
- Contradiction
- Ambiguous Statements
- Lies

People and larger entities use deception for many reasons. The three main motives for deception include avoiding punishment or protecting someone or something to keep relationships intact and to preserve the aggressor's self-image. On top of those motives, things like propaganda and media acts of deception can oftentimes be linked to larger goals. For example, a country might put out propaganda to trick the people into believing that everything is okay, or that another country is the enemy when there is no truth behind it. A media outlet may put out misleading or half-truths to broaden their base of supporters for a specific cause or political candidate.

In today's political market deception can be found across party lines, both in the media and directly from the sources. It is a game of back and forth, telling mostly half-truths for you to draw your own conclusion based on your predetermined political ideals. These half-truths can lead to separation of the people and battles back and forth within the community based on political thoughts and notions.

On a smaller level, deception from person to person can lead to broken relationships, financial loss, loss of property, and even death. There are also forms of visual deception. They come in both natures and through human-made efforts. Disguises are another form of visual deception. As you can see, many of these types of deception are for survival purposes. It is when they move into personal gains or selfish reasoning's that they become dangerous across the board.

Detecting deception can be difficult, especially when the deceit has no real grounding in physical proof. You could have him/her battle, and the only proof is the words being spoken. How then is one supposed to know which side is deceitful and which is telling the truth? Oftentimes these decisions come down to your personal viewpoint and how well you know the people that are telling you the possibly deceiving stories. Other times, as it is with media and propaganda, research can be done to find out what the entire truth is.

Beyond the boundaries of nature, psychologists have studied deception for many years. They have cataloged, listed, and researched the different types of deception and what the psyche behind it holds. Those with a high likelihood of using their dark psyche often turn to deception for personal gain and to hold onto the lifestyle they have created.

The Psychology of Deception

Deception, boiled down, is essentially lying. Whether the truth is only half the truth, or the information is twisted to fit an agenda, it is a lie. But how often do we find ourselves lying? While no one likes to admit that they have lied or lie regularly, it is a regular part of life.

Bella DePaulo, Ph.D., a psychologist at the University of Virginia, conducted a study in 1996. The study used 147 people ranging between 18 and 71 years of age. Each person was asked to keep a journal of all the lies that they told during the course of one week. The study had the following findings:

- Most people lie once to twice a day.
- Men and Women, equally, lie in a fifth of their social interactions that last more than ten minutes.
- In the course of one week, both sexes deceive thirty percent of the people they interact with face-to-face.
- Some relationships attract deception more than others.

While we grow up being taught that lying is bad, and telling the truth is always the best way to go, as adults we don't follow that rule at all. Even some of the most influential professions such as lawyers, accountants, and politicians lie and deceive on a regular, or even daily, basis. Oftentimes, lying keeps you from receiving punishments. For example, if you are late to school, telling them that you overslept will give you detention, but telling them there was an accident will usually let you off the hook. For such small insignificant occurrences, we are pressured into lying not to pay unneeded penalties when nothing is changed by our lateness.

DePaulo's study also included breaking down the types of lies, and the types of relationships most affected by them. She found that couples that are dating lie to each other about a third of the time.

Most couples lie from the beginning about things like prior relationships and sexual history. Within marriage, the lies go down to about ten percent, and usually about small everyday things. DePaulo stated, "You save your really big lies for the person that you're closest to."

There are other types of lies as well. The small lies we tell others to avoid hurting their feelings. When we tell someone we like their new haircut or the color of their new magenta shoes. We tell people that they are good people that their mistakes don't define them when we know they often do in our society. People with extroverted personalities tend to lie more, especially when under pressure. We also, when facing mental health issues such as depression, tend to lie to ourselves. Those lies can go either way. We can deceive ourselves into thinking everything is fine, or we can further dwell in our own pits of self-loathing, creating lies about ourselves that drag us down further.

The cold hard truth is that we, as a society, have set boundaries and expectations that are rigid enough that every single person lies. Most people, put under enough pressure and fear, will lie about anything. Some deceive to hurt others. Child custody court is a very good example. The father gets up and makes up complete untruths about the mother to discredit her. The only thing the judge listens to are the words from both parents and has to decide which one is being deceptive and which one is not. This can often highly affect a child's life.

With all the ways around things these days, what is the real reason that we lie? If there is an easier way to avoid discontent and deception, everyone should use it, but we don't. We use lies to put out the fires in our lives quickly, only to find out those lies often start new ones. It is an endless cycle that everyone has gone through in their life.

Top Ways to Effectively Deceive

If you really want to know how to be an effective liar, the answers are all over the place. First, sit and think about a time you have been lied to, but the liar was terrible. Think about the things that were dead giveaways to you. It might have been body language, it might have been their inability to repeat the lie, it could have been filled with absolutely ridiculous information that anyone would have known was a lie. Whatever it is, take note of that. Those are things you do not want to make the mistake of doing. Beyond knowing what not to do, there are several things you want to make sure you always have in line before lying.

Reasoning Is Everything

By reasoning, we don't mean your motive. Reasoning means, is it worth it? Pathological liars have a mental condition that triggers something in their brains that is almost a reward for telling a lie. Most pathological liars no longer have any idea what they are saying, and whether it is truth or lies. They will lie about anything at any time for no reason. To be good at the deception you basically have to be selective. Keep your lies to a minimum. This wills not only save you from having to remember all of your lies, but it will also create a persona of trustworthiness so when you do lie, no one will really question it. Pick the best times to lie, the times you will get the most out of it.

Have Your Story All Laid Out

There is nothing worse than telling a lie and then having someone ask questions, especially when you don't have the entire story and all the details laid out ahead of time. Making spur of the moment decisions on your stories can often lead you down a bad path. Things don't line up, timelines are off, and lies don't seem to fit together. On top of that, all of the lies you told spur of the moment now have to become cemented into your mind. You have to remember what story you told. To have a fluid deception, you have to lay out your story from the beginning to the end. Look at it from an outside perspective and think about all the questions that could be asked. Integrate that information into your mind and then test it for inaccuracies. Compare it to any proof that might be brought forward.

Create a Lie That Is Not Completely a Lie

There are always some truths to lies. One way to get around getting caught in a lie is to tell the truth but leave it short storied. Allow the other person to conclude based on how your lie is told. Give a false impression when you tell your truth, one that pushes the other person in the direction that you want to see them go. Creating a lie from a truth will also help to avoid questions that can significantly increase your ability to carry out your venture successfully.

Chapter 10: Narcissism in a Relationship

Making a sweeping generalization about human characters can be improper due to the random nature of humankind. Spotting a narcissist needs a keen eye since such persons hide the real faces behind humor and empathy. They can easily attract with first impressions like good looks and conspicuous kindness than can be felt by anyone. This could however be a welcome to a very stressful relationship, a relationship full of emotional sabotage and deceit.

Contrary to what somebody might think, narcissists can fall in love just like other people do. The true identity of a narcissist in such a case unleashes itself slowly as time goes by. The relationship will then get more toxic from time to time, giving a partner a hell of experience. A partner can lose self-esteem due to mistreatments coming from the narcissistic better half. For this reason, narcissistic relationships are prone to breakups.

Some of narcissism cannot be hidden, its toxicity can easily be observed. Individuals in this class have their real faces on. They behave as their reasoning, so they are as they should be. Such individuals have been seen to be attracted to sensitive and empathetic people against the odds. This could be against the will of a person in the question, but that is a natural fact as far as narcissistic relationships are concerned. The observation is, however, quite ironic on how someone will fail to identify the narcissist to prevent bad experiences in a precious lifetime.

The manifestation of narcissism in a relationship can vary according to the factors such as, when both people are narcissists, another factor is when one partner is behaving in a way that can cause damage to his/her better half. The first factor can rarely be seen but it can happen, partners cannot just simply let go of the factors besides true love. The latter can actually be observed in many cases now; it is evidenced by myriad abusive relationships that have been witnessed among the couples. Bad things done by a narcissist could be being center-minded, putting his/her needs before the better half's significant needs.

Signs of Narcissism in a Relationship

They Often Make One Feel Guilty

They are good at manipulating, and will often try to make you feel discouraged and guilty for reasons brought about by them. They have a way of making you feel sorry for things they have even done themselves or minor reasons. They will blame you for reasons that would just have themselves to blame, they are also known for looking for small faults and making it look like you really did a big mistake.

They Are Manipulative

A narcissist is a kind of person who will have nothing standing his or her way in acquiring what they want. Such people would want to make you fit in a position in assisting them to achieve their goals. Making you serve roles that you wouldn't have wanted for your personal reasons. Such manipulation automatically comes upon the narcissists because they regard themselves as special and as people who are full of confidence in themselves.

Entitlement

Narcissistic disorder seems to grant some of its victims a strong belief that they will have somebody do what they ask. That they can command and through you, all that they want will be accomplished. They find their own needs more important than those of their partners and should be met without any delay. That forms abusive relationships over time, making their partners experience dreadful experiences in love life.

They Seem to Defy Some Rules That Apply to Everyone

Due to so much felt self-importance, narcissists act like some rules should not apply to them. They are seen to push ahead of their colleagues regardless of the gatherings at public places like they do not value the rest. Under this factor, they are also known for standing against anyone regardless of the ranks. To elevate their esteem, narcissists step on everyone in the manner in which they do things, they consider themselves special and thus they should have their power and control validated.

Frequent Threats

This is also a true sign of a narcissist; it is associated with a high temper. Somebody who pours threats like 'I didn't need you anyway, you can leave me alone' could likely not be so promising in the long period relationship.

Externally Impressive

Narcissists have a common way of making themselves appealing, be it in their social lives, possessions, or in their general body appearance. They often do a thorough cover-up of their true selves, they can blaze in the eyes of beholders but deep down they are enormous social misfits. This factor relates to the others above in a sense that most narcissists have a feeling of self-importance, making them feel above others. They make this feel like it should be an acceptable fact by making themselves look quite impressive. It however does not alter anything about them.

They Believe They're Very Special

If somebody thinks you cannot live without him or her, then beware you could be in a relationship with a narcissist. Narcissists value themselves with a high degree of specialty compared to others. Such guys believe that nobody can do something better than them. The worse aspect of this factor is that they expect you to feel them equally as they feel about themselves. They do not want to feel challenged or underrated, so they can only go a long way with partners who can comply with this, even if by pretending.

Hot and Cold

They are good at seducing people to win something they need. They can sweet-talk through compliments and other possible means to win favor from you. Feeling great through praises is how many people's hearts are won. The narcissists however can switch from being so good to a nasty mood, to make you feel discouraged and guilty, to have you carry blames for some things you didn't do.

Narcissistic Abuse

This is the abuse associated with the relationships of a narcissist. It is a form of emotional abuse from narcissistic individuals to people who are close to them. Besides psychological and emotional abuse, there are other forms of abuse grouped as financial, spiritual, sexual, and physical. The following are relationships in which the above mentioned narcissistic abuse manifests itself.

Workplace

Research shows that abusers often get an easy way of getting up the ranks at the place of work, winning the trust of their colleagues. Their impressions give them an upper hand in achieving such since most of them are considered smart, thus more deserving than their co-workers. Gaining dominance over others is what narcissists go for; they follow this up regardless of the path they use. They are psychopaths who can play workmates against each other, they then stand to gain favor from all the directions to reach where they want to in the company. Such a trait has been observed to be dominant among the managers than the rest of the workers of the lower rank.

After achieving their 'deserved positions' in the company through the co-workers, they then use intimidation and harassment to push others down. Undermining others is also another way they use to put down the rest of the workers, earning a feeling of overpowering them. As far as Workplace Bullying Institute is concerned, these are the sources of domestic violence at the place of work where an individual with narcissism trait is the only beneficiary. Their acts conflict with the morals, but they often seem not to care as their objective to clinch the positions of power.

Parent-Child

Family relationships keeping people together as parent-child or among siblings makes the perfect environment for narcissistic abuse. For instance, a parent who is a narcissist will demand power to control and feel self-validation, which will be imposed on their children. A child's misbehavior is seen as outrageous disobedience of the parent's direct orders. The parent feels utterly neglected the slightest provocation, developing hard feelings, which is associated with bad things such as corporal punishments.

Love Relationships

Narcissism is born from self-esteem and a feeling of entitlement of an individual. In the case of a narcissistic partner feeling less admirable to their partners, they will in turn demean the looks of their partners. They belittle the looks of their lovers to make them feel better or just above them. Their natural ultimate goal here is to boost their ego over their partners, and this is how to make themselves suit their standards.

Their annoying tactics go as far as humiliating their partners in public places. They enjoy the emotional reaction from their victims when they make them feel guilty and humiliated. They can literally behave like sadists, in this case, practicing what is termed as gaslighting, making their victims feel at fault and annoyed even before the gatherings. This is their way of how to take and seal control and power over the rest of the people that are their partners involved.

A narcissistic love partner will demand to be valued highly, to have his or her grievances addressed in good time, and be well-attended to. Frequent threats to the partner is another outcome of a narcissistic relationship. The partner with narcissistic traits will want often to have the other partner feel guilty and discouraged, even for the wrongs they have caused. They are associated with turning the guilt to their partners; they dig the dirt on a partner to make them look bad.

Fear and anxiety will always be a portion of a partner in narcissistic relationships. The behavior of a narcissistic partner is unpredictable, good times are just but a short lift, they make one feel wanted and well valued but then, they can still bring regrets in the next minute. They're often regarded as bright and classic people, judging from how present themselves socially, physically, and economically. Ironically, they are people who are not able to create and guard strong social relationships even with their own lovers.

As explored earlier in this article, narcissistic individuals tend to disrespect their mates by putting their needs before others' needs; in a love relationship, they will obviously make a partner feel intimidated. They will be felt as uncaring and too many toxic partners for a smooth relationship. This is a reason why a person in a relationship with a narcissistic individual will often be advised to abandon the relationship as soon as possible.

Narcissism and Healthy Relationship

The traits of a good relationship can vary from one couple to another. It is fitting to bring a contrast between a relationship full of conflicts and that of a healthy relationship in this article. Some features of a healthy or rather what could be termed as a good relationship are discussed.

Respect for Each Other

People in a relationship need to show positivity to build a good relationship. Treating each other well is the core of this factor; this should be despite frustrations somebody could be going through. Differ peacefully if you must differ to allow room for a better tomorrow of a relationship. This is to avoid the distress that is associated with narcissistic relationships easily.

Chapter 11: Setting Boundary Not to Be Manipulated

By now, you must have the ability to know the value of setting limits for both personal and relationship growth. Many people will have a hard time establishing and maintain boundaries because of some misconceptions. Because they are scared of the repercussions, such borders can have on their values and their lifestyle.

For instance, some individuals hesitate about losing all their friends when their limits appear to be too high and unrealistic. It is essential to handle common boundary myths and accept reality to set limits effectively.

Misconception #1: I May Look Self-Centered If I Set Boundaries

This misconception or objection is frequently raised by people who believe or feared being considered as self-centered or self-indulgent when they set boundaries. Many people are scared of being accused of doing not have issues for others when they set borders. Hence they offer upsetting such limits. In reality, setting boundaries does not make you self-centered; setting limits will help you take care of others, while you safeguard yourself from being at the receiving end of every misgiving. Individuals who set boundaries the most are typically the most caring ones in the world because they have discovered that through borders, their requirements have been taken care of; for this reason, they have lots of energy and time to take care of the needs of others.

All our needs, desires, and selfishness only consider our desires, whereas borders think about our needs. When we concentrate on our desires, we might lose focus and balance, and somewhat of pursuing our healthy goals through setting limits, selfishness might force us to work to please others. Trying to satisfy our needs does not make such requirements bad.

Misconception #2: Boundaries Are Symptoms of Disobedience and Un-Submissiveness

Many people are scared that setting boundaries or limits will signal to their partners, co-workers, friends, or bosses that they are disobedient and rebellious. Some people think that saying "No" to something good just implies they are unresponsive. Thus they take part in every social event or take whatever that is thrownat them. Doing everything that comes, your doing has no spiritual or psychological worth. When you do things out of your inner voice, however, your heart is not in it, and then you are wasting your time and trying to please others. Focus on setting borders in whatever you do so that you don't do too much.

Outwardly need something when we mean No merely makes you a liar. If we state No to great things only because of our self-centered desires, then such a limit makes you disobedient.

Misconception # 3: Setting Limits Indicates I Am Always Upset

For many novices who are just setting borders, they may realize that they suddenly begin to tell the truth and take responsibility for all their actions. These people may feel that some type of "anger cloud is surrounding them," many especially when they become conscious where their limits are being violated. When you start setting boundaries, you might fear that you can be offended easily, and this might get you confused. This is simply one of the essential things you may experience at the beginning of setting a limit; however, you will overcome it when individuals start to understand what you stand for. Borders do not cause anger in us; however, if you see the limit set as the source of your passion, and then you misunderstand your emotions. Your emotions must be the signals that need to tell you about something—for instance, your fear ought to advise you to move away from a dangerous situation, while anger needs to ask you to challenge an imminent risk.

You ought to remember that a mad circumstance is a warning that you are in imminent danger of being attacked or injured. For this reason, anger ought to be viewed as a positive indication that you will be manipulated, or your boundary will be violated. While your worry might tell you to withdraw from a situation, anger will help you advance and protect your fence. There is no reason to be scared when your boundaries are being breached; instead, the violence should help you not to be violent; however, affordable way to inform the violator to stop breaking your borders.

Don't simply let your anger out; instead, you need to discover to protect whatever is yours more properly without showing unfavorable feelings.

Misconception #4: When I Begin Creating Borders, I Might Be Injured by Others

When you set limits with people who do not regard constraints, it is frequently complicated. Indeed, many people don't like it when we present our arguments and viewpoints, and may snap at us or simply withdraw from connecting with us. However, this does not mean you need to treat people gently always because they don't appreciate your border. You should not refrain from reality, because those who enjoy the truth will quickly want to associate with you. It is essential to be liked by people who understand the fact than to be disliked by many who wish to oppress and take advantage of you.

Ask yourself the question; what if the person who hates you for your borders is your spouse? Will you then abide by no boundary guidelines just to maintain peace in your relationship? Or will you just endure his wrong sides and let him breach your borders and still abandon you. If you hesitate to the survival of your relationship and keep allowing your partner to maltreat you, then you might not have the guts to set the boundaries. It is ideal to discover the hidden character of your partner and solve all fundamental problems instead of preventing the problem.

You will likely get hurt from setting borders; however, your relationship will likely end up being deeper.

Misconception #5: When I Set Limits I Might Injure Others

You may end up frustrating other people occasionally when you set boundaries, particularly when you value the happiness of such people. Some of the cases where you might hurt people when you set a limit to consist of:

- When a friend desires to borrow your car when you need it
- People might call you for a social gathering preparation, which is when you are physically down, or
- When a relative enters into a difficult financial situation; however, you can't loan him the specific quantity because you have some monetary responsibilities to care for.

Depending on how you see boundaries, you might harm or might not injure others. However, nothing can be much better than knowing the truth, and the truth is that setting borders around your treasures is the only way you can safeguard them from being taken, ruined, or trampled with. When you set boundaries for the wrong function or motive, then you might hurt the ideal people. Still, you need to remember that saying No for the best reason will not cause injury to other people, although it might trigger discomfort, and they need to look elsewhere for the same favor.

It is not your responsibility to meet the requirements of everyone; though you must do everything possible to help others achieve their goals (however not at the hindrance of your happiness). You should help others quickly when you have the resources to do so, and even when somebody dares to have a problem. You might have other more significant issues to compete with, for this reason; you need to try to fix the most critical problems in your own life before thinking about meeting the needs of others. Sometimes you might be the one who gets declined; hence, you need to develop some supportive relationships where you do not enslave yourself because of others.

Misconception #6: Boundaries Might Become Difficult to Accept

Some people hesitate to establish boundaries because of the bad experiences they had in the past regarding previous borders that were set for them. Obtaining to accept the limits set by others can be unpleasant. Given that nobody likes to be declined, you need to prepare your mind for unfavorable answers you get when you cross the boundaries set by others. You may ask yourself, why is it difficult for people to accept bounds?

- During your youth, you may have been hurt by certain unsuitable limits set by people. When parents set borders around their kids, for example, the kids might feel some sense of not being wanted, and this may follow them through their adult years, and often feel unaccepted when the word "No" is said to them. The bright side is that old problems don't have to stick in your memory correctlywhen you discover to accept other people's limits.
- Individuals who were gravely injured by borders in their youth typically attempt to leave from the harmed by satisfying the same bounds against others. Setting boundaries on other people cannot allow you to impost hatred on them because they will just move away from you for the best reason. Never predict your old feelings from the boundaries set for you, for your kids, good friends, colleagues, and other people around you.
- The inability to accept limits set by others, specifically in your marital life, might tend to do with your objectives of unfaithfulness to your partner.
- If your emotional satisfaction will always depend on your spouse's being on your side at all times, then something is

not right about the relationship because you are the only one who set borders.

- Failure to accept boundaries may show somebody has problems in taking responsibility. Often, many people are accustomed to counting on people to save them from problems they deliberately induced themselves. These people believe the duties of their well-being remain in the hands of others; for this reason, they feel dejected when their recipients do not satisfy such requirements. When you learn to take responsibility for your own life, you will be positive about setting limits.

Misconception #7: Boundaries May Result in Feelings of Guilt

This is another misconception many people can't comprehend, the factor being that the sense of responsibility may become an obstacle for them in setting borders that can be advantageous. It is difficult to say No to somebody who has helped us in the past, particularly with money, effort, and time. All you need to do is show thankfulness for what has been done for you, instead of setting boundaries. Many are not comfortable taking gifts because we always think sometimes we need to pay in return. And some people do not wish to accept presents any longer because they do not want to fret about repaying in the future.

Some people do not give selflessly; however, they give for future purposes. You can discriminate between these people by the way they respond after you thank them for their gesture—Kind givers don't also wait on you to thank them because they need nothing from you. If the giver is outraged by doing you a favor, then the person sees the present as a financial investment. If your appreciation is enough, then he or she probably wants absolutely nothing in return.

The concern of thankfulness and borders should be kept different because limits must not be nullified sense of appreciation; thus, this misconception holds no weight.

Chapter 12: NLP for success

NLP Techniques

Neuro-Linguistic Programming (NLP) tells you that emotions and experiences is what guides people in their view of the world. That what you currently see is not the real world, but a distorted representation based on your beliefs, perceptions, values, and other variables. Use NLP strategies will help you build on aspects of your life and help you improve your quality and understand how people work. Discover how to use these NLP methods to improve the communication skills and emotional intelligence that you can use to control your life and mind.

The technique of anchoring in NLP is necessary to pull up a certain emotion or to place you into a certain mental state. That can also be used on yourself, or someone else. This works by integrating emotion with a physical movement and is dubbed the anchor laying. For instance, if you decided to pull the excitement feeling, then you would start by thinking about times you've been euphoric. You would like to tell the account of what went on in your head that led to this moment. Talk about how it feels and goesinto a great deal of detail. Remember the moment, the emotions.

First, keep in your right hand your left index and middle fingers. There are two squeezes you want to give them. Talk about your special moment on the second squeeze and strive to add the sensation. Describe once again how you feel, how you think, and twice click your hands. Let the warm feeling double when you click the second time. Do it five times. You could use those gestures later to regain your feeling of happiness. You could use a quick touch of the arm to secure them if you were to do this to another man.

Meta Model

The methodology of the meta-model of NLP is often used to make you understand the concerns of other individuals. It could also be used to support others better understand their issues. The aim is to dismantle the discussion, help you achieve the root cause of the issue, and fix it. The response is consciously or unconsciously understood when someone has a question, but often the simplest solution is something that they do not like. The lack of uncertainty allows the crisis to persist, anticipating that there will finally be a new solution. You can help them develop a way by deconstructing the way someone explains their question.

Mirroring

One of the most relevant NLP strategies you should learn is mirroring. It will be very beneficial to be good at mirroring, as it is hard to hate someone who knows how to do this act. It is the replication of the individual you interact with that individual's behaviors. Subtle and typically subconscious, this simulation is complete. Copying somebody's speech patterns, body language, vocabulary style, speed, rhythm, pitch, voice, and volume are ways that you can do this.

Framing

The technique of NLP framing is used to affect the increase or decrease of the emotional feeling significantly. It's a great way to use it, along with most of the others. You're going to experience good and bad moments in life. These should enable you in your life to be able to learn and grow. Nonetheless, memories have no feelings connected to them. Such separation is because in different parts of the brain, there exist memories and thoughts. So at present, you will experience feelings, and then you will be able to remember them. The hippocampus is the brain part that is responsible for long-term memory storage. The amygdala is the brain's portion that regulates feelings. The amygdala will give you a quick little reminder of the feelings you feel when you recall a memory from the hippocampus. Just because of that, the sensation that is important to a specific memory can be modified.

Pattern Interruption

Interruption of the pattern is often used to preserve words in a listener's subconscious mind. One great technique to pair with others is this technique. To do this, you have to draw the thoughts of the listener into a series or pattern form. When the model gets out of control, before finishing the form, you take them out of the template for a critical juncture. The unconscious mind of the listener is supposed to embody the pattern, while the conscious mind is overwhelmed at the moment. You can change the way you think, look at the past, and view your life with a new way of thinking by learning NLP. It can help to improve your communication skills and enhance your emotional intelligence. It's a way to regulate your mind, which helps you handle your life better.

Manipulation through NLP Techniques

Getting to understand NLP techniques will help you in manipulating people for a positive impact on your life.

The Eye Cues

It is necessary to calibrate your NLP eye accessing signals while communicating with someone to ensure that you perceive the signals appropriately.

Left-handed people tend to turn left and right, but note that they don't depend on their left/right-handed choice.

When eyes move to the right side, it means Visual Construction (VC) - The person is taking a picture about something they have not seen. While there may be some aspects of the image from memory, other elements are being created (envisioned).

When the eyes move up and to the left means Visual Remembered (VR) - Here the person is recalling an image of anything.

When the eyes move on the right, there is Auditory Constructed (AC) - Here, the person imagines something they've never seen before. This is likely, in my opinion, the least experienced access cue.

When the eyes move on the left means there is Auditory Recalled (AR) - Here, a sound from memory is recalled by the user.

When the eyes move down or right, Kinesthetic (K) means that the consumer relies on an internal emotion. When the eyes move down and left Auditory Digital (AD) means in their ear, the client listens to the conversations going on from the inside.

When you have mastered the list for processing NLP eye signals, the best thing is to look at people for some time to see if their facial expressions make any sense to you.

For example, when people keep speaking about their new ride and how to flash it was, they kept glancing up and left, implying that they were taking photos. Does this seem highly likely to be so?

But just be vigilant with your assumptions: If a right-handed individual says they have submitted a letter to you, but their eyes go up and left, most people would assume they're lying. You can't know for sure, of course, without measuring. All this knowledge informs you (guessing you know by gazing up and left they recall visual recollections) is they're creating an illustration. We can make up a picture of them uploading the letter or imagine anything completely different. They may not have published the letter by themselves or imagine the message being published.

In this case, an easy way to configure might be to ask what you believe they will understand and see whether or not their eyes are heading the same way. And note that this has to be done slowly and informs you only if the picture was remembered or created.

It takes a while to start noticing these often subtle signals and ignore the noise when you start trying to watch NLP eye accessing signals. When projecting the image with a much more visible look, the eyes of many people can move very quickly to reach a memory. For example, when you ask someone to remember their tenth birthday, they'll certainly look up and on the left side quickly, look at a point on their timeline and see the picture there.

Such accesses sometimes occur in pairs, and the logic of what someone has to do to answer the question is worth considering. For example, what is likely to be the eye movement when you ask somebody to reflect about a moment when they feel at ease?

Will the individual react by looking down and to the right to the feeling (K)?

Or are they trying to imagine the location they felt the ease (VR)?

The response is they're going to do both, almost certainly. They will probably reach the emotion, then just go back to their memories, searching for and imagining the corresponding moment.

Also, importantly, if you begin to ask intelligent questions about the images and sounds that they make as they think, you will finally find somebody who will pledge falsely that they are not making any images in their minds.

You may find that their eyes move exactly as you would be expecting when you ask them the important questions. You may be concerned about what that means.

Okay, first of all, you should note that they are not lying-they are just dealing with what they're aware of, but they are forming mental images.

Anchoring

While using the anchoring technique; the concept is simple, you should get a client or consumer into a particular mental condition, and establish a relationship with it so that the condition can be re-activated at will.

In this post, we're going to deal with the more delicate NLP anchoring strategies you can do in a corporate environment, instead of the type of anchoring that is often used with NLP customers in which you can create a very strong state and continue reaching it purely because the client is happy to follow your instructions.

There are four skills needed in a covert method of anchoring:

- Connect a powerful union
- Recognize when and how to set the anchors
- Anchor the state as precisely as possible
- Fire the anchor if necessary
- Connecting to a powerful union

First, determining which state is being anchored is critical.

When you try to sell, probably you would like your customer to be in a desirable buying state. The easiest method of accessing a system is to make the customer identify when they were in that position: "Do you remember a time when you first saw something and decided you had to have it?" "Have you ever seen something did an impulse buying?" These kinds of questions pressure the customer to remember a time that suits the state and to activate it.

This is important for the effectiveness of your NLP anchoring strategies. Other strong states that you might want to have connections with also include anger about your competitors, transparency, and obstinacy if you have come to see a friend who wants to ignore them.

Setting the NLP Anchor

Some NLP anchor strategies work by having the consumer access some of their memories. The ideal time to anchor the system is to reach the memory-connected state. So have a close look at the eyes and watch every small motion of the body. When they simply fall off or even calm or even become sensitive and enthusiastic in some situations, this will be the time to start putting the anchor.

Chapter 13: When the Opponent Is a Manipulator

If the negotiating partner is a genius of communication, then it is best to find a way to make him or her replaced with a less talented one. Of course, this is possible in the sense that this person is not the decision-maker.

You can discredit. You can look for the possibility of transferring such a fellow to another project—preferably in another city. You can find him other life concerns.

Another good way is to find someone who can influence him. Now, I will write in more detail.

Golden Key

Someone is influencing each of us. Sometimes, someone's opinion is important; sometimes, the attitude; sometimes, the wishes—head, wife, lover, friend, a famous magazine, public opinion in the person of "Aunt Tasha," the cleaning lady.

If you can figure out people whose opinion is important for your future interlocutor, consider that you have already practically prepared the ground for negotiations—unless, of course, you can influence them.

And when they tell him about ten times from different sources how wonderful you are, how good it is to deal with you, how important it is to listen to your opinion and go towards you, you just have to appear and voice your proposal.

Become a Mythical Person

Experienced negotiators collect all available information about the other side. So make sure that all available information about you plays on you. Rumors, gossip, stories, legends—create a myth about you! And make it available to the masses. Plus, the reputation, of course, has not been canceled.

Let your opponents get conflicting, sometimes erroneous, mysterious information about you. Or they just gain the belief that you need to be friends, you need to be taken care of, cared for, and cherished.

Arouse Emotions

If you control emotions in a conversation, you control enough. You may have gaps in the argument and stretch in the logic. You may not have any normal rationale at all. If only it depended on you what the interlocutor will experience.

The ability to arouse interest, delight, joy, pleasure, curiosity, attraction, fear, doubt, insecurity, anger, disgust—this is all that is necessary for success in negotiations. If it is, the rest will follow.

If the interlocutor does not see the logic in your words, but he likes your ideas, he will come up with the logic himself. If the opponent does not agree with your arguments, but at the same time feels sadness and regret, he will be able to convince himself. Control your emotions, and you will succeed.

The State of the Interlocutor

It became clear that the creators were sitting here in the morning—in their eyes smoldered the light of the indescribable stupidity that the brain always emanates, exhausted by hours of brainstorming.
—Anonymous.

It can also be influenced. Directly and indirectly. If you think of negotiations for your interlocutor's deadline, and he just doesn't physically have time to look for other options, his condition is good for you. Especially if you manage to pull the time politely. If this morning he was "accidentally" poured with mud over his car, he will not be very comfortable. If during a meeting with you they called him and told him the good news, he will be more generous. If he holds a cup of roasting coffee poured to the top, part of his attention will be riveted to her.

Biorhythms, state of health, "random" meetings, background music, lack of sleep, day of the week—all this and much more affects the physical and psychological state of the interlocutor. And if you competently think about how to use all this, you can "make" even the best negotiator.

Pain Points, Weaknesses, Fears, Doubts

"Sir," a student asked, thinking, "How did you find out that she loves nuggets so much?"

"Learn to use the Internet, Daria," I explained. A fool in the "interests" is everywhere written in plain text.

Any friends of his, old and new, information about the psychotype, observation of behavior and reactions—any strength has a dual weakness, so even laudatory reviews will tell you a lot. Just collect the information. We analyze. We are looking for optimal methods of exposure—because it would be wrong to use this information head-on. Only leave as a last resort.

Play on Weaknesses

Regrettably, the vast majority of people are cars. In the sense that they live quite mechanically. There is a stimulus—there will be a reaction. Press the button—you get the result. Already on this alone, you can build a huge number of effective manipulations.

Now, it is important for us that when you click on some buttons, people completely automatically give out stormy experiences. It is necessary to shout at someone, threaten another, praise the third, admire the fourth, show the fifth to the sixth, show the "sex-friendly" object, take the seventh away—of course, different things affect different people. Therefore, if the interlocutor did not give a significant reaction to one provocation, you need to move on to another.

To do this, you need to know the list of basic human weaknesses. For example, I offer these:

- Superiority
- Greed
- Pity
- Sex
- Patriotism
- Masculinity
- Femininity
- Fear
- Wine
- Generosity
- Envy
- Jealousy
- Justice
- "Weak?"

Over time, you will learn to determine by eye what this or that person will do. In the meantime, you can just do a bust. Or even switch to another way to set your interlocutor off balance for your antics to work.

We Are Not Robots; Robots Are Not We

Information collection is standard. We are looking for patterns in the spirit of, "In the situation 'X,' he acts 'U.'" Accordingly, we can provoke the "U" we need by creating the corresponding "X." For example, when they praise his car, he blurs with a happy smile. Clearly, what needs to be done to make him smile? If he agrees only to the third proposal, the first two cannot be soared. And the third is to make it profitable for us.

On the other hand, if we know what external signs are responsible for what internal reaction, we actually "read the thoughts" of the interlocutor—which is convenient. Look for patterns!

Territory Development

They say that Special Forces differ from ordinary well-physically and psychologically trained troops in only one: the completeness and quality of information about the enemy and the place of the future massacre. Under this information, a model of the future theater of operations is built. Then tactical combat schemes are planned and practiced to be automatic. Therefore, special forces and can destroy many times superior enemy, and even on its territory.

If the information is false, the Special Forces are doomed. And no hand-to-hand combat with mark shooting helps them—foreign territory.

The funny thing is that many people go to important "meetings" with them, not even having mastered their own territory. What really does fit into any framework, you should still propose to master it.

The Best Alternative to Negotiations

If negotiations fail, what will happen to you? Where are you going to go? Who to contact? A simple fact: if the alternatives you have are the sea, you are calm, like a boa constrictor, easily take risks, and can play on the verge of a foul. And the attitude arises—that same game. If you have a rich choice, you will not put up with the inconvenience. If there is no choice, you will have to come to terms. If you have nothing to fear, you will not use harsh and ugly methods. People pressed against the wall are capable of any meanness.

Look for alternatives! Expand your selection! Explore the market. Offer to many. And when the price of defeat falls, there will be significantly more victories.

Let the Walls Help You

"Maybe I should not go to the palace?"

- How to walk! Sorrel raised his voice. "I will need a henchman."

- A henchman?

- Well, yes. One who listens to me—errs, cast spells—and admires them: the very first degree of apprenticeship.

It is good when it depends on us where we will meet with the interlocutor! After all, we can make everything play for us. Or a lot. The ideal situation is when the territory is fully developed by you but is not familiar to him at all. Then you have almost won.

If everyone around you shows honor, the interlocutor inevitably imbues with respect. If the music helps to create the right mood sounds, it's also good. If it depends on you what will be served on the table, you have an advantage. If everything that happens does involuntarily distract his attention, and you are used to it, everything is just wonderful.

The appearance and disappearance of certain people. Calls to mobile, Shine, Music, and Furniture. Create an atmosphere! And do not forget about your own convenience. Let your acquaintance psychologist sit next door—he will tell you how to behave and point out mistakes. Let convenient access to the Internet be nearby if you need quick reference information. Let your friend be here, next to whom you will be "knee-deep in the sea of affairs." The territory is a creative affair.

Who Is Around?

If your support group is around, with an approving hum that meets all your remarks and is ready to boo any creep in your direction, the opponent will be hard.

Anyway, no matter who is nearby, it is sometimes more useful to influence the interlocutor through the audience. Very often, speakers do not turn to the opponent, who will object anyway, but to the public, which will support it sooner. Let your words and actions look beautiful. Attractive. And well, if he himself will be shy of his actions. Witnesses determine!

Therefore, by the way, it can be useful to invite rude negotiators with their wives—for a dinner party, for example. And then, they automatically lose all the advantages of the usual style of communication—against the background of a man who, in theory, should have played on his side.

Leeway

Everything is clear here: we create the maximum margin of time for ourselves and adjust to the minimum margin for the other side. Then we are calm, and time plays on us. And the opponent twitches. Because time is playing against him.

Where Is the World Heading?

Where are oil prices moving? What is the situation with the labor market? Where does the political course go? What major competitors will enter the market soon? And if you know what market is, political, cultural, etc. situations will play on you at some point, you can guess.

Chapter 14: Creating Strategies for Manipulation

Steps 1 - Define Your Goal(s)

This is the objective of your deception technique. Without an objective, you run the risk of pointlessly manipulating people. One important consideration for your goals is to decide if they are something you really want to accomplish. There is no point in saying that your goal is to rule the world if you are not willing to make an effort; who wants that kind of power, anyway?

It is also better to define goals to which there is already a clear path. Take the target and break it down. The first thing you mightneed is management expertise.

Career success is not the only type of goal for which this methodology works.

You could set the goal of carving a niche at work that gives you more free time and allows you to work with less stress. You could set the goal of seeking a caring partner. It doesn't matter the target itself, as long as you really want it.

Don't forget to set a date for your goal as well. Now take note of all your goals, long-term and short-term, large and small, and order them right away.

Remember your targets every single day. You do this by concentrating your attention on a mission. Think of a time when you reached a high level of achievement at work, school, or college. Think about what it takes to do something that makes you proud of yourself. Was it just a modest number of hours, or did it include going the extra mile? Were you dreaming about the project night and day, running it through your brain until you went to sleep and structuring it in your mind? Of course, you were. That is exactly what made the difference.

Through concentrating your attention on a mission, you have devoted all your energy to a high level of achievement. The more attention you have paid to deception, the more you are going to be able to gain and the more likely you are to succeed. Of course, it is also best if you keep all of your ambitions a secret for now.

Step 2 - Chart the Paths to Success

Now that you have the targets, and you have planned how to achieve them, it is pretty easy to find a path to success. If your goal is promotion, you are going to need a manager to support you. If your goal is to find a loving partner, you are going to have to find someone suitable and convince them to get married.

Consider alternative paths to success as well. If you want to take the position of your supervisor, there might be a way for them to get fired or they could be hired in another position, leaving a vacancy open for you.

Map as many directions as you can and find all the options for now.

Once you have done this, it is time to set up the parties involved. Who would be in charge of the decision-making process of your promotion? Who are the potential contenders? How is the information flowing between these people?

In the case of promotion, your strategy of manipulation should be to ensure that the people who have the power to promote you and your brand will want to do so. Did you see the movie Inception? Unfortunately, it is not an option to actually hack into someone's dreams. You need to start understanding their goals and behavior to manipulate your target.

Step 3 - Collect enough Information

Consider the objectives of the people you need to influence—those who will decide whether or not you will be promoted. Note down all their activities from now on, and as much of their previous behavior as possible. Look for patterns and try to relate each of their actions to what you see as their goals. Then look for ways they don't align and reassess their goals to see what matches.

Get to know all the parties involved, including those who have the power to promote you, your competitors, and anyone on the trajectory of your path to success. Include their goals in your notes, record their actions, spot patterns and link them to their goals. Keep the notes organized with all this information and hide it from everyone.

The goal here is to give your brain as much information as possible. Only visualize the brain as a tool again. It has the greatest chance of producing the right outcomes (actions) if it has access to the best inputs (information) and the more you can logically arrange this information, the easier it will be to make smart decisions rather than irrational instinct-based decisions.

After a while, say a few days, you need to start building a picture. Take a little more time if you feel like you need it. Nonetheless, you don't need to have a complete understanding of the situation to begin the next stage of gathering information, which is to recognize the key figures amongst those you are observing. These may well be the ones who have the power to promote you.

You will continue to gather information indefinitely, even as you begin to manipulate others. Make it a habit, and you will improve your speed and accuracy in identifying the expectations and behavioral patterns of others.

Focus on understanding where the power lies, how the parties involved make their decisions, and try to identify what causes them to take action. Please relate this back to your own goals.

Step 4 - Identify Opportunities and Threats

This is where the time has come to use your brain. Every day, you will talk about your ambitions and develop a deeper understanding of the dynamics of your scenario.

Opportunities

Remember the goal you set yourself. So note that your main goal is to want the people in charge of your appointment to support you. What did you learn about their goals? Consider a standard example to be that they want to achieve good numbers—they want to improve the efficiency of your company by increasing their profits.

Relate what you learned about the parties in the scope of your goals back to the paths you mapped out. Begin using that information to determine the likelihood of success in each scenario. Is it more likely that your current team leader is going to be fired or promoted? Weigh up the options against each other.

Suppose you have a reason to believe that your current team leader is under-performing, and you want them to be terminated rather than promoted in their line of duty. In this instance, you need to be careful about timing. The right opportunity will present itself, and when it happens, you need to be in pole position.

Influence

As a candidate in pole position, you are considered to have the most power to help the potential new supervisors (those who would appoint you) achieve their goals. You have even learned that your current boss, the team leader, is facing the sack. This is almost definitely because they are considered to lack the power to help their direct subordinates accomplish their goals. They haven't been sacked yet, though, and this could be for many reasons. They may not have had enough opportunity to prove themselves, or their bosses may not be convinced that you are the best substitute.

Persuasion

Forget going to those with the power to promote you and giving an epic speech about why you are the perfect candidate to be the next team leader. This is not a Hollywood movie. More to the point, the universe is not just going to bend to your request if you ask for it.

Deception

What you can do is act to control the flow of information that hits the subordinates of your employer. The goal, in this case, is to lower their opinion of the authority of your boss and get your boss fired quicker.

The ways you could do this are too many to count. How close are you to the people you need to influence?

Just consider, who do they listen to? Possibly someone on their team. Maybe someone who you are observing. Now you have the opportunity, far enough from yourself, to indirectly influence people directly above your boss.

To recap, this applies to someone approximately your age, working for a team at the same level as your own, who depends on the actions of your colleagues. Immediately begin profiling this individual, their goals and actions.

Bear in mind that this is a hypothetical example, but it gives you an idea of the kind of person you might be able to influence. You will have to analyze your own situation and develop a strategy based on these ideas.

Remember that so much of what is involved in successful manipulation is choosing who to control. You are likely to exploit everyone at some point, to some degree. Right now, you are formulating a plan to exploit a specific situation by exceptional means.

Threats

A potential hazard is that the manager can regain his prestige (perceived power) and escape the danger zone. Remember, anything that may help to interrupt your path to success is a potential threat.

Always look for threats and use the same principles to avert them. Also, act in secrecy to reduce the power of any faction that tries to undermine your plans.

Step 5 - Take Action

Setting the threat aside, refocus on the current example. There, an excuse has emerged to establish a deception. It may well be the case that you have a close relationship with the designated person to facilitate the flow material, in which case it may be possible to conspire. If your manager is truly useless, your task team is genuinely focused on improving the performance of your staff, and your objective is to see this happen, you may potentially agree to work together to promote any knowledge that will damage the reputation of your manager.

You have admitted to another human that you want to conspire. This will affect your reputation and your trustworthiness.

Your partner may change their mind, in which case you will have sabotaged your opportunity to trick them by disclosing your ambitions.

Your partner may change the plan to meet their own goals and undermine your strategy.

For deceit, you are just running the risk of being found out yourself, and it is quite easy to try and lie, which you can reasonably deny if necessary.

For the purposes of this example, say that you are on friendly terms with this person and that you can eat lunch or have coffee with them approximately once a week. Show active interest by asking questions. Add in questions about their job with a natural, personal interest in the subject. Try to focus on pursuing lines of conversation that they are willing to talk about. There is a good chance that this will be related to their interests, which will be linked to their objectives.

Chapter 15: Self-Confidence and Self-Love

Self-confidence is a very important skill, and it gives you the ability to judge your own personal and social standing by your environment and also gain great satisfaction out of it.

Many factors influence self-confidence such as work environment, upbringing, as well as the drive or the level of commitment and enthusiasm towards pursuing a cause. Self-confidence is an essential element in developing and improving business ties as well as your personal life.

Just like the popular saying reminds us, as you begin the journey of your professional life, always have high confidence in the abilities you possess because you have yet to prove your abilities.

This saying has been in circulation as far back as the evolution of modern human society, yet the context couldn't be more accurate than it is today. More so than ever, in the present times that we live in, which are very competitive, self-confidence becomes a great asset, a source of strength, as well as self-sustenance for us.

But first, let's talk about self-confidence, why we need it, and how important it is in our lives.

Why Do We Need Confidence?

Knowing your strength and being confident about it can help you draw in courage and firm determination when things get difficult in life.

Self-confidence helps provide perspective and gives you the courage to carry on when everyone else might view the road ahead or the task at hand to be almost impossible to carry out in the required time.

People who are confident have the ability to see and recognize what their limitations are and understand how to make up for their limitations with strength and resolve.

All that said, what you should understand is that self-confidence basically depends on your ability to handle actions, so let's talk briefly about the actions that can help in developing self-confidence.

1. **Self-confidence Shows True Acceptance and Self-love**

People with low self-confidence will mostly rely on the acknowledgment of others to make them feel important or get a sense of pride in themselves.

Self-confident people don't need to get anybody's approval before they feel happy or proud of whom they are. Self-confidence will help you realize or develop an attitude that no matter what challenges you face, or how difficult things get, you have promised yourself that you will always be there for yourself. It is like an unconditional acceptance of who you are.

2. Self-confidence and Positivism

Negativity or a negative mental attitude is toxic to both the physical and emotional well-being of the body. It can also affect the people around us and lead to us pushing them away.

Nobody likes to hang around someone who always blames others for their own mistakes yet will never see their error, or ways to improve.

Self-confident people are typically optimists because they are very confident in themselves, their skills, and their abilities because they think positively and are not easily thrown off-track. They are confident about their course and are sure of succeeding, therefore they don't allow anything to hinder them or worry about negativity.

3. Self-confidence Shows Maturity

When we pay too much attention and get too engrossed in the opinions of other people, we hinder our own path to happiness. When we start caring more about what we want and what we think and let our opinions and decision guide us, then we can enjoy life better in ways we planned to, or the way we want to live it.

One of the major signs of adolescent age is interest and expectations. According to the American Academy of Child and Adolescent Psychiatry (AACAP), adolescents usually appear sad, tearful, and mostly irritable, and there is a decrease in activities they used to be interested in.

They become very sensitive to how people feel about or perceive them.

Self-confident people are usually more emotionally mature, and people who are emotionally mature are mentally healthy, make better rational decisions, are well attuned, and display a highly positive mental attitude towards themselves, their work, and other people around them.

Actions That Help Develop Self-Confidence

Self-confidence does better in an environment where you receive constructive feedback, while the focus always remains on the positive.

As a confident person working in such an environment, you will be able to practice your skills and abilities far and above expectations. Meaning, you will be opportune to set goals, move beyond past mistakes, and learn new and exciting things.

Meanwhile, an environment where the expectations are impractical and you are always in comparison with others can gravely impede your self-confidence. When people are set as rivals to go against each other according to their performance in the game of numbers, self-confidence is harder to find.

Such circumstances can force you to develop or nurture a competitive mentality that is rather unhealthy. By making use of unjust and iniquitous means to achieve success, you could become ruthless in judging your self-performance, taking after unworthy people as role models, and even underestimating or doubting your capabilities.

Such an atmosphere will create a workplace that is basically unhealthy due to the stress and pressure to outdo someone else's performance, instead of combining your energy as a team and work together while you help and assist each other to succeed. Some organizations actually do practice such a method of pitting staff against each other and it works well. However, it peaks for some time, but most assuredly crashes.

High Self-Confidence

The approach people with high self-confidence employ to tackle problems is usually different from that of other people. They perceptually understand that building relationships is important and therefore, they have a knack for meeting new people, making new friends, and they get to share ideas and learn new things. This quality that they possess is one of the main reasons that they are so likable. Additionally, these highly self-confident people are always prepared to engage in conversations that highlight and grant mutual respect and equal importance to everyone that participated in it.

Another point about people who have high self-confidence is that they are fond of expressing what they think, as well as their ideas in the presence of others. This is because they are secure emotionally to the point that they can easily handle constructive criticism and rebuff the emotional ones. Meanwhile, that is not to say they are arrogant–quite the opposite, they are open and they present everyone with the opportunity to air their views. Nonetheless, they are courageous enough to hold on to their decisions against all the antagonism to their ideas, especially when they believe and are convinced that they are doing the right thing or are on the right track.

Once you have made a decision and it is set in motion, there are two possible outcomes, which are that you have either made the right decision (success) or you made the wrong one (failure). But what distinguishes confident people from others is that when they succeed, they don't throw it in the faces of all those detractors.

Also, highly self-confident people are humble enough to admit to their mistakes and use that opportunity to learn from their failures. They have an objective mindset and approach with regards to both failure and success. That characteristic makes people with self-confidence respectable as well as lovable.

Low Self-Confidence

People who have low self-confidence have an awfully harsh and judgmental view of themselves, which when compared to the highly self-confident people means they are separated by a very wide gap.

People with low self-confidence are susceptible to making emotional decisions instead of thinking rationally. They are more of the "let me stay in my corner" type in place of meeting new people, making new friends, and sharing new ideas. They avoid meeting new people or having company.

People with low-confidence are inclined to feel that they have nothing new, constructive, or consequential to contribute to any process. All these feelings combined with low self-worth and the total denial or avoidance of accepting changes make people with low self-confidence very prone to be undervalued and mistreated.

People with low self-confidence are mostly hesitant to share their views, thoughts, and opinions about things because they think they might be publicly mocked for their views. Naturally, it meanstheir past interactions and experiences with others have little to no impact in enhancing their self-value and self-confidence in any way, therefore their views remain the same about their importance and productivity.

Like we mentioned earlier about the productive environment, this is where it comes into play. Everyone is bound to learn from their environment. The kind of people you meet and the type/quality of discussions you engage in with them directly affect and influence your self-confidence. On one hand, people who are very self-confident mix and interact with others and learn from those from who they can learn from. On the other hand, low confident people believe they can't be who they are and that they will remain undervalued no matter what they try.

The Effects of Low Self-Confidence

People need role models who they can look up to and idolize as a compass to guide themselves and measure their own talents and skills, achievements, as well as compare their progress to to help them constantly improve themselves. That is exactly how people who are self-confident behave.

High self-confident people choose to interact with others, and in that process, they share their views publicly to gain new perspectives; they keep improving on their skills, and they expand their knowledge constantly.

When people stop doing exactly that, what happens then? Well, without an anchor in their lives to hold them and stabilize them when they are drifting away, and without a model to tether on, they begin to lose focus. Without interaction with society, people will become extremely self-centered and only think about what concerns them, and it will be even more evident in how they take criticism. Everything will appear personal, and even when constructive criticism is aired about their work, it will be assumed to be a personal attack.

The effect of low self-confidence will make people with such personalities think that they are less talented with inferior skills and abilities to handle and complete any assigned task. They feel unworthy to receive compliments and be appreciated. It gets even worse when honest compliments are given for their efforts—it becomes a surprise or shock to them; hence they tag it as false, pretentious, or fake appreciation.

Chapter 16: Victims of the Narcissist

You have finally found someone that appears to be not just wonderful, but amazing. The first couple of months are nothing short of magical. You have a seemingly perfect relationship. Of course, there are a couple of bumps here and there that appear to be red flags; however, you let it go, as to whom in the world doesn't have a bad day. You don't believe that they intend to be so mean. Aside from that, they apologized. However, it appears that you have been the one doing most of the apologizing.

It is difficult for you to pick out what it is you did wrong; nevertheless, you apologize anyway since that's easier. They tell you that you activate their moodiness, but they never let you know exactly what it is you did not do, nor do they tell you why it had them so upset. You notice that they appear to be quite secretive about a lot of things.

Before you know it, things escalate. They get furious for no discernible reason, and you two break up. You ask for another chance, or they might beg you. The relationship is back on, and then it all begins all over again. This individual is an emotional parasite. This is the sort of person who takes advantage of the kindness you have and hopes to exploit it in the worst way. You know deep down that this person is not for you, but it is difficult to leave, as you feel the desire to stick with someone that has previously been through a lot.

The truth is, none of this is your fault at all as narcissists are best at emotional predating. You have likely heard of Narcissistic Personality Disorder; however, the truth is an individual does not have to exhibit the full traits of Narcissistic Personality Disorder to have the traits of narcissism. These types of people are dangerous to be around. It might even seem that you did not get involved with them; they more likely got tangled up with you. Onemoment you are flirting with a person you believe is excellent andthe next thing you know you are involved in an extraordinarily committed and intense relationship, with no way of discerning how exactly it happened.

This is because narcissists are known to be survival masters. It is almost as if they can sense and identify people that are more likely to fall prey to the side of them that is charismatic. They are also able to sense people that are likely to hang on and ensure that they are taken care of especially after they have revealed their true repulsive selves. This is where knowing how to handle a narcissist will help you to eradicate their existence from your space.

The question is, how do you identify the signs associated with Narcissistic Personality Disorder? If you are able to recognize the characteristics listed below in yourself, it could be that you have a higher likelihood of being besieged by a narcissist.

The truth is: "There Is Something in Your Possession That Narcissists Want: Power, Money, Lifestyle, and Position."

When it comes to a relationship that a narcissist is tangled in, there is usually an inimitable dynamic in play. It always begins with a catch, a dream perhaps. It is often one that you believe is about you; however, it is solely controlled by the narcissist.

There are times when the narcissist might appear to be helpful, only for things not to work out, and they flip the script on you. The moment you catch on to their tricks or attempt to make them accountable is when tension escalates. Having learned that, below are the kinds of individuals narcissists love to prey on:

Conscientious people

One of the most noteworthy qualities that narcissist search for is the capability of being conscientious. Conscientious individuals are preoccupied with the well-being of others, and they are likely to see through any obligations they have to others. Considering decisions are made using their morality, they are more likely to accept as true that the narcissist operates on their own moral compass. This causes them to believe that the narcissist will see through their obligations as well. Narcissists understand that when their targets are sufficiently conscientious to concern themselves with the well-being of other individuals, they are able to take advantage of that quality for their own selfish purposes.

Malicious predators understand that a conscientious individual is bound to believe them, even if they appear unsure and are more likely to give them another chance. They also know that these conscientious individuals care about the needs of the narcissist, even if it is at their expense. This type of caretaking, narcissists recognize, is linked to the responsibility that is created by a romantic relationship. This causes them to trust that these individuals will go out of their way to fulfill their obligations to them.

People with Empathy

For a narcissist, having a target that is empathetic can never be understated. A narcissist can't receive a steady dose of resources, attention, praise, and more from any individual that lacks empathy. While narcissists lack empathy themselves, they search for targets that have a hefty dose of empathy. Narcissists use an empathetic individual as emotional fuel to make themselves feel in control and powerful. If they do not get this emotional fuel, they begin to starve and search for a new source.

This trait is used to take power away from victims in a cycle of abuse. Narcissists count on the fact that you can see their side or their view, even if they are abusing you. This is what keeps the abuse cycle going. An extremely empathetic individual is an ideal candidate to listen to their pity ploy of abusive events.

Narcissists believe that once they provide a fake apology or a sob story, the abuse can be erased. This is because they understand that you, being an empathetic individual, will rationalize their conduct and make justifications for them. They depend on you being able not only to forgive but empathize with them, especially after the terrible events of mistreatment. When they appeal to your empathetic side, they can evade being held accountable for their behavior, every single time.

Empathetic individuals tend to rethink their decision to have the narcissist held accountable, as they feel an inordinate amount of culpability the moment the narcissist is being punished. What they do instead is to be compelled to try to protect the narcissist rather than have them deal with the consequences of their true self being exposed.

People with Integrity

An individual who keeps their promises can be a desirable proposition to a narcissist. People like that have a host of characteristics that narcissists believe they can selfishly exploit. This is because it is not like an individual with integrity to cheat in a relationship preemptively.

Narcissists tend to feel almost no regret for causing their victims harm, however, their victims, due to their morals, feel apprehensive when it comes to retaliating or relieving themselves of the obligation or making a conscious effort to betray the relationship. It is this integrity that offers them a benefit when in a relationship with like-minded, empathetic individuals that becomes ammunition for the narcissist. It is what they use to destroy any iota of trust they have in the world.

People with Resilience

Being resilient is being able to recover from an abusive event. This is something that strengthens the emotional bond of a victim with the narcissist. Individuals like child abuse survivors are known to be resilient, and they have provided an infinite source of victims for narcissists as they are capable of withstanding quite a lot of pain. While this is a beautiful trait to have in life when it comes to confronting everyday adversity, in an abuse cycle, that resilience becomes a weapon wielded by the narcissist to ensure that their victim remains ensnared in their world.

Afterward, highly resilient individuals are not likely to pack up after abusive events, even though they might have an increased ability to recognize abusive threats. They usually choose to ignore any instincts they have and instead fight to save the relationship. This stance causes them to adopt a fighter or savior mentality while they attempt to save an extremely unsustainablerelationship. They might even choose to measure the love they have by how much cruelty they can withstand. This could also be down to the type of trauma bond they have developed with the abusive and toxic person.

Extremely Sentimental People

An individual who is not only sentimental but loves deeply is one that appeals to a narcissist, as they can use excessive praise and flattery to groom their victim. This is done to appeal to the individual's desires and needs easily. Narcissists choose to idealize their targets very early in the relationship, and this enables them to use their target's need for love to gain their trust. Narcissists love to create memories that are happy early on, as they know those memories will be romanticized and used for comfort during the relationship's abusive periods.

A narcissist enjoys messing with their target's emotions. What they do is to intensely mirror the emotions their targets show before they start to withdraw. This is done to create a faux soulmate effect that leaves their targets drained and addicted. Empathetic and sentimental individuals are the perfect candidates for narcissists to manipulate, as they have to exploit the target's need for a proper relationship.

People Who Were Raised in Dysfunctional Environments

It is important to note that one's previous experience can make it quite challenging to recognize boundary violations the moment they happen. This can cause you to disregard your instincts when your trust is violated. Narcissists do not like limits. If you are unable to set them or keep them, this is a weakness that a narcissist can exploit to their benefit. There are times when narcissists will act like heroes; however, instead of encouraging empowerment or independence, they use that as a means to builddependency.

People with a Frantic Need to Be Loved and Are Lonely

A narcissist lives by the motto; look for a need and fill it. An individual that has low self-confidence can be controlled easier than someone that is extremely confident. Initially, the intensity will feel great as it is confused for passion; however, a narcissist is unable to be transparent. The initial intensity begins to wane, revealing a cold and calculating disposition that makes you wonder what you did wrong and how you could locate the loving individual that you met at the beginning of the relationship.

People Who Accept Blame Willingly

As the relationship begins to wane, narcissists begin to guilt-trip you and claim that you are the delinquent one in the relationship.

Sensitive and empathetic individuals are very vulnerable to blame due to their naturally reflective disposition. When a narcissist redirects your attention to something you seemingly did wrong, they divert attention from their own unhealthy behavior.

Chapter 17: What Is Covert Emotional Manipulation

How Will a Manipulator Target?

Human beings have various personality traits and types such as warm, passionate, adventurous, loyal and dependable, idealistic, analytical, fun-loving personalities, and many others. Our personality traits are greatly influenced by the biochemical processes ongoing in our bodies. These processes affect how we behave at a given time, making some persons have unpredictable natures and sudden mood swings. Despite all these inconsistencies of the human characters and lives, you still need to learn ways to manipulate and persuade people to get what you want from them.

There are various ways of manipulating a person through persuasion, but you can persuade and influence using your body language and manners of speech respectively. Let us look at some ways to manage and control people like:

Polishing and Improving Your Manipulation Strategies

You can clean your skills for effective manipulation of others through mastering the art of public speaking, theatrical displays, creating parallels and correspondences, exhibiting charismatic traits by displaying self-confidence, and learning from the experts.

Applying Various Methods of Manipulation

Getting what you want, will not be possible if you do not know how to use some techniques of manipulating people like using rationality and logic to present your requests to a person, you can even act like a scapegoat and the victim in dangerous situations. These tactics will subconsciously compel your target to give you what you desire without any restraint. Another way to get what you want from a person is by using a bribing pattern like offering a person something in exchange for what you want from him or her.

Using Manipulation Techniques on Your Friends and Acquaintances

Your friends and acquaintances are the best persons to manipulate to get whatever you want. This is because they must have known you and your personality traits and probably despite your faults will continue to stick to you no matter what happens. To achieve this, you will play on their emotions because your friends should have feelings for you, and most importantly, they commit to help you and make you happy or comfortable if it is in their power to do it. Play on their conscience by reminding them how you have been helpful in the past, and this will motivate them to offer you whatever you desire.

Theories on Successful Manipulation

If you get caught, you will not only completely blow your chances at success in that conversation, but you could end up spoiling your reputation. People do not tend to take lightly this type of situation, as no one likes the idea of being under mind control or brainwashing. To avoid this type of disaster, you need to know how to prevent yourself from getting caught. Getting caught can potentially destroy your success at mind control, as well as any relationships you have used this strategy in. When people catch wind that you are attempting to brainwash them, or that you have effectively done so, they will no longer trust you and this mistrust will spread across your network extremely quickly. People do not appreciate being subjected to brainwashing and mind control, and so they do not want to know that someone they have grown to trust is using it on them.

Practice Regularly

The more you practice, the stronger your mind control game is going to become. You want to make sure that you practice often, preferably in every single conversation you have. Even if you don't actually want anything significant from someone, knowing how to get them to say or do certain things you want will help you practice brushing up on your technique. It could be something as easy as getting someone to touch a certain area on their body, say something in particular, or do anything else small and seemingly unimportant. The more you learn to use these techniques to get what you want, the better.

Take Your Time Expanding Your Skill

It cannot be stressed enough how important it is for you to slow down when it comes to practicing your skill. It may seem like a good idea to embrace many of these techniques at once and create a conversation that will help you get what you want, but this can lead to you being caught, quickly. When you put this type of pressure on yourself in a conversation without having any practice, you essentially infuse the conversation with a lot of unnatural and uncomfortable feeling. This is because you are not practiced at the techniques, so you are attempting to recall them and use them on the spot, and you are doing it with too many at once. People are going to see through you, and they are going to catch you in the act.

Start Small

Sometimes, starting with large goals is honorable. When it comes to learning how to use mind control and not getting caught in the process, it is actually inefficient and an excellent way to get caught, quickly. The best thing you can do is start small with things that are seemingly unimportant and irrelevant. This allows you to practice getting people to say yes or do what you want them to do, with very little pressure on the situation overall. Once you get regular results in getting your smaller goals met, you can start practicing getting larger goals met. This will give you the best opportunity to really get natural in your talent and feel confident when it comes to setting out larger goals and accomplishing them.

Be Choosy about Who You Brainwash

You must be choosy about who you brainwash. Remember, just as you have the opportunity to learn about mind control, so do others. Many people in this day and age are somewhat knowledgeable about the art of mind control. While they may not be masters of it, they may have general knowledge around some tactics such as deceit and manipulation. You must learn to identify those who are more likely to comply with your attempts and those who are more likely to be resistant to mind control.

Be Selective about Phrasing and Actions

You must be careful about the phrasing you use and the actions you carry when you are using mind control strategies. If you use the wrong phrasing, are too forceful or obvious in your phrasing, or have fidgety or otherwise uncontrolled physical movements, you are more likely to be caught. People will recognize that you have something "off" about you and will be less likely to trust you or believe you. This means that you are going to ruin your attempts and even more people will be less likely to believe you because mind control and manipulative types of reputations tend to be exposed and shared on a mass level to prevent other people from becoming manipulated. You need to be very careful in your actions and phrasing, ensuring that you are intentional and that you are behaving in a way that is not going to expose you and let others know what you are doing.

- What are some of the motivations of a manipulator?
- The key to manipulation is using the goals of others to further your own.
- When would I need to manipulate someone?

Most times, you may not get what you want in life if you are not ready to take some necessary steps in manipulating other people involved in the process. It is challenging to get what you desire if you are not exactly a careful manipulator. Therefore, you need to learn the necessary steps to use in manipulating people. These steps will surely give you an edge over others because you will know how to appeal to their conscience and mentality without being caught in the act, which may annoy them.

Let us make an analysis of these steps, which involves using body language expressions and spoken words such as:

Manipulative Looks and Stares

Manipulative looks and stares include wearing of stony faces suggesting displeasure and anger over an incident or something else, death stares used for intimidating others, sexy looks and stares intended to seduce and lure a person into sexual intimacy, maintaining eye contact with someone without saying anything, rolling of eyes, and many others.

Shouting Down on Someone or Yelling

Insidious or manipulative persons have a way of using these tactics to cow and frighten their victims. Shouting down on someone or yelling at people is a manipulative tendency aimed at making the other person or persons shut up in fear and condescend to your whims and caprices unconsciously. Mostly, bosses use this manipulative tendency or traits in the offices to suppress anger and maintain control or leadership of the firm. In some cases, the staffs are never comfortable whenever the boss is around; everybody whisks away in fear of the next reprimanding action that may happen.

Manipulations by Avoiding you at All Means

When someone avoids or ignores you, by all means, something is possibly wrong in your relationship with that person. This type of attitude manifests in so many ways such as when someone leaves a meeting when you enter, if a person does not acknowledge your presence in a place but acknowledges others, no response to your e-mails, phone calls, and messages. Moreover, if a person avoids eye contact with you, you should know that something is fishing and beware of interactions with such persons.

Preferential or Silent Treatment

One of the ways to manipulate someone to give what you want is by showing them unusual, preferred, or silent treatment. After giving them this type of attention and care, the chances are that they must succumb to your wishes and desires.

Playing on the Emotions

Master manipulators like to play on your emotions to coerce you to give them what they want from you. They know that if they can make you have a feeling for them, you will surely respond to their requests. Therefore, they look for words and expressions that can captivate your feelings and thoughts to give them a leeway into your heart. These manipulators may use words such as "I love you," or anything that can endear them to you. This attitude is to get what they want from you.

Chapter 18: Victims of Manipulation

Three Ways of Becoming the Victim of a Controlling Manipulator

We have looked at the character of the controlling manipulator, but what of their victims, how do they become ensnared? It might surprise you how much we are all manipulated in our daily lives.

There are situations where any one of us could find ourselves being easily persuaded. Every day we are bombarded with advertisements, all urging us to buy their wares. Extolling the virtues of one product over another. Building a discourse where not buying certain goods is almost seen as unthinkable, out of sync with the zeitgeist.

1. Sales Tactics

This is the obvious example of such a situation. It seems to be the acceptable face of social manipulation. Commercial products always seem to carry some type of manipulative tactic. All in aid of getting the public to buy the goods. The worse of it is that we are aware of the scheming maneuvers, and yet we still fall prey to them.

When marketing is done well, it works. That's why advertising is a multi-million-dollar enterprise. Companies do not have huge advertising budgets for no reason. For example, how often do we succumb to their "Buy One Get One Free" offers or half-price sales? They seem like a real bargain, saving our hard-earned bucks. Often, we are coerced into buying products we might not even need or ever wanted in the first place. The offer tempts us with generous words, such as "Free" or "Reduced." Yet, it is a marketing ploy to manipulate customers to empty out their purses and wallets. It even has its own acronym, known as BOGOF. Customers are seduced by attractive false pretenses. Are the stores or companies really being kind in giving us free products? How can they afford that? The truth of it is that they are not giving anything away for free.

Economist, Alex Tabbarok,* informs us that there are many ways that these offers can seduce us. The cost of a product is seemingly reduced, giving the customer an offer that's too good to refuse. Most likely the price of the product is increased before the offer, so the customer pays more in the first place. Most larger shops buy their goods in bulk. This means that the price they pay for an individual product is far less than the price they charge their customers. That is acceptable because they are a business after all, and must make profits to keep going.

You may also note that the BOGOF temptation is used on a lot of perishable items. If the stores have a surplus and the sell-by date is fast approaching, it makes commercial sense to reduce the price, or use BOGOF. If you are coerced into buying this type of bargain, make sure you can eat it all before it expires. Some have argued that this practice of promotion has led to an increase in food waste. The stores and shops refute this theory completely.

Such commercial practices are seen as choices that adults can assess intelligently. No one is forcing us to participate in the offers. We all have individual agency and should take responsibility for our actions. Yet, somehow, we are blinded to the persuasiveness of such marketing methods.

We live in a consumerist society. The need to own the latest gadget or have the latest model can become crucial to the buyer. Not only for their standing in society but also their sense of self. Advertisers take advantage of our weak areas and offer us unmissable deals at supposedly low rates. If customers cannot afford it, no problem, they will be offered credit for their purchase.

It should come as no surprise that advertising has such a powerful impact on our lives. Linked to the massive increase in consumerism over the last few decades is a similar increase in marketing efforts. In the 1970s, it was believed that the average person viewed around 500 adverts, which has now increased to 5000 ads, in a single day. Whilst that might seem excessive and may not apply to everyone, it does show the pervasive nature of advertising in everyday life. Advertising is proven to work, overtly manipulating the shopper and often tagging into their emotions to coercing them to purchase the product in question. Though it may not work every time and on every person, it is successful often enough to make it a profitable venture.

Of course, no one is physically or mentally abusing customers, or attempting to ruin their lives. It is a business tactic, not a personal ploy. Even though it is done subtly, it can have a powerful effect on the lives and well-being of individuals.

Some people are far more vulnerable to manipulation than others. Some are very impressionable, and sometimes vulnerable too. A classic target for scammers and strong-armed sales personnel are the elderly. They are easy to confuse when a strong character is knocking on their door. This part of the population is perfect for the controlling manipulator. Their weaknesses can be taken advantage of. Such people will not fully comprehend what is being put to them. Even if they do understand, they may fear to say "no." That makes them the perfect target for unscrupulous manipulators.

2. Working Environment

Anyone who is vulnerable is a potential target of a manipulator. It is not always the obvious people that can get ensnared. Already we have learned that such a character will initially behave with impeccable manners. This false front is performed to impress and gain trust. If you do not know this person already, it may be hard to recognize that you have become their target. That is until it is too late. On a personal front, this type of relationship can occur at work, or even in intimate relationships.

Consider your place of work. Do you have a boss that makes your life a misery by demanding work at higher and quicker levels constantly? Browbeating you to meet impossible targets. Warning you of a reduction in your salary or canceling any bonuses. Could even threaten to sack you. At that point, you become trapped. This person knows we all have responsibilities, such as mortgages or rents, and families to support. We cannot walk away. In such a situation, any of us could become this vulnerable person. This is the victim of a controlling manipulator.

Here are some typical manipulative tactics of this character. See if any sounds familiar in your current work situation. "Careerizma" is a career website that provides useful guidance and resources. In a relevant blog article, they cover this exact topic.

Fake Praise

The boss said they liked your idea and think you're a great person, but then they go with someone else's idea instead. What was the point of the pretense in the first place? Like many manipulators, they like the feeling of control. By leading you astray, it gives them a sense of power over you. This is about building a person's confidence up with false praise and then crushing them. At this point, they may belittle you or devalue your work. Diving in with the kill to make you feel worthless. Now they have you like a puppet under their control.

Stealing the Credit of Your Talents

Using you to write up their own reports, and then taking all the credit for it. This is a classic manipulative strategy. They tell you that you're perfect for the job. Show you how they trust in you as the best person to get the job done. All that encouragement was a complete front for their real plans. Once the job is completed, they claim any praise for themselves. Now you are left on the sideline, feeling well and truly exasperated. Should you question them about it, they'll claim your report was a total mess. It's better now because they spent all morning putting it right.

Embarrassing You

Putting people down, in front of others, makes these characters feel powerful. Say that you put forward an idea, they may laugh and ridicule the very thought of it. After a while, you no longer believe in it yourself. Were you to confront them about their behavior, they' would come back at you with sarcasm, "Hell, man, can't you take a joke?" Cruel jokes and sarcasm all will be done at your expense.

Blame Shifting

Whatever has gone wrong is everyone else's fault, but theirs. Never would they admit up to their own shortcomings and mistakes. Not only that, they'll often deny any negative things they might have done. Should you attempt to explain the wrong they did, they would only claim that your version of events is wrong. Typically, they will say, 'I don't normally behave like that, only when I'm around you." This is what Freud called projection. They are projecting their own misdemeanors onto someone else.

Belittling

Making others feel irrelevant. Such as, if you walk into their office, they don't stop whatever they're doing to greet you. Instead, you get a wave of the hand to come in. They know you are there, but take an age to get to you. It leaves you sitting there feeling insignificant, which is exactly how they want you to feel.

Quite often they will bring irrelevant information into an argument, especially if they are losing. Moving goalposts whilst in a discussion is a classical way to make them look good. These people must have the last word, always.

Unappreciative of anything you do and pushing you to your limits are all signs to watch out for. If you hear these bells, you are working for a manipulative controller.

Working with such people can be a game of survival, and not everyone has the strength of character to win. Some, once they've identified them, will stay clear of such people. Their tactic is to keep them out of their lives by avoiding them. That can be difficult if the person doing the manipulation is your employer or your partner. Others may stand up to them and confront them. This is risky but done in the right way could result in the manipulator moving on to another target. Most of the time we have no choice other than to put up with them. We all have our own strategies on how to deal with people we don't like, but the handling of narcissistic manipulator takes courage.

Working with a controlling figure can make your life unhappy; living with one can make your life hell. Have a look at some of the signs to look out for, to know if you are in such a relationship.

3. Personal Relationships

This is a terrible situation to find you in. Being in a relationship whereby your supposedly loving partner keeps you on a leash. When someone wants to control everything that you do, it can become a dangerous situation to find yourself in. This type of partner might tell you it's for your own good. They are keeping you safe under their protective wing. Yet, being on the other end of such treatment does not feel safe. It is a suffocating experience that comes with other serious problems, such as sexual, physical, and mental abuse.

Chapter 19: Attraction and Manipulation - Put This in Correlation

Some people are natural at reading others, but they couldn't tell you how they know what they know. That's because they are intuitively reading others' body language, but they don't have the knowledge to define why they are such good communicators. More than 70% of the messages we send and receive are through non-verbal language. Not only are the greatest percent of our messages non-verbal, but that non-verbal language is more honest and genuine than the words we speak. Our bodies don't sugarcoat the message; we just respond and react without being conscious of doing so.

If people are saying one thing, but their body language is delivering a different message, put more stock in what you see than what you hear. However, to make sure you are reading the person correctly, let's discuss all the different non-verbal messages we send. We'll cover the non-verbal signals and what they might mean, but keep in mind that different cultures and countries might attach a different meaning to your body language. When you're confused about the non-verbal message that another is sending, then listen to the words and take the signals in context with the phrases they use.

Another way to determine the message is through the tone, pitch, and volume of another's voice. It gives truth to that saying, "It's not what you said but how you said it." When all these things are examined during your analysis of others, you'll find clarity in the message. While we're at it, there is one more thing—pay attention to the other person's required personal space. If you are questioning whether the message they are sending is positive, negative, or benevolent, step inside their personal space and be aware of their reaction. Their feelings will then be quite pronounced. If the message was meant to be off-putting, they will immediately step back or adopt a space-claiming stance that will let you know their feelings in no uncertain terms.

Facial Expressions, Features, and Head Movement

Playing with Hair and Moving the Head

If someone slides their fingers through their hair at the temples and tosses their head back, this is an indication they might be flirting with you. On the other hand, if they are running their fingers through their hair from their forehead through the top of their crown, that is a sign they are confused or frustrated. Tilting the head and twirling the hair is also a flirtatious mannerism, indicating interest combined with a little nervous tension.

When people nod their heads, it matters how many times they do so before stopping. For example, public speakers who are attentive to their audiences know that three nods mean interest and attentiveness. However, if you observe a group of people conversing, you'll notice the person who nods their head only once is eager to leave and will probably be the next one to make a quick exit.

If someone is interested in what you're saying, they will often tilt their head in your direction. They could be showing curiosity or questioning what you are saying when they bring one ear closer to make sure they are getting every detail of the conversation.

Eye Movement

People usually blink six or seven times a minute, but those who are stressed blink quite a bit more. If someone covers their eyes with their hands, excessively rubs their eyes, or closes their eyes, they could be hiding something or feel threatened. When the eyes are shifty or rapidly moving from one person to another, it reflects some scattered thoughts that are going on in their heads. If there is a flickering interest between two people when this is happening, then it can also be a way for people to prevent detection as they were checking out the other.

If someone has a habit of not making eye contact or looking down as they speak, it can show shyness or can also be a cry for empathy. They are waiting for you to ask what's wrong and open the way for them to share their feelings. Investigators have come to realize that a sustained glance from a person, who denies involvement in a crime, may mean they are lying and trying to over-compensate by looking them straight in the eyes for a long time to show they're telling the truth.

If you have asked a question and the person you asked looks upward, they are most likely trying to picture something they saw. On the other hand, if they look to the side toward their ear, they could be trying to recall a message they heard. If they look downward after your question, they are connecting your question with something negative and trying to find a way to avoid answering or revealing their feelings about the matter.

Eyebrow Movement

If individuals raise their eyebrows, it usually means the person is curious about or interested in your conversation. A quick pop-up of one eyebrow could be a flirtation, and if the eyebrow is raised a bit longer, it often means that the other person doesn't quite buy into what you say.

If the brows furrow, you can almost bet that person is having second thoughts about what is being done or said. It most likely indicates a negative emotion like fear or confusion, so it might be time for you to back off a bit.

Lips

Of course, a smile sends a universal message, if it is truly a smile. We've all been at the other end of a fake smile, which is one that doesn't travel all the way to the eyes and makes them wrinkle in agreement. We call those "Red Carpet" smiles. They are Hollywood smiles given by people who are trying to be friendly to their fans but just want to get inside, sit down, and make it through the night.

Individuals, who plaster a smile on their face almost all the time, are usually nervous. If it's in the workplace, they could feel out-of-their-depth or incompetent. There's a good chance that foreigners who smile a lot don't understand a blasted thing, so they just smile and nod.

Another thing people do with their lips is to suck on them and bite them. Sucking or biting the lip is a reaction by those who need to settle themselves down. Like a newborn, the action soothes them and offers a bit of comfort in a stressful situation. If one clamps down on their lips or purses them, it can mean frustration or anger.

Body and Limb Movements

Body Positions

If there is a group of people standing and talking and one or more people open their bodies to you, that is an invitation to join the conversation. If they just turn their head, you might want to choose another group. You will know if you have captured the attention of a love interest because he or she will turn slightly toward you and point their feet in your direction, to indicate they are interested in finding out what makes you tick. If you step into the group and the person beside you touches your shoulder or arm, this is a direct ploy to show you they are interested in exploring the relationship a bit further.

When you step into the group, if the person beside you leans in to you, they genuinely like you. If their head retracts backward, perhaps something you said surprised or offended them. If they physically lean away from you, they've already made up their mind that they're not going to listen to or like you. If they turn their head in the opposite direction and follow it with their shoulder, you just got the cold shoulder. So, forget about it!

Standing Positions

If someone is standing with legs about shoulder-width apart, it often is a sign of dominance and determination, as if they needed to stand their ground against something or prove a point. If they stand with legs together, front forward, they will hear you out, but you need to make your point quickly. When the person you are speaking with is standing and shifting their weight from side-to-side or front-to-back, it might indicate several things. They could be bored, or they are anxious and need to soothe themselves with this rocking sort of movement. To determine their feelings, it is necessary to look further at what they are doing with their arms as well.

Arm Positions

Don't assume that crossed arms always mean that the other person is upset. Not so! Some people will stand or sit with their arms crossed because it is just a comfortable position. You can distinguish the other's emotions by looking further at their facial expression. If they have furrowed eyebrows, their mouth pursed, and their arms crossed, chances are they are angry or upset about something. Crossed arms can also be a sign of protection or a closed attitude to the ideas you are presenting.

If someone is talking with their arms flopping around, it can mean they are excited and agreeable, or it can say that they are out of control. Again, you'll need to couple your observations with other non-verbal messages to be sure. Typically, people who are overly animated are less believable and have less control over their emotions, as well as having a lack of power. They flail their arms to gain attention as if to say, "I'm talking now, so would somebody please listen to me?"

Leg and Foot Positions

People whose toes turn inward could be closing themselves off to your comments, or they could just be pigeon-toed. To determine if there is a physiological issue that causes their toes to point it, you might need more background information. Don't rush to judgment, just wait, observe more body language, and listen to their words. Some people, who began turning in their toes because they were insecure or awkward, might have created a habit that they find difficult to break. The only message they are sending is one that says; I have a physical issue that is impacting my body language.

Sitting Positions

If a person is spread out all over your couch, they have a feeling of self-importance. On the other hand, they probably have a good deal of confidence as well. Legs open, leaning forward with elbows on knees shows an in-charge attitude that is still open to hearing what you have to say.

If a person is sitting next to you and crosses their legs at the knee, pointing their foot toward you, they are permitting you to approach them. If, however, they are sitting next to you and angle their body in the opposite direction, you're probably not going to engage or connect with him or her. If that same person is fidgeting, quickly moving their ankle or foot, they are looking for a way out. Excuse yourself; both of you will probably feel more comfortable.

Chapter 20: Brainwashing

A lot has been said about brainwashing, from its applications in the armed forces to its use in science fiction sleeper agents. The truth lies somewhere in between. Brainwashing first entered the public consciousness during the Korean War, where a group of American GI's were captured and then reportedly brainwashed by their captors. Millions looked at their TV sets in horror as American soldiers denounced their own country and refused to be rescued. Many speculated that they had been brainwashed using ancient oriental techniques—but in truth, the men were probably just tortured. When they were later examined after their release, examiners found all the traditional symptoms of PTSD but no lasting evidence that the men were brainwashed. What the men were suffering from was a combination of trauma and conditioned fear. Still, it had all the hallmarks of what we now consider as brainwash.

Following the war, the US government would start a secret research program called MK ULTRA, which would last for about a decade. In 1973 an FOIA request saw the release of hundreds of documents related to the program, each talking about how the government experimented with LSD, hypnosis, and other brainwashing techniques. Experimental subjects ranged from soldiers to drug addicts and prostitutes. MK ULTRA routinely disregarded basic human experimentation rights and was quite the scandal at the time.

Whether any conclusive technique for brainwashing was discovered by the US government is unknown. But we do have reason to believe that brainwashing, in whatever capacity, is certainly possible and has been used since the 20th century at least. The question becomes not if brainwashing is possible, but what does it entail, and how does it relate to the techniques used. What is the difference, if any, between brainwashing and propaganda? Or brainwashing and religious indoctrination? In all these instances, the victim may act in a certain way that fulfills a greater agenda. During the cold war era, for example, there was mass hysteria and inoculation from communism in the United States. Ordinary citizens were made to hate the foreign ideology of communism—a sentiment that exists even today.

Then there are cases like Patty Hearst; a woman kidnapped in 1974 by a terrorist group calling themselves the Symbionese Liberation Army. By the time she was released from her captors, she was a wanted criminal for several crimes. There is a famous CCTV recording of her and other members of the SLA robbing a bank with long guns. What followed was a public debate about whether Patty was a bonafide criminal or an unwilling participant in a crime. There was also talk that she had been brainwashed by the SLA, similar to how young Arabic men are radicalized by Islamic terrorist groups today.

For whatever reason, we are more likely to accept "radicalization" than we are to say "brainwashing." Both things point to the same general phenomena, which is an extreme form of depersonalization that results in a radical shift in behavior.

The Cultish Brain

Why on earth would hundreds of people willingly drink Kool-Aid laced with cyanide poison? Why would the same people willingly force their children to drink it as well? The answer is probably some combination of brainwashing, deception, and plain old coercion. People who follow cults tend to have a similar psychological profile to each other. It is a deadly mixture of helplessness, gullibility, and trustfulness.

In a way, the cultish brain has already been softened up for indoctrination. Nothing in the cultish brain tells the follower that what they may be doing is wrong. Couple this with the superficial charm of cult leaders and their false goodwill towards others and you have a situation of extreme misdirection. Whenever the cult leader lashes out or punishes someone, it is accepted. Everyone is so deluded in the Utopian vision of their leader that they never realize who the true psychopath is.

The washing of the cultish brain is perhaps the ultimateapplication of dark psychology techniques. Everything from charisma, manipulation, and deceit are used to trap followers.

Should we consider these people as brainwashed? Most certainly so! And they got into that state simply because they fit a certain psychological profile and a malicious attacker decided to take advantage of it.

There really isn't any magic to it. There is no ancient oriental technique needed, even if it existed. Torture and violence go hand in hand with it but are also not required. A psychological profile and the will to power are all that is needed.

Brainwash, Abuse, and Stockholm Syndrome

The dark psychological technique of using operant conditioning (positive and negative reinforcement) is often likened to brainwash. In it, the victim's behavior is tailored through a series of rewards and punishments. Again, there is nothing mystical or science fiction about making a dog salivates with the ringing of a bell (as per Pavlov's experiments). But the end result is something akin to what is popularly described as brainwash.

Now, within this framework, there is the possibility that the victim is "in on it." People who knew Patty Hearst said that the Patty that they knew was kind and warm-hearted. Never did they imagine that she was capable of terrorism. So, when the audiotapes of Hearst admitting to joining the SLA were aired on TV, her closest friends and family did not doubt that it was some form of brainwash. As with the captured soldiers during the Korean War,

Hearst was likely subjected to torture. She would later admit that the SLA sexually abused her and, in her words, "brainwashed" her.

Others have pointed out that the Patty Hearst case may have been caused by Stockholm syndrome—a positive relationship formed between a hostage and their captors. Clearly, Patty Hearst showed all the signs and symptoms of Stockholm syndrome. This included denouncing her own family and aligning her own belief system with that of the SLA. One can only wonder why Patty Hearst acted in such a way. She even donned a different name amid all the confusion. Assuming a different personality is a common denationalization technique.

It could be that Patty Hearst was simply trying to stay alive in a time of duress. Ultimately, it was the nature of the hostage situation that granted her a presidential pardon by Bill Clinton

A Recipe for Brainwashing

A potential formula for brainwashing someone (controlling their behavior) can be sourced by using dark psychological techniques. The first and perhaps most important step is to select a target who already fits the psychological profile, someone who possesses a cultish brain, for example. If the target does not have that attribute, any attempts to brainwash with this recipe will fail. The cultish brain can either be acquired or inherent. Many of the hallmarks of the cultish brain are just defense mechanisms against previous traumas.

Depersonalization

The first step is to breakdown the target's personality little by little. Gaslighting techniques can be used to attack their sense of self and their belief system. Changing the target's name or insisting that they use a nickname often helps. At the same time, the target needs to have a high sense of dependence. Over time, they must be isolated from their closest support groups and family members. Gaslighting and other forms of deception can pit the victim against such support groups. Discord within these groups (whether real or imagined) will push the victim away. They will seek salvation somewhere else, like the arms of an attacker.

Acclimation

A depersonalized victim does not put up a fight. They do not object when given manufactured truths. They are willing to accept any new identity that you form for them. During the acclimation phase, the victim will require more attention from the manipulator. Brainwashing, in this way, is not a simple solution. It requires dedication over many weeks or months.

Acclimation is completed when the target is no longer their former self. In the case of Patty Hearst, this was the period when audiotapes were recorded of her denouncing her family.

Acclimation can manifest itself as a rejection of commonly held beliefs like religion and nationalistic doctrines—a denouncing of ideas and the common belief system of the target. If you do not know what these are, then you cannot gauge their level of acclimation.

Conditioning

After the acclimation phase, the victim is in a very vulnerable state. They are rejecting things that they used to hold as sacred. They are slowly reinventing themselves, with the careful guidance of their manipulator. All that follows is conditioning their behavior in whatever way the manipulator chooses.

Positive reinforcement results in more complicit subjects. The victim is rewarded for their actions, either in the form of attention, money, power, sensual gratification, love, or whatever else it is they require. Positive reinforcement creates more trusting relationships between the manipulated and the manipulator. The downside is that positive reinforcement may not always work. The subject is motivated primarily by their needs. Once those needs are reasonably met, they have little motivation to take risks.

Negative reinforcement is more effective but crueler. It can be done with emotional or even physical abuse. Anything that is punishing enough. Negative reinforcement is like placing the subject in between an anvil and a hammer. The source of punishment is usually their manipulator. It is also possible to construct a situation where the punishment comes from an outside or internalized source.

Once the three phases are completed, the subject is far gone from their former selves that they won't recognize their own actions. If done correctly, the change should be dramatic, like a middle school kid acclimatizing to high school and from high school to college. At each one of these stages, there is a radical shift in the maturity and belief system of the student.

Hypnosis

It originated out of a belief that all humans and beasts were controlled by a force called "animal magnetism." And just like regular magnetism, animal magnetism could be manipulated using some form of magnetic force. The father of hypnosis, Franz Mesmer, influenced the term "mesmerize." The type of hypnosis he practiced consisted of hand movements across the body that served to make "mesmeric passes."

Though back then it was widely rejected that hypnosis had anything to do with mysterious forces. The most likely conclusion was that the phenomena were caused by the placebo effect and the participants' own imagination. To hypnotize someone, they had to be looking to be hypnotized. It is used in clinical practice to help psychotherapists unlock suppressed memories in their patients through the power of autosuggestion.

Normally, hypnotherapy takes years to study. A skilled hypnotist can induce a trance-like state in their patients that lie somewhere between waking consciousness and REM sleep. Inside of the hypnotic trance patients are susceptible to the power of suggestion, which the hypnotist may bring attention to. By uttering certain words or phrases, they can make the patient thinkand even do certain things. The connections that the patient makes are largely on a subconscious level.

Chapter 21: Being Proactive

Finally, it's going to be incredibly crucial for you to be proactive. The biggest failure that you will have as a leader is simply not doing anything at all. Even If you make the wrong decision and have some mistakes. That's still better than sitting around and just hoping that everything changes. It is up to you to take action and get the things that you want from this life. Lead by example. Always reflect and grow and make sure that you motivate your team by listening to them and building their emotional intelligence.

Leading by Example

The best method of leadership that you are going to want to use is to lead your team by example. You can't tell people what to do, only for you to not follow the same rules in return.

Not everything that you want your team to do is something that you need to tell them directly by using your words. You can show them how to act by the way that you perform. What we need to remember about leading by example is that they are also the one who's responsible for actually teaching people how they should be responding and respecting you in any given circumstance.

Make sure that no matter what happens, you are never afraid to get your hands dirty and do the hardest tasks of the day. While you don't have to do this every day, if you are always giving everybody else the challenging things that they don't want to do, then it makes you look bad as a leader. Many people assume that just because they are the manager, they've earned their rank and that means they no longer have to do some of the most laborious work there is. While this is true, in some cases, you do still have to make sure that you are willing to get down and dirty with the rest of your team.

It doesn't mean that you won't be doing the most laborious tasks all the time, but remember that even though you do have a higher rank, you are still getting paid more in the end. For many individuals, it is their business as well. So, if you are a leader who owns their own business, then you can't expect people to work for you and do some of the hardest things. When you are the one making the most money and not as willing to participate in these more challenging tasks, remember that what you act on is always going to be more of a sign of who you are and what your character is, rather than just the simple words that are coming out of your mouth. Actions will always speak louder than words.

Make sure that you are practicing active listening as well. Too many individuals aren't willing to fully listen to others, and will instead do all the talking. You need to open the door for communication for your team, which means actively hearing what they have to say while sharing important information as well. Every conversation should include two people; it shouldn't just be one-sided. It is not just about telling things to other people. Make sure that you are always giving people freedom, as well. If you want to create independent and thoughtful team members, then you have to be the type of person who lets them take the lead every once in a while and take action for themselves. This is going to create autonomous and responsible adults, who, when put together, will make an incredible team for your company. Always be the person that you want your team to be. Always show who you are in a way that makes your team able to see exactly who they should be. You are a leader, which means that you will have followers. You aren't just the boss telling people what to do. It is up to you to keep the team together. You are the strong independent glue that holds everybody along with your high morals and integrity.

Reflecting and Growing

Hopefully, by this point, you have a higher ability to be able to self-reflect.

That doesn't stop there. However, your journey is not over. It is just the beginning. Every day going forward, you should have a period where you can self-reflect. Maybe it is why you are taking a shower, as you fall asleep, or when you are driving to work. Wherever it just takes a minute to ask yourself a few questions to make sure that you are really creating an objective perspective of yourself.

Ask yourself what your biggest mental challenges might have been recently. Are you more stressed than usual? Is anxiety getting the best of you? Do you have trouble managing your anger? What is it that you've been struggling with? Make sure that in the same breath you criticize yourself; you also ensure that you are looking at the benefits of your skills. Is there anything that you are proud of about what you have accomplished that has made you a better person?

Are there things that you've achieved that you never thought you would? Also, make sure you reflect on your relationships. Are you a good friend? Are you the right partner? Are you putting in the same work that other people are? Is there anything that you need from other people? Are there things that other people might need more from you? Look at yourself, reflect, and find things that help you to understand better the way that you are interacting with yourself with this world, and with everybody else that you know.

Motivating Your Team

As a leader, it is also your job to make sure that you are the one who's motivating your team. We should all be teaching our team how to drive themselves, but at the same time, we must ensure we know how to do those ourselves.

No matter what you do, always thank your team. Make sure that they feel entirely appreciated and that they know how thankful you are to have them there.

Whenever somebody has a new idea or concern with you, always take it on with enthusiasm. Be incredibly appreciative that they trust you and those they feel open to expressing their true feelings to you. Have open communication and make sure that everybody can say what's on their mind. You need to use enthusiasm and compassion with them as often as you can. Be excited that they have new ideas.

There are a few essential things that you can do to ensure that you are consistently motivating your team and other ways. Make sure that you give them tasks that might be a little bit harder than what they're typically used to. Encourage them to do this and tell them that you will be there to support them along the way. Give them all the tools that they need to complete these tasks successfully. By giving them harder things, you were showing them that you trust them and that you believe that they are intelligent and capable human beings and make them feel good. It helps provide them with a little boost of confidence. Ensure that you are also giving them the chance to be creative when possible. While the task might not involve total creativity, it is also something that they might be able to put their own personality or voice into. Throughout this entire process, make sure that you have one-on-one time with them. If you never really get to know somebody or speak to them face to face and they can feel disconnected from you. You want to allow them to form a healthy and robust bond because this is what is going to keep them motivated and connected to your workspace.

Increasing Listening Skills

You are going to be managing people and delegating tasks. One of the most important things that you will do as a leader is listening. Listening is easy. All you have to do is sit there and hear the words as they come into your ears. However, not everybody is an excellent listener. Too often people are planning what they'regoing to say next, rather than listening to what somebody is saying.Now, to be the best listener possible, remember that it is not just about hearing what words they're saying. You also have to look at the context of the situation. Consider their emotions and personality. What might they be thinking versus what they feel comfortable saying to you? There's always going to be a deeper meaning and unspoken words that should be part of the overall truth. Here are a few listening tips that will make it easier for you to show others that you care about what they're saying.

Ensure that all distractions have been put away and that you are facing them one on one, maintain eye contact, and let them know that you are there to listen to them and support them. Repeat what they're saying back to them to make sure that the way that you comprehend it is the same way that they are trying to express themselves. Don't overdo the attentiveness. You don't want to stare at them directly in the eye the entire time. You don't want to have frigid body language. Be open and relaxed and have it be a casual conversation that you might have with a friend.

Make sure that you restrict any judgment. Even though you might not be saying things, it might show in your face if your brow is scrunched up, or if your mouth is open, or if you have a generally confused look on your face. You don't want to scare them into keeping things from you because they feel as though you are judging them too harshly. Give them a chance to have a moment of silence before you respond. Sometimes they might not be done. Or they might want to reflect a bit on what they just said to make sure that it is actually what they genuinely move. Ask more questions to pull as much information as you can from this. You don't want the conversation to earn and have to revisit it later on by asking questions that should have been discussed the first time around. If you have to take notes, it will actually show them that you really care about remembering the things that you are talking about. If you are managing a large team, you might forget individual small bits of information that are shared throughout the day, especially if you have multiple meetings at a time. Taking notes means that you can reference things, that you have a record that you were listening to, and it shows them that you care about the things that they're sharing. Actions will always speak louder than words. So always remember to consider that what they're saying is critical, but what they're doing is also something that we have to evaluate.

Chapter 22: Identifying Manipulator Types

Have you ever felt a sudden lack of self-confidence or, worse, this curious and agonizing impression of not knowing how to communicate? Have you ever been deafened by doubt about your skills or qualities? Have you ever been inhabited by that feeling of inferiority that paralyzes you, chills your blood, and prevents you from reacting normally? If you have ever experienced this kind of situation, it is because you have been the victim of type III manipulation and placed in the line of sight of a manipulator.

We remember that the second type of manipulator is a selfish or egocentric person who thinks only of his interests, without worrying about the consequences. But the type III manipulator, which is also called the manipulator, has a very different characteristic intention. His only goal is to destroy. Everything he undertakes is meant to kill you, to ruin what you do, or to destroy an aspect of your personality that does not suit him.

The manipulator is characterized both by his will to harm and by a formidable ability to conceal. This is why many people do not trust him or take him for another.

The manipulator does not display distinctive signs and his perversity does not necessarily read on his face. He is a true chameleon that hides behind deceptive appearances to destroy better. He can take the appearance of a parent who is "overprotective" and who, out of selfishness, prevents his child from becoming independent. The manipulator could be a nice grandmother who, secretly, gives money to her little girl who is in rehab to, supposedly, "help her hold on." It can also be a mistress, a lover, a boss, a neighbor, a teacher, or a long-time friend. In the cozy atmosphere of the offices, it is the collaborator willing to do anything to take your place or that colleague who seeks to devalue you because your expertise is shady.

He intends to destroy. Sometimes it may bring him something, but in this case, it's a secondary benefit because what he's essentially aiming for is the destruction of who you are, what you do, or the other of your behaviors.

Illustration

It is through these situations and testimonies that we will examine the harmful activity of a type III manipulator.

A man wanted his son, Jean, to succeed him by also becoming a doctor at all costs. When Jean announced his desire to leave school to become a musician, his father did everything to break that dream and bring his son back to what he thought was the right path. He tried to persuade his son that he was right in seeking to destroy this vocation. "I did it for your sake, you'll thank me later," he told him then. But what he put his son through was a terrible ordeal that almost drove Jean to suicide, as he felt rejected, devalued, ridiculed, humiliated, and disavowed deep within himself.

A husband insidiously belittles his wife, Christelle, so that she stays at home. He has nothing against her. He simply does not want her to become independent because it's not how things are done in his family and he earns enough to make her happy. As she does not agree, he will do everything to prove (by demeaning and humiliating her) that she is unable to do without him. From his point of view, he thinks he is acting justly and in the interest of his wife. But one can easily imagine that Christelle does not see things in the same way.

A department head, who confronts and belittles a better-performing collaborator than himself, does not necessarily feel particular hatred toward this person. He is simply trying to break the person because he feels they are a danger to him and the only way he can defend his own mediocrity is to belittle them, to diminish them, or to put him in his place so that he does not do not encroach on the department head's work. He destroys what seems to him to be a threat that could prevent him from continuing to dominate the situation. In return, the employee can talk about bullying.

The type III manipulator is a weak man who, when he feels he is in danger, tries to diminish others. He advances masked. Where a normal person tries to surpass himself to become stronger (than whatever threatens him), the manipulator has no other resource than to weaken or treacherously destroy everything that worries him.

He destroys for the sake of destruction. He is mean and does not allow others to exist on their own. He wants to control everything. We cannot impress him. It makes you feel that you are small, weak, and shabby; it turns you into a "mop," it tramples you and makes you incapable of any development.

He destroys you by giving you the impression that it is for your good, but we feel very bad in his presence. We cannot win. We are not recognized for what we would like to be. He does not listen to you, and his criticism is never constructive. When he says something, it's always negative. With him, one feels humiliated, discouraged, and degraded. He is a "mental assassin" and life with him is like slavery.

This test separates the appearance and truth of the situation and highlights the perverse maneuvers that the manipulator uses against us.

Harassment and Concealed Manipulation

Type III manipulation often goes unnoticed by those who experience it. This is called harassment or hidden manipulation. A large number of victims are thus abused and destroyed without their knowledge by the deceit and duplicity of a manipulator. After two pregnancies, Chloe cannot seem to get back to the weight she was as a young girl. She explains her fight against the pounds:

"When I discover a new diet, I hasten to try it. I am sure this time it will be the right one. I do what it takes, and I feel good. I have a clear mind, I am dynamic. Sometimes I even go back to playing sports. I do everything I can without effort and I start losing weight. And then, brutally, without my understanding why, I fall back into the fog. I have no courage, I ruminate on the same black thoughts, I do not do anything, I am exhausted, and I spend my time sleeping. Then, seeing all the tasks accumulating around the apartment, I feel guilty and without realizing it, I start eating again. I call myself names while looking at my belly and my thighsin the mirror of the bathroom. Every day, I decided that, the next day, I will put myself firmly on the diet and that this time I will getthere. Today, I am completely desperate because despite all my attempts, every time I get on the scale, I can see that I still gained weight."

While a hidden manipulation is hardly perceptible from the inside, this is not the case when we observe it from the outside. This is what a friend of Chloe tells us about her weight problems:

"I have known Chloe for many years. She was always a little concerned about her weight, but it almost became an obsession from the moment she met Guillaume, her future husband. He is a charming boy, but he attaches great importance to appearances. Since Chloe gained a little weight, having had her children, he frequently comments on it. He always comments nicely, in the tone of the joke, but I think it comes a little too often. I also see that Chloe is touched, even if she pretends to laugh with the others about her 'little bulges' as she says. But I can see that deep down she is hurt when he makes fun of her in public. Moreover, in the days that follow, she regularly buys clothes that are too small, claiming that she is going to lose weight. The other night, I was at home and he did not stop criticizing a common friend who had grown enormously. He told multiple bad jokes about his plumpness and talked about the contempt he had for people who do not know how to control their weight. When Chloe came out of the room with tears in her eyes, he suddenly changed the subject of conversation. Everyone was embarrassed, but he did not seem to notice. The worst part was that he seemed satisfied with what he had just done as if it were a good joke. I thought about Chloe and it was really awful to see how happy he looked."

A manipulator can be extremely pleasant and user-friendly. By appearing charming, playing on someone's guild, or using a respectable or simply authoritarian position, he creates a mirage that deceives his victims and prevents them from seeing that behind his disguise of the moment, hides a purpose that is invariably destructive and harmful. Moreover, it is very difficult to blame him for the behavior because he always has an excuse to justify himself: "I am only following the instructions. I do not have the right to disobey. I only did my duty. I acted believing it was the right thing to do. It was a joke."

To be sure, we can examine (below) the two sets of symptoms that signify the presence of a manipulator. The first contains the essentials of what one feels when one is a direct victim of a manipulator and the second enumerates what one perceives as a mere observer of a hidden manipulation.

Internal Symptoms of Concealed Manipulation

These are the main internal signals that can be seen when one is a victim of type III manipulation. These symptoms are far more indicative of the presence of a manipulator than the analysis of his words or deeds:

- I alternate moments of enthusiasm and discouragement. I often feel a sense of guilt or doubt.
- I find it difficult to defend myself or counterattack. I feel a sudden loss of confidence in myself.
- I sometimes feel that I am "drained" of my energy. I feel physical or mental discomfort in the presence of someone.
- That person belittles me one way or another. It is impossible to impress or affect her.

- There is always a form of ambiguity between what she does and what she says. I am not well in my head or my body when I am around that person.

If you have at least three symptoms there is a good chance that you have been the victim of such manipulation. When all five symptoms are reached, manipulation is certain and you should focus on finding out for sure who the manipulator is and how he proceeds.

Do not hesitate to ask for advice or help!

Generally, someone with an outside perspective can find out much more easily because they will often notice things that one who is a victim and who lives things from within misses.

Chapter 23: Seduction of Dark Psychology

Seduction is persuading someone to have sex with you or make them more excited to do so. Seduction is often simply part of attraction between two people, as it sets the stage for the sex to come. It may include a woman wearing lingerie to greet her partner after his long day at work, or a man buying his date a fancy dinner and whispering in her ear how beautiful she looks in her dress. Among good-intentioned people, seduction is a normal, specific mode of communication appropriate for indicating desire and hoping the person of interest feels the same way. Ideally, the process of seduction is never dishonest or misleading. The person being seduced knows what their pursuer wants, and they can have a mutually satisfying sexual encounter or start a romantic relationship.

How does seduction fit into dark psychology then? Seduction can be to help the person being seduced, to hurt that person, or to benefit the person doing the seducing. All three of these motives have one thing in common though; all seduction, to some degree or another, requires at least some affection of the desired person's mental state.

Why Use Dark Seduction?

Dark psychology seduction is often an effective seduction technique because it can make the person of desire feel intrigued and excited. In some ways, it is almost a form of persuasion. At its most ethical, persuasion is beneficial to the person being seduced, and the persuader has good intentions. At its worst, the persuader causes harm to their victim and only thinks of possible rewards to them. The same goes for seduction.

A person with good intentions may use dark psychology seduction techniques to get the most out of their love life. They harbor no will to harm others but know how to have fun. When this person decides to marry, it will most likely be a happy marriage, as they have created excitement and joy in their partner.

Someone who seeks to harm through dark psychology may choose to do so because of the thrill they derive from letting someone down so spectacularly. When this harmful person seduces someone, usually a vulnerable person, they feel pleasure in watching the partner's excitement turn into fear and anguish. This person has no regard for the person they have seduced and is often promiscuous, with a long trial of failed relationships and angry exes behind them.

If someone is completely self-serving with their dark seduction, then their results will fall somewhere between those of the good-intentioned seducer and of the maniacal seducer. The completely self-serving seducer may cause harm, but mostly out of selfishness and lack of awareness. In general, this person will often be dissatisfied because their intentions lead them to neglect their relationships with those whom they seduce.

Using some dark psychology when trying to seduce someone is not innately good or evil. Instead, it simply a tactic that has proven more successful than others. The only absolute truth about this method is that it is an efficient way to seduce someone that maximizes one's chances of finding someone they find attractive and enjoyable. With that said, dark seducers are more likely to get what they want because they know what they want. Dark seducers usually get the most attractive, most successful partners because they see what they want and go for it. They are not wishy-washy, and they do not settle out of convenience or loneliness.

Dark Seduction Techniques

There are many techniques to dark seduction, but at the core of this method is creating excitement and joy in whoever you wish to seduce. Be sure to entice this person, make them want you. These techniques are all about creating witty banter and showing off how fun and attractive you are in a suave, smooth, swoop.

The Friendly Opener

This technique involves doing anything but asking "what's your sign" or "come here often?". In this technique, an open-ended question is best. Something like, "Hey there, could you help my friend and me? We disagree with who the most overplayed artist on the radio is right now." See what's happening? The seduce asked a friendly question that opened the floodgates for a funny, friendly conversation. The person being seduced does not feel overpowered or intruded upon. Instead, a friendly stranger asked an interesting question.

The strength of this technique is that it simply invites friendly conversation without mentioning any sex. It is impossible to be rejected because this is not even a sexual advance. It is simply a way of meeting a new person and having some fun banter.

This also works because it avoids coming on too strong. The object of your desires is less likely to feel defensive, suspicious, or intruded upon if you present yourself in a friendly, non-aggressive way. You will not seem overtly sexual or creepy, so this person will not feel the need to avoid you or shut down the conversation as soon as it ends.

Show Off (A Little Bit)

This tactic is all about demonstrating, not just bragging about, social capital and success. The first step is to simply look the part—wear a nice, noticeable watch or jewelry. Dress unlike everyone else, as it is a sign of a confident, independent thinker. Another important way to show off is not to seem too desperate for company; show up to a bar with a group of friends, or flirt with two women at a time who are friends with each other. This demonstrates to both women that you are not only a bit of a challenge but also that you are a friendly, confident person in general.

Be Mean (But Again, Just a Little Bit)

If the person you are trying to seduce is acting a little bit haughty or clearly playing hard to get, pretend you are about to walk away. They will be wowed by this one because they expected you to keep playing along with their little game. Showing that you are not so desperate that you will put up with game playing from them show you are confident and not in need of their attention because you can simply seek attention elsewhere. Once they want your attention back, you have practically won, because now the person you are interested in feels like they are working a little bit extra for your attention, not the other way around.

Send Mixed Signals

It can work in your favor not to seem too interested. Do not pick up their call every now and then. Maybe once whoever you are interested in seems to reciprocate, hold back just a little bit and cut back contact. Why? Seeming just a tad aloof can create a sense of depth about you, leading your target to wonder even more about you or maybe even become fascinated. This is all about creating an air of value for you. Everyone wants what they can't have. Playing just a little bit hard to get can make someone's interest in your pique.

Give the Ego a Nice, Long Stroke

To stroke someone's ego, do not simply flatter them until you turn blue in the face. Instead, agree with them a lot—go along with what they say, get to know them, and come to understand how this person's emotions work. In doing this, you will comply with the person's belief that they are the main character of their own story. Everyone believes this about themselves because it is true; each person, in their own story of their life, is the main character of that story. By playing along with someone else's story of their own life, you satisfy and validate them, making them trust you and enjoy your presence.

Be a Little Bit Taboo

Most people are, at least to some extent, thrill-seeking. This does not mean that we all seek out dangerous situations or abuse hard drugs to feel alive, but rather that we all crave a little bit of excitement, and the taboo inspires this in us.

Another important facet of dark psychology is to know that you miss one hundred percent of the shots you do not take. Why is this important? A little bit of arrogance and psychopathy is useful here. Most people suffer from an overwhelming fear of rejection when they are trying to flirt. They are so afraid, in fact, that they will avoid going after those they find attractive because they fear how much pain they may feel as a result of rejection. The dark seducer knows a secret, which is that there are billions of fish in the sea, and rejection is not all that bad.

Simply put, learn to take rejection—avoiding it simply makes flirting an even more daunting prospect and adds even more anxiety to dating. Instead, flirt enough that you get some practice with rejection. Once you survive it a few times, it will seem way less intimidating. The dark seducer knows rejection is a blessing in disguise because it simply frees up time in the future to pursue other, more interested prospects.

Rejection creates resilience and will let you figure out what your flirting and seduction style may be. Some people go for a more structured approach, by asking questions and knowing the emotions to evoke in a specific order in the object of their desires. Others, however, may like to go for it more organically by asking an open-ended question or "going with the flow"—of course, projecting confidence and ease throughout the interaction.

While you may have already made up your mind about dark seduction, you must ask, "When does dark seduction turn cruel and unethical?" Dark seduction becomes malevolent when it involves dishonesty, deception, and coercion. There are many ways one may wield dark seduction morally dubiously but knowing what this looks like can prevent you from experiencing a great deal of pain.

Of course, not everyone can be lucky in love. Some people were raised in chaotic households and find themselves in dysfunctional relationships as adults because they were not taught as children how healthy relationships function. Others are young, naïve, and impulsive; the prospect of love is so tempting to them that they are willing to ignore obvious red flags about their dates and dive headfirst into sex and relationships.

There is a different type of serial dater, though. This person does not seem naïve and has a string of failed relationships behind them. Many of us know someone like this—an uncle on his fourth wife or a friend who dates men for short periods, all of whom seem similarly deferent and meek, before discarding them and finding the next one. The serial dating dark seducer, unlike a normal person who has simply dated many people, will often take no responsibility for why their past relationships failed. This is the guy who says, "All my exes are crazy," or "I won't break up with her now even though I don't like her. I'll leave her when I line up someone else to date afterwards." Avoid this person. They discard people callously and use dark seduction to either harm others or benefit only themselves.

Chapter 24: The Dark Core of Personality

Dark psychology is human consciousness as well as constructive study regarding the human condition and human personality since it relates to the nature of psychology where people prey on others.

The character is often motivated by the psychopathic and psychopathological criminal drives that usually lack purpose as well as general assumptions of instincts and drive. It is also driven by evolutionary biology as well as social sciences theory.

All humanity can victimize humans as well as other living creatures successfully.

Although many will restrain from this character, some will take action on their impulses.

Dark psychology is also defined as the art of manipulation as well as mind control. Although psychology is known as the study of the human character and it's central to human thought, interactions, as well as actions, the word Dark Psychology is a great phenomenon where people use various tactics in motivating and persuading others to get what they want.

Dark psychology is also an overview of the existing psychological persuasion that humans have over other people. In the current world, dark psychology is a powerful force that's used in several sectors.

Great influencers across the world also utilize it. Those who aren't aware of the risks of this dark force may have it used against them in different scenarios. To be safe from such harmful elements in society, you need to familiarize yourself with the effects of dark psychology in the community, including families as well as different individuals.

While some people restrain this character, some will take action upon their feelings, thereby delving into certain characters.

Dark psychology also seeks to comprehend the different thoughts and feelings, as well as perceptions that may lead to existing human predatory behavior.

It assumes that the production is natural and purposive and carries some rational and goal-oriented elements at that time.

The remaining percentages under the umbrella of dark psychology refer to the brutalization of the victims without any purposeful intent, coupled with a reasonably defined science as well as religious dogma.

In the next century, there will be predators as well as their acts of different actions of theft, violence, coupled with abuse.

It'll become a major global as well as an international epidemic that will affect society. There will also be cyberbullies and sexual predators that will harm different people.

Just as portrayed in the study of dark psychology, abuse is going to become an international phenomenon that will affect every part of the earth.

As such, the theory of predators takes up the same framework. However, it revolves around the abuse as well as the assault of different people using information and communications technology.

With that said, egoism, psychopathy, sadism, as well as spitefulness are some of the traits that have been standing in for dark psychology.

Results from a project show that was spearheaded by various scientific researchers also indicated that these traits stand for the dark sides of the human personality.

They are defined as the dark core.

Therefore, if you have one or more of these traits, you are likely to possess others as well. In the world of history, life is full of perfect examples that people are using to exude their characters while acting mercilessly towards others.

Most of these individuals are not only selfish but self-centered.

They are barely supporting their friends and relatives in handling their projects. For that reason, there are different names for such traits.

Some are known as psychopaths, while others are better defined as narcissists.

While at first glance these traits appear to be well defined such that the differences can be seen, and they seem more acceptable at first glance, they also appear to be a bit confusing for learners who are seeking to understand the effects of dark psychology in the community.

As such, most dark traits have been misunderstood by people seeking to learn more about psychology and understand their friends as well as relatives.

New research on the same indicates that other traits that can be categorized in this discipline are such as sadism and spitefulness.

Many dark traits can be comprehended as a major flavored manifestation of the common underlying issue that directs researchers to disposition.

With that said, the dark core of a person's personality is what is defined as dark psychology.

It implies that if a person is known for tending exuding these dark traits; they are also likely to have a strong, viable additional trait.

According to research, the common denominator, in this case, is the D-factor which can also be defined as the general main tendency of a person's ability to maximize their utility by disregarding and accepting the disutility of other individuals.

This is usually accompanied by the belief that serves as a justification. In other words, it implies that dark traits can easily be traced back to the tendency of putting one's own objective as well as interests over other people's preferences.

This act is usually to the extent of rejoicing when another person encounters any misfortune in life.

The main intention is to hurt others while pleasing one.

The research-based on this study indicated that dark traits come along with certain justifications that can generally be understood as different instances of the common core.

While these aspects may be different in different ways, they all sum up to one major trait that is known as dark psychology.

The justifications point to narcissism since there's an aspect of provocative characters. A psychology professor known as Ingo Zettler has demonstrated how the common denominator applies in the study of dark psychology.

Here are a few factors he pointed out towards egoism, moral disengagement, self-interest, spitefulness, psychopathy,

Machiavellianism, and psychological entitlement. These are some of the important elements he realized that needed the input of trained professionals in deciphering the truth behind their effects on humanity.

In a different series of over 2,000 individuals, moderators realized that most people who were asked to what extent they agreed to disagree with sentiments such as it's challenging to delve into projects without being manipulative here and there, and, it's worth the struggle of trying to find out what the project really entails exuded tendencies of aggression as well as impulsivity.

These are the main measures of selfishness, as well as unethical characters and behavior.

The researchers also mapped out the main D–factor, which ended up being published in the academic journal of psychological reviews.

The subject can largely be compared to the works of Charles Spearman, which were published more than 100 years ago when he stated that people who often score highly in a certain type of intelligence test would most likely score highly in a different test. This is because there is a general aspect of both cases.

In that same way, it was established that the dark elements of the human brain and personality have a certain common denominator which implies that one can easily say that they are in the expression of the dispositional tendency.

For instance, in a person, the dark factor is usually manifested as narcissism and psychopathy.

It may also be any other form of a dark trait such as a combination of the two. However, with the correct mapping of the common denominator, one may easily ascertain that a person has the dark factor in their brain.

This is because the element indicates how likely an individual is to engage in different behaviors linked to one or more of the dark traits.

An individual who exudes some of these traits is likely to carry some elements of malevolent behavior, too.

They are likely to humiliate other people by cheating, lying, as well as stealing. The updated nine dark traits aren't the same.

They may also result in various kinds of characters. Nonetheless, at the core of these traits, every trait can majorly result in certain kinds of behaviors that end up setting them apart from the rest.

The dark traits in a person are not the same for everyone.

Every element in those traits differs in different persons.

At the core of the characters, the dark traits have common elements that may end up setting them apart.

Knowledge regarding this dark core can also play an important role in the life of researchers as well as therapists who often work with specified people in assessing the existing dark personalities in individuals.

As it may be, the dark trait and factor that affects various types of reckless as well as malicious person's behaviors in addition to actions have often been reported on media. For instance, it has been seen in extreme cases, that many of these cases involve people who lie and manipulate others, thereby ending up killing them.

It has also been established that some of these people with the D-factor of characters have ended up deceiving officials in the public sector.

Here, vast and extensive knowledge regarding a person's D-factor can be a useful tool in assessing a person's traits in the long run.

Also, it's going to be used against them in order to prevent them from taking more actions against humanity.

A Major Fact Box of Dark Psychology

Dark psychology is a powerful force that works in the real world today. It's one of those factors that majorly control the world in many ways.

It's used by the world's most powerful influencers to control most of the actions taking place in different scenes, including politics, the health sector, and the entire economy generally. It is also one of the main forces behind different industries across the world.

Dark psychology has been applied by professionals who are aware of its implications in the world and its economy.

You should not be at risk of receiving the actions of those people who understand this game better.

As such, many people are encouraged to find the real meaning of this subject before associating with other people in different matters.

It seeks to identify the traits involved in dark psychology while addressing some of the impending issues that need to be dealt with.

In the long run, these also address some of the main applications of dark psychology not only as a subject but a trait in many people who would like to manipulate others.

In the subject of dark psychology, ideas are usually illuminated using various examples to make the duty of comprehending the actual factors slightly easier.

As a learner, you're likely to come across different studies that analyze the application of dark psychology in matters of real life.

You will also have a clear understanding of the issues affecting the center of humanity, especially when it comes to seeking the truth about how people treat each other.

People with dark market traits are often considered to be callous, cold, dishonest, as well as impulsive in every action they take.

At their workplaces, these individuals can easily endanger the eventual success of their teams while seeking to become the best versions of themselves to be identified as winners in the long run. Also, one other popular conception is that they may risk the lives of their team members without their knowledge.

Chapter 25: Understanding Emotions

Emotions are key in emotional intelligence and as such, we should be able to understand them better to know what we feel. Not only emotions are vital to emotional intelligence, but they play an essential role in how we behave and think. What we feel every day can compel us into taking action and influencing our decisions that have to do with our lives, no matter how large or small.

For you to truly understand emotions, you must first understand the basic components of emotion which are the following:

- How you experience an emotion - the subjective component
- How does your body react to emotion - the physiological component
- How you behave as a response to an emotion - the expressive component

Emotions can last for a short amount of time, such as a fleeting annoyance at your coworker, or they can last for a very long time such as sadness over the loss of a meaningful relationship. However, what is the role of emotions and why do we feel them?

To start with, emotions can motivate us into taking action. For example, when a student has to deal with a difficult exam, he or she may feel a lot of stress and anxiety about whether he or she will do well at the test and how this test will impact the final grade. Due to these emotional responses to stress and anxiety, the student may have a higher chance to study hard for the exam. Since the student experienced a certain emotion, he or she had been motivated to take action and make a positive step to improve his or her chances of having a good grade.

People also take action to experience positive emotions and lessen the risk of feeling negative emotions. For instance, you may wish to go out and socialize or indulge in hobbies that offer you happiness, excitement, and contentment. On the other hand, you most probably avoid getting yourself in situations that might lead to anxiety, boredom, or sadness.

Emotions are also able to help us avoid danger, thrive, as well as survive. According to Charles Darwin, emotions are adaptations that permit animals and humans to reproduce and survive. For example, when we are angry, we are more likely inclined to deal with the source of our anger. When we are afraid, we are more inclined to get away from the threat. When we feel love, we are more inclined to find a mate and reproduce.

Emotions are also able to help us make decisions. Our emotions greatly influence the way we decide whether it is what to eat for breakfast to which candidate should we vote for in elections. Also, according to research, people who suffer from certain types of brain damage that affect their ability to experience emotions face difficulties to make good decisions.

Even during the times when we think that our decisions are made based on rationality and logic, our emotions still play an important role, as is the case with emotional intelligence that has been shown to play an essential role in decision-making.

Emotions are also the ones that allow other people to understand us. When we interact with others, it is important to offer them clues so as to help them understand the way we feel around them. Such clues may have to do with body language, like the use of facial expressions that are connected with the certain emotions we feel at that moment.

In other cases, we may directly express how we feel. For example, when we tell our family members or friends that we are frightened, happy, excited, or sad, we offer them important information they can use to take action and respond to us.

As a result, emotions are also used as a way for us to understand others. In the same way that emotions are used by other people to understand us, emotions are also used by us to understand others. Social communication is part of our everyday life and relationships.

As such, it is essential to be able to understand and react to the emotions other people project. It offers us a way to appropriately respond and create more meaningful and deep relationships with our friends, family, and other important people to us. Emotions also allow us to indulge in ineffective communication during different social situations, including our work. Charles Darwin has also suggested that displays of emotion also play an important role in our survival and safety. For instance, if you were to encounter a spitting or hissing animal, you would understand that the animal is defensive and angry and as a result, you would back off to avoid any potential danger.

Our emotions exist to serve a wide variety of purposes. However, completely understanding them can be a tricky business. The way we feel our emotions and the different ways we react to them makes us unique.

Psychologists have tried to identify the various types of emotions people experience. Throughout this process, different theories have emerged that explain and categorize the emotions that people feel. Psychologist Paul Eckman during the 1970s he proposed six basic emotions that as he suggested were experienced universally in all human cultures.

These emotions are:

- Happiness
- Disgust
- Sadness

- Surprise
- Fear
- Anger

Another categorization of emotions was created by psychologist Robert Plutchik, who presented the "wheel of emotions." According to this theory, emotions can be combined to form different feelings in a similar way that colors can be mixed to produce different shades. The basic emotions act as building blocks while more complex emotions are only blends of these basic emotions.

To both theories, basic emotions remain the same. For this reason, let us take a closer look the some of the basic emotions as well as analyze their impact on our behavior.

Happiness is maybe the only emotion that people strive to achieve the most. It is often defined as a pleasant emotional state that includes feelings such as joy, satisfaction, well-being, joy, and contentment. This emotion is often expressed in the following ways:

- The pleasant tone of voice
- Facial expressions like smiling
- Body language most commonly with a relaxed stance

Even though happiness is believed to be a basic human emotion, the things we consider it will create are influenced by culture. For instance, the influence of pop culture emphasizes getting things such as having a high-paying job or buying a home as ways of attaining happiness. However, in reality, the various things that will contribute to being happy are more complex and have to do with each person separately.

For example, for a long time, people believe that happiness and health are inherently linked with research supporting the fact that happiness can play an important role in mental and physical health. It is linked with increased marital satisfaction and longevity.

On the other hand, unhappiness has been linked to various poor health outcomes. For example, depression, loneliness, anxiety, and stress have been connected to lowered immunity, decreased life expectancy, and increased inflammation.

However, severe and prolonged periods of sadness can lead to depression. Sadness can be expressed in the following ways:

- Quietness
- Dampened mood
- Lethargy
- Crying
- Withdrawal

The severity and type of sadness varies and depends on its cause, as well as how people cope with these feelings. Sadness is known to lead people in indulging in various coping mechanisms such as ruminating on negative thoughts, avoiding other people, or self-medicating.

Such coping mechanisms will actually enhance the feelings of sadness and prolong the situation.

Fear can be a powerful emotion that plays an important role in our survival. When we come across some sort of danger, we experience fear and our bodies start a process known as the fight-or-flight response.

During this response, our muscles become tense, our mind is more alert, and heart rate, as well as respiration, increases, preparing the body to either run away from the danger or fight it. This is the response that helps us make sure that we are ready to deal with threats in our environment effectively. Fear can be expressed in the following ways:

- Facial expressions like the widening of the eyes
- Physiological reactions like rapid heartbeat and breathing
- Attempts to flee or hide from the danger

Fear is not experienced by people the same way, with some being more sensitive to it and also particular objects or situations being able to trigger this emotion easier than others.

Fear is our emotional response to an immediate threat. We can also have a similar reaction to expected threats or thoughts that have to do with potential dangers. This is what experts commonly refer to as anxiety. For instance, social anxiety has to do with an expected fear of social situations.

On the other hand, some people actually seek out situations that will cause them to be afraid. Take extreme Sports for example and other similar things that can induce fear. This is happening because some people seem to enjoy and thrive when under such feelings. However, when we are exposed to fear repeatedly, it can lead to acclimation and familiarity, which can reduce feelings of anxiety and fear. This is the basic idea behind exposure therapy, during which people are exposed in a safe and controlled manner to the things that scare them the most. As timepasses, the feelings of fear will start to decrease.

Another basic emotion as described by Eckman is disgust that can be shown in the following ways:

- Physical reactions like retching and vomiting
- Turning away from the thing that disgusts us
- Facial expressions like curling the upper lip and wrinkling the nose

The revulsion we feel during disgust can come from various things such as an unpleasant smell, taste, or sight. According to research, this emotion was developed as a reaction to foods that may have been fatal or damaging. For instance, when people tasted or smelled foods that have gone bad, their typical reaction was disgust.

Another example can be that a disgust response can be triggered by poor hygiene, blood, death, infection, and rot since this may the way our body is telling us to avoid such things that may carry diseases.

People are also able to experience moral disgust as they observe other people involved in behaviors deemed evil, distasteful, or immoral.

Anger is another powerful emotion that includes feelings of agitation, antagonism towards other people, hostility, and frustration. As is the case with fear, anger can also play a part in the fight-or-flight response of your body. The threat can generate feelings of anger, and as such, you may feel inclined to protect yourself when you fight off the danger. Anger can be shown most commonly through:

- Body language like having a strong stance
- Facial expressions like glaring or frowning
- The tone of your voice like yelling or speaking gruffly
- Aggressive behaviors such as kicking, throwing objects, and hitting

- Physiological responses like turning red or sweating

Conclusion

This information gathered by our senses is crucial in the decision-making process of every individual. To gain access to this, one must learn how to read body language cues effectively. Moreover, manipulators take this opportunity to blur the lines by utilizing statements that either limit or expand the choices you see about a particular decision that you have to make.

Other people often pose hurdles to us. They may try to hurt us. They may lie to us, or detect our lies, and try to get us in trouble. They may say no to something that you want or need. But dark psychology allows you to plow through the blockages and hurdles that others create so that you can get anything that you want. You now know how to get your way, no matter what anyone tries to tell you.

Your knowledge of dark psychology is something that most people won't want you to have. You can use this knowledge to become an absolute monster if you so choose. Hopefully, you will use your conscience and avoid employing these methods for evil. Instead, you will use these methods for good. You will become a ninja at getting your way, and you will always have good intentions. You can use these methods to build healthier relationships, bring about organizational change at work, and influence people to do right rather than wrong. You don't have to use them for evil purposes and destroy lives with them. Of course, it is entirely up to you how you use what you have learned.

However, you choose to use this knowledge, you now have a lot of power over others. You can get your way in any situation, with any person. You can influence and change people, molding them into your slaves, metaphorically or literally. You can change your life and pave the way to your own success. How you choose to use this power can affect your karma, so be careful.

From here on out, resolve to treat yourself kindly by associating with kind people, and being decent yourself. Surrounding yourself with positive people who are not high in dark triad traits or cutting off relationships with those who use CEM tactics can be the biggest favor you ever do for.

Using a mix of psychological tells and body language, you will never be at a loss as to what people are thinking. The key part of successful lives is relationships, and now you have the skills to form them. Employ these skills and your friends and work colleagues will notice the change immediately.

Put the techniques that you have learned into practice out in the real world. Find a target that you want to manipulate and try some of your favorite techniques out, whether that means trying to control the narrative, attempting to manage your target's expectations, or making an effort to manipulate your target's beliefs. Do not expect to get everything right the first time and do not be afraid of failure; if something goes wrong, simply learn what you can from the experience and move on to the next target. Learning a new skill is always a process, and that includes learning how to manipulate people in the world around you.

DISCOVER DARK PSYCHOLOGY

How to read People Through Body Language. Learn the Darkest Techniques of Manipulation and Persecution, How toUse Them and How to Defend Yourself from Them

By

Jake Bishops

Table of Contents

Introduction 266
How Dark Psychology Is Used Today? 266
Dark Psychology Tactics That Are Used regularly 267
Love Flooding 267
Lying 268
Love Denial 268
Withdrawal 268
Restricting Choices 268
Semantic Manipulation 268
Reverse Psychology 269
Who Will Deliberately Use Dark Tactics? 269
Narcissists 269
Sociopaths 270
Politicians 270
Salespeople 270
Leaders 270
Selfish People 271

Wide, Practical and Theoretical Observations 271

The Code of Hammurabi 273

Chapter 1: The Art of Persuasion - NLP 275

Which Side of the Brain Their Subject Uses? 278

Which Sense Is Most Important to Them? 278

How Their Brain Stores Information 279

When They Are Lying or Making Things Up 279

How to Make Someone Drop Their Guard 280

How You Can Condition People Without Their Consent/Knowledge 280

Listen and Watch 281

Building Rapport with Others 282

Chapter 2: Body Language 283

Lower Body 284

Legs Touching 284

Pointing Feet 285

Smarty Pants 285

Shy Tangle 286

Upper Body 286

Leaning 286

The Superman 287

The Chest in Profile 287

Outward Thrust Chest..288

Hands 288

Control..289

Greeting..289

    Dominance...*290*

    Affection *290*

    Submission...*290*

Holding... 291

Chapter 3: Mind Control Techniques 293

Recognizing the Art of Manipulation...................... 294

    Persuasive Language.. *294*

Techniques Used in Mind Control 295

Chapter 4: Stop the Manipulators 300

Chapter 5: Persuasion and Influence 308

The Six Weapons of Persuasion 309

    Reciprocity...*309*

    Commitment and Consistency 310

    Social Proof.. 311

Chapter 6: Psychology and Dark NLP 316

Personality Does Not Go Away................................319

What You Need to Know 321

Play on Hope and Fear 322

Insult Someone Subtly 323

Chapter 7: Thoughts and Actions 325

Link between Thoughts, Decisions, Actions, and Results   325

Thoughts 326

Feelings 326

Behaviors 327

Chapter 8: What is Emotional Manipulation? 332

Specific Types of Emotional Manipulation 333

Lying 333

Lying by Omission 334

Denial 334

Rationalization 334

Minimization 334

Selective Attention and/or Inattention 335

Diversion 335

Evasion 335

Covert Intimidation 335

Guilt-tripping 336

Shaming 336

Blaming the Victim 336

Playing the Victim 336

Playing the Servant 337

Seduction 337

Projection 337

Feigning Innocence 337

Feigning Confusion 338

Peer Pressure 338

Signs That You're Being Manipulated 338

Specific Examples of Emotional Manipulation 340

Chapter 9: Dark Criminals among Us 344

Criminal Mind vs. Cybercriminal Mind 346

The Role of Psychology in the Legal System 346

The Roles of a Criminal Psychologist 348

Clinical 348

Experimental 349

Advisory 349

Actuarial 349

Profiling 350

Applied Criminal Psychology 352

Chapter 10: How the Mind Works When It Is

Manipulated 354

Using Isolation to Get What You Want 354

Criticism 356

Alienating the Target to Get What They Want 359

Using Social Proof as a Form of Peer Pressure 360

Chapter 11: The Role of Defense 361

The Steps to Raise Self-Esteem 361

Acceptance 362

Increase Awareness 364

Detach with Love 366

Chapter 12: Toxic People 369

How Negative and Toxic People Affect Your Life. 374

Managing Negative Thoughts 374

Chapter 13: How to Fake Your Body Language 376

Concentrate on the Eyes - Eye Conduct Can Be Telling   376

Look at the Face - Body Language Touching Mouth or Smiling 377

Focus on Vicinity 378

Check Whether the Other Individual Is Reflecting You   378

Take a Quick Check at the Other Individual's Feet 379

Watch for Hand Signals 380

Look at the Situation of the Arms 381

A Wrinkled Brow Can Occur in a Brief Instant and Uncover Negative Feelings.. 382

Chapter 14: Undetected Mind Control..........385

Undetected Mind Control Tactics 386

Finding Those Who Are in Need 387

Media Control with Images 388

Restricting Choice 389

Media Mind Control with Sound 391

Chapter 15: Effects of Narcissism in Relationships 393

Why Am I Attracting Narcissists? 395

Caregiving Spirit.. 396

You Fall for the Name-Dropping Charm 396

Flattery Is Your Undoing 397

Hovering for a Second Chance 397

You Sustain the Drama..................................... 398

You Are a Hopeless Empath 399

Why Empaths Attract Narcissists 400

You Are a Natural Healer................................. 401

Chapter 16: Brainwashing 402
What Is Brainwashing?... 402

Methods 402
Techniques That Are Used in Brainwashing 403
    Isolation 403
    Chanting and Singing 403
    Love Bombing 404
    Barratrous Abuse 405
    Fatigue and Sleep Deprivation 405
    Activity Pedagogy 405
    Lifton's Process 406
    Assault on Identity 406
    Guilt 407
    Self-Betrayal 407
    Leniency 408
    Compulsion to Confession 408
    Challenging of Guilt 408
Self-Rebuilding 409
    Progress and Harmony 409
    Final Confession and Rebirth 409

Chapter 17: Covert Hypnosis 411

Techniques 412
    Covert Hypnosis and Media 413

Covert Hypnosis in Fiction 413

Learning Covert Hypnosis 414

Get into the Right Learning Mind Frame 414

Build Rapport 415

Look for Trance Signals 415

Understand Hypnotic Language 416

What Hypnosis Is and Is Not 416

Advantages of Covert or Conversational Hypnosis 417

Covert Hypnosis Is a Simple Way to Convince People 418

Research-Based Evidence on Use and Utility...420

Covert Hypnosis Explained...............................420

Getting Ready for Covert Hypnosis 420

Chapter 18: How to Use Dark Psychology to Succeed at Work 421

Chapter 19: Knowing the Woman's Mind 429

How Women Process Attraction 431

Chapter 20: Characteristics of Manipulative People 435

How Manipulators Select Their Victims................ 436

Signs of a Manipulative Partner 438

How to Know You Are Being Targeted...................440

How to Deal with a Manipulator............................441

Chapter 21: Victims..................................444

Traits of a Victim.. 444

Empathetic 445

Caregiver 445

Codependent.. 446

Grew Up in Dysfunction 447

Low Self-Esteem.. 448

Signs of Abuse or Manipulation............................ 448

Self-Sacrificing or Martyrdom......................... 449

Self-Sabotage 449

Fiercely Protective of Abuser 450

Mental Health Issues 450

Being Distrustful.. 451

Fearful Behavior 451

Paranoia 451

Chapter 22: Deception 453

The Types of Deception 454

Lies 456

Equivocations.. 456

Concealments 456

Exaggerations 457

Understatements *457*

Untruthful *457*

Identity *458*

Relational *458*

Instrumental *458*

Simulation *459*

How to Use Deception 460

Chapter 23: Distance in Communication 461

Chapter 24: When "No" Means "Yes" 468

Chapter 25: Subliminal Persuasion 476

Cold Reading 479

Conclusion **484**

© Copyright 2020 by Jake Bishops - All rights reserved.

This book is provided with the sole purpose of providing relevant information on a specific topic for which every reasonable effort has been made to ensure that it is both accurate and reasonable. Nevertheless, by purchasing this book, you consent to the fact that the author, as well as the publisher, are in no way experts on the topics contained herein, regardless of any claims as such that may be made within. As such, any suggestions or recommendations that are made within are done so purely for entertainment value. It is recommended that you always consult a professional before undertaking any of the advice or techniques discussed within.

This is a legally binding declaration that is considered both valid and fair by both the Committee of Publishers Association and the American Bar Association and should be considered as legally binding within the United States.

The reproduction, transmission, and duplication of any of the content found herein, including any specific or extended information, will be done as an illegal act regardless of the end form the information ultimately takes. This includes copied versions of the work, physical, digital, and audio unless express consent of the Publisher is provided beforehand. Any additional rights reserved.

Furthermore, the information that can be found within the pages described forthwith shall be considered both accurate and truthful when it comes to the recounting of facts. As such, any use, correct or incorrect, of the provided information will render the publisher free of responsibility as to the actions taken outside of their direct purview. Regardless, there are zero scenarios where the original author or the publisher can be deemed liable in any fashion for any damages or hardships that may result from any of the information discussed herein.

Additionally, the information in the following pages is intended only for informational purposes and should thus be thought of as universal. As befitting its nature, it is presented without assurance regarding its prolonged validity or interim quality. Trademarks that are mentioned are done without written consent and can in no way be considered an endorsement from the trademark holder.

Introduction

Psychology is going to underpin everything in our lives from advertising to finance, crime to religion, and even from hate to love. Someone who can understand these psychological principles is someone who holds onto the key to human influence.

This is not an easy task which is why most people don't possess it. Learning all the different principles of psychology is not necessary. Start with the lessons on these pages, and you'll have a solid foundation. You have to be able to read people, understand what makes them tick, and understand why they may react in ways that may not be normally expected. And even then, you may need to spend time taking classes and reading through countless books to gain a complete understanding. It depends on how far you want to go with this.

So, if only a few people understand psychology and how the human mind works, why is it so important to know what this is? It is because those who do know what it is and how to use it can choose to use that power and that knowledge against you.

How Dark Psychology Is Used Today?

While some people are going to use these dark psychology tactics to harm their victim, there are times when you may use these tactics without the intent of negatively manipulating another person. Some of these tactics were either unintentionally or intentionally added to our toolbox from a variety of means that could include:

When you were a child, you would see how adults, especially those close to you, behaved.

When you were a teenager, the mind and your ability to understand the behaviors around you were expanded truly.

You were able to watch others use the tactics and then succeed.

Using the tactics may have been unintentional in the beginning, but when you found that it worked to get you what you wanted, you would start to use those tactics intentionally.

Some people, such as a politician, a public speaker, or a salesperson, would be trained to use these types of tactics to get what they want.

Dark Psychology Tactics That Are Used regularly
Love Flooding

This would include any buttering up, praising, or complimenting people to get them to comply with the request that you want. If you want someone to help you move some items into your home, you may use love flooding to make them feel good, which could make it more likely that they will help you. A dark manipulator could also use it to make the other person feel attached to them and then get them to do things that they may not normally do.

Lying

This would include telling the victim an untrue version of the situation. It can also include a partial truth or exaggerations to get what you wanted to be done.

Love Denial

This one can be hard on the victim because it can make them feel lost and abandoned by the manipulator. This one includes withholding affection and love until you can get what you want out of the victim.

Withdrawal

This would be when the victim is given the silent treatment or is avoided until they meet the needs of the other person.

Restricting Choices

The manipulator may give their victim access to some choices, but they do this to distract them from the choices that they don't want the victim to make.

Semantic Manipulation

This is a technique where the manipulator is going to use some commonly known words, ones that have accepted meanings by both parties, in a conversation. But then they will tell the victim later on, that they had meant something completely different when they used that word. The new meaning is often going to change up the entire definition and could make it so that the conversation goes the way the manipulator wanted, even though the victim was tricked.

Reverse Psychology

This is when you tell someone to do something in one manner, knowing that they will do the opposite. But the opposite action is what the manipulator wanted to happen in the first place.

Who Will Deliberately Use Dark Tactics?

Many different people may choose to use these dark tactics against you. They can be found in many different aspects of your life, which is why it is so important to learn how to stay away from them. Some of the people who can use some of these dark psychology tactics deliberately include:

Narcissists

These individuals are going to have a bloated sense of their self-worth, and they will need to make others believe that they are superior as well. To meet their desires of being worshipped and adored by everyone they meet, they will use persuasion and dark psychology.

Sociopaths

Those who are sociopaths are charming, intelligent, and persuasive. But they only act this way to get what they want. They lack any emotions. This means that they have no issue with using the tactics of dark psychology to get what they want, including taking it as far as creating superficial relationships.

Politicians

With the help of dark psychology, a politician could convince someone to cast votes for them simply by convincing these people that their point of view is the right one.

Salespeople

Not all salespeople are going to use dark tactics against you. But it is possible that some, especially those who are really into getting their sales numbers and being the best, will not think twice about using dark persuasion to manipulate people.

Leaders

Throughout history, there have been plenty of leaders who will use the techniques of dark psychology to get their team members, subordinates, and citizens to do what they want.

Selfish People

This could be any person that you come across who will make sure that their own needs are put before anyone else's. They aren't concerned about others, and they will let others forego their benefits so that they can benefit. If the situation benefits them, it is fine if it benefits someone else. But if someone is going to be the loser, it will be the other person and not them.

This list is important because it is going to serve two purposes. First, it is going to help you be more aware of the people who may try to manipulate you to do things that you don't want to do, and it can be there to help out with self-realization.

Wide, Practical and Theoretical Observations

Murder, rape, incest, abuse, all words that can send chills up your spine. As a culture, we have saturated ourselves with negative ideals for entertainment purposes. We sit and watch horror movies, crime shows, and reality shows diving into the minds of the deviant. The darkness within these becomes an obsession for some, and though they don't reenact or find the actions preferable, there is a connection that few want to recognize outwardly. While the majority of human beings have a buffer in their mind, knowing fact from fiction and right from wrong, some lack it.

Imagination is one thing. Combing through the worst fears of people to find what scenario can be the scariest and most grabbing is something that fiction writers and creators do. Often though, when watching these dark psyches at work on the screen in front of you, the human mind finds certain recognition of why the predator or villain did what they did. Some movies and books even prey on the idea of the worst human condition. Depraved and distraught, the father who witnessed his family's murders climbs out of his ominous depression to wreak havoc on those that committed the acts to begin with. There is a satisfaction for people in the revenge of heinous acts. But then, doesn't that apply the same dark psyche to the perpetrator, regardless of the reasoning behind it?

Dark Psychology has no pointed targets and cares little for the reasoning behind the actions. It is the actual act of manipulation, deceit, and harm that carries the weight within the dark psyche. The idea of revenge has been around a very long time, and at some significant points in history was considered a requirement of honor if the wrong was done to you. Very clear examples of the "eye for an eye" concept are still in existence today. The death penalty is one such example, though the root of it is wide and doesn't currently encourage private actions of one person to another. The federal organization as a whole is in charge of carrying out the punishment. But long before that, laws were erected in civilizations that based themselves on the idea of revenge.

The Code of Hammurabi

The Code of Hammurabi dates back to Babylonian times. Around 1760 B.C., the king of Babylon set forth a stone pillar inscribed with the laws of his kingdom. They are considered the oldest discovered set of laws in our history as human beings. What is so significant about the Code of Hammurabi? It is the fact that it is set in the pure idea of revenge. King Hammurabi believed wholeheartedly in the idea of an eye for an eye and set forth over thirty laws of Babylon based on that specific theory.

Through time, this code has shown its influence through almost all judicial and legal systems. Even the American justice system is predicated on the idea of an eye for an eye. A punishment system where retribution for a crime is equal in severity to the crime committed. What was not expected or understood was the fact that this revenge system is actually internally governed by a specific part of our brains called the dorsal striatum. This sector controls the idea of revenge within our minds. For victims of crime, the dorsal striatum is more active. So ultimately, with a society of an eye for an eye, we are taking the actions of a dark psyche and melding a new one from their actions.

One very prominent case of revenge on a large scale would be the St. Bartholomew's Day Massacre. This massacre occurred during the Protestant Reformation in the sixteenth century. During this time, a new sect of Christianity had been created, and the Catholic Church stood to lose control and power over people, land, and money. In August 1572, the French Protestants flooded Paris for the marriage of a Catholic woman to a Protestant aristocrat. When the wedding was over, King Charles IX ordered that the aristocrat be killed for his crimes to the church. To make it as easy as possible, he also ordered the murder of the Protestants within the town and then outward into the French countryside. That case of revenge cost society between thousand and four thousand lives.

Chapter 1: The Art of Persuasion - NLP

Perhaps you were considering being hypnotized yourself and you wanted to know more about the process. Or maybe you have always considered a career in psychology, in particular, hypnotherapy.

Many people wonder if hypnosis can be used to persuade people—to win arguments, negotiate purchases and sell people things, and so on. The truth is that hypnosis truly is meant to be a therapy. That is, the field of hypnosis originated with psychologists whose goal was to help people change undesirable attitudes, fears, and behaviors. With hypnotherapy, a therapist can delve deep into a person's subconscious and reprogram how that person thinks and reacts in their waking state.

Yet there are other ways to use the subconscious.

Hypnotherapy uses several different techniques. Among these are the ideas of mirroring and leading, strategies that are part of another area of psychological study called neuro-linguistic programming, or NLP, as it is commonly called. NLP is a method of changing how we communicate with others to create more favorable outcomes for ourselves and those we communicate with. That is, if you understand NLP you better understand how people think and behave, and you better understand how to have productive interactions with people—interactions that accomplish goals, both yours and theirs.

We will talk briefly about NLP, teaching you a few concepts that you can use in your everyday life to have more beneficial interactions with other people. You can also use these tips if you go into hypnosis practice to build a better rapport with your subjects and to best help them achieve their goals.

NLP is a way of reading body language and mood and using this information to lead the other person where you want them to go. When you properly implement NLP, you can communicate better with your partner, be a better parent, work better with your colleagues, communicate more effectively with your boss, and more. When you learn NLP, you learn to know yourself better, to read what other people are thinking, and to have a direct impact on the world.

Psychologists and laypeople have used the practice of NLP for decades. Somewhat similar to hypnosis, NLP is both an art and a science, an idea that is founded on sound observation and research, yet a skill that is developed through practice and mindfulness. Put simply, NLP is a type of subconscious programming (just like hypnosis!); it's something that we all exhibit every day. For example, if someone says something that upsets you, you may subconsciously tighten your jaw and your body muscles, staying very still as you process the information.

This is a subconscious response, part of our fight-or-flight tendencies, which first tell your body to freeze as you access a situation.

Many therapists use NLP techniques in counseling their clients, as NLP can be a very effective way to manage phobias and anxiety. NLP counseling can also help people who have had a difficult past (perhaps with abuse or trauma) to move on and learn to manage their memories. NLP has been used by dating coaches to help instill confidence in their clients and by marketing professionals to better reach their target markets. NLP can also be used on one'sself in a very simple way but with profound outcomes. Let's look at a few of the most fundamental NLP concepts, and how you can use this subconscious programming to benefit you and others in everyday life.

NLP has been used in alternative medicine to treat illnesses like Parkinson's disease. It has also been used in psychotherapy, advertisement, sales, management, coaching, teaching, team building, and public speaking. Yes, each one of these categories is a form of manipulation to some degree. You can't go to a class, the grocery store, or even a restaurant without being subject to some form of manipulation. No matter where you are, you can't escape it. It's present in advertisement posters, the tactic of that business sales clerk that stops you at the mall, the product placement in the movie you're watching, and everywhere else. However, instead of being afraid of this knowledge, you can use it to your advantage and redirect that manipulation as the wielder.

But some skilled individuals can harness this power to give them an unbeatable advantage. The techniques are best used in a one-on-one or small group environment. The fewer people involved, the easier it is to read and apply NLP methods.

NLP is a complex subject and is often taught over years. That's because it takes practice to learn the range of reactions people can express. But the promise of learning people's inner secrets makes this technique especially attractive to con artists and law enforcement.

A skilled NLP user can determine:

Which Side of the Brain Their Subject Uses?

People fall along a spectrum between creative and analytical. New science shows that brain function is distributed across the brain. But it is still helpful to think of people through this lens.

Word choice, sentence structure, and associations all reveal details about the person that uses them. Left-brained people often use words that elicit emotions or experiences. Right-brained people like to include things outside their experience or expertise.

Which Sense Is Most Important to Them?

We have more than the five senses (sight, sound, taste, touch, and smell) most people know about. We also have a sense of order, balance, morality, and a host of others, and each of us has one or two that are more important than the rest.

How Their Brain Stores Information

Our brains are the most complex computers we have ever come across. They store and process billions of bits of information for a second. Each one functions a little differently. One of the biggest areas of divergence is in how people store information.

Some individuals have a memory like a sponge, soaking up everything near them. Others are more like a filter that catches big chunks and allows everything to pass through. NLP techniques help people discern the difference and to what degree.

Over time, NLP users get better at keeping track of information. With enough time, users can improve their information tracking abilities to near-genius levels. This gives us an advantage over anyone who isn't as experienced or naturally gifted.

When They Are Lying or Making Things Up.

People perform specific behaviors when they make things up called "tells." NLP users like me can pick up on these tells and be able to call out the liar as they lie. Some people are better than others at lying, but everyone has at least one tell.

Skilled liars understand that for someone else to believe their lie, so must they. So they convince themselves of it first. They often don't display all the signs of dishonesty because they truly believe the lie as they tell it.

Practice can help people fall for their lies, but the process demands a selective memory. This feature is more reliably detected than the oft-cited slight downward glance. It also proves to be a more consistent indicator of ingrained deception than awkward looks. Power imbalances also make a refusal to make eye contact less reliable as well.

How to Make Someone Drop Their Guard

When someone likes you, they want to include you in their lives. Listening to what they say often provides deep insight into what controls their lives. People offer up their darkest secrets willingly, believing that I truly understand them.

How You Can Condition People Without Their Consent/Knowledge

Let's face it; people don't like finding out someone was manipulating them. It violates the idea that we are in control of our lives. But sometimes the truth is hard to take, and we need someone to help us see the way without calling us out on it.

We all manipulate those around us to one degree or another. This can be as simple as breaking a bad habit or establishing new relationship rules with a toxic family member. By steering them in the right direction, we can help them respond to how we prefer.

NLP doesn't brainwash someone (that's covered elsewhere) or cause them to do something out of character. But it does reveal the strings that control each of us. What you do with those strings once you have them is up to you.

Listen and Watch

This is the most time-consuming step, as it is the basis of building the structure for the more intimate relationship you'll build later. Body language is essential to NLP practices. Not only is it vital to the beginning, but knowing how to read body language comes into play throughout the NLP process and any other psychological process. Luckily, the longer you build a relationship with someone, the easier it will be to know they tell, as they are developed from habit. Some people may be guarded around you, which will appear as tense or straight shoulders and back, not holding your gaze, or even fidgeting. This is a sign you aren't building a vital rapport. Before moving any further, this person needs to feel relaxed and warm around you. Watch for an open face, a relaxed smile, and some easy-going interaction such as light laughter. Stay away from heavy topics until this person is comfortable with you.

Building Rapport with Others

Every day we use our communications to try and influence others. Unfortunately, most of us are rarely successful because we don't know what we are doing—we don't understand the psychology of other people. We don't know how to get into another person's subconscious mind.

One important aspect of getting on well with others is the building of rapport. First, let's consider what rapport is. Rapport is simple, it is the magic that happens when two people are getting along really well and communicating on the same level. When you have a rapport with another person, you are each understanding the other; you are listening better, and you are accomplishing something.

You do not have to think the same way as another person or agree with everything they say to have rapport. You simply have to be communicating similarly. One way that people show rapport is when they mirror each other, that is to say, they have similar body language. People who have a good rapport use similar body language, including posture and eye contact. Imagine in your head that you are talking and laughing with a friend. Likely, you are both standing with your feet a comfortable width apart, your arms moving animatedly as you speak, you are both smiling, and your eyes make frequent contact.

Chapter 2: Body Language

Being able to communicate well is extremely important when wanting to succeed in the personal and professional world, but it isn't the words you say that scream. It is your body language that does the screaming. Your gestures, posture, eye contact, facial expressions, and tone of voice are your best communication tools. These can confuse, undermine, offend, build trust, draw others in, or put someone at ease.

There are many times where what someone says and what their body language says is different. Non-verbal communication could do five things:

- **Substitute** – It could be used in place of a verbal message.
- **Accent** – It could underline or accent your verbal message.
- **Complement** – It could complement or add to what you are saying verbally.
- **Repeat** – It could strengthen and repeat your verbal message.
- **Contradict** – It could go against what you are trying to say verbally to make your listener think that you are lying.

We are going to cover:

- **Gestures** – These have been woven into our lives. You might speak animatedly; argue with your hands, point, wave, or beckon. Gestures do change according to cultures.
- **Facial expressions** – You will learn that the face is expressive and able to show several emotions without speaking one word. Unlike what you say and other types of body language, facial expressions are usually universal.
- **Eye contact** – Because sight tends to be our strongest sense for most people, it is an important part of Non-verbal communication. The way someone looks at you could tell you whether they are attracted to you, affectionate, hostile, or interested. It might also help the conversation flow.
- **Body movement and posture** – Take a moment tothink about how you view people based on how they hold their head, stand, walk around, and sit. The way people carry themselves gives you a lot of information. Non-verbal communication could go wrong in several different ways.

Lower Body

The arms share a lot of information. The hands share a lot more, but legs give us the exclamation point and can tell us exactly what someone is thinking. The legs could tell you if a person is open and comfortable. They could also who dominance or where they want to go.

Legs Touching

When a person is standing, they will only be able to touch their bottom or thighs. This can be done seductively or they could slap their legs as if they are saying "Let's go." It might also indicate irritation. This is when you have to pay attention to the context of the conversation. This is very important.

Pointing Feet

Look at the direction of a person's feet to see where their attention is. Their feet will always point toward what is on their mind or what they are concentrating on. Everyone has a lead foot, and it all depends on their dominant hand. If a person is talking that we are interested in is talking, our lead foot will be pointing toward them. But, if they want to leave the situation, you will notice their foot pointing toward an exit or the way they want to go. If a person is sitting during the conversation, look at where their feet are pointing to see what they are truly interested in.

Smarty Pants

This is a position where someone tries to make them look bigger. They will usually be seated with their legs splayed open and leaning back. They might even spread their arms out and lock them behind their head. This is normally used by people who feel dominant, superior, or confident.

Shy Tangle

This is usually something that women do more than men. Anyone who begins to feel shy or timid will sometimes entangle their legs by crossing them under and over to try to block out bad emotions and to make them look smaller. There is another shy leg twirl that people will do when they are standing. The actual act of this movement is crossing one leg over the other and hooking that foot behind their knee as if they are trying to scratch an itch.

Upper Body

Upper body language can show signs of defensiveness since the arms could easily be used as a shield. Upper body language could involve the chest. Let's look at some upper body language.

Leaning

If someone leans forward, it will move them closer to another person. There are two possible meanings to this. First, it will tell you that they are interested in something, which could just be what you are talking about. But this movement could also show romantic interest. Second, leaning forward could invade aperson's personal space; hence, this shows them as a threat. This is often an aggressive display. This is done unconsciously by powerful people.

The Superman

Bodybuilders, models commonly use this, and it was made popular by Superman. This could have various meanings depending on how a person uses it. Within the animal world, animals will try to make themselves look bigger when they feel threatened. If you look at a house cat when they get spooked, theywill stretch their legs and their fur stands on end. Humans also have this, even if it isn't as noticeable. This is why we get goosebumps. Because we can't make ourselves look bigger, we have to come up with arm gestures like putting our hands on our waist. This shows us that a person is getting ready to act assertively.

This is normal for athletes to do before a game or a wife who is nagging their spouse. A guy who is flirting with a girl will use this to look assertive. This is what we call a readiness gesture.

The Chest in Profile

If a person stands sideways or at a 45-degree angle, they are trying to accentuate their chest. They might also thrust out their chest, more on this in a minute. Women do this posture to show off their breasts, and men will do this to show off their profile.

Outward Thrust Chest

If someone pushes their chest out, they are trying to draw attention to this part of their body. This could also be used as a romantic display. Women understand that men have been programmed to be aroused by breasts. If you see a woman pushing her chest out, she might be inviting intimate relations. Men will thrust out their chest to show off their chest and possibly trying to hide their gut. The difference is that men will do this to women and other men.

Hands

Human hands have 27 bones and they are a very expressive part of the body. This gives us a lot of capability to handle our environment.

Reading palms isn't about just looking at the lines on the hands. After a person's face, the hands are the best source for body language. Hand gestures are different across cultures and one hand gesture might be innocent in one country but very offensive in another.

Hand signals may be small, but they show what our subconscious is thinking. A gesture might be exaggerated and done using both hands to show a point

Control

If a person is holding their hand with their palms facing down, they might be figuratively holding onto or restraining another person. This could be an authoritative action that is telling you to stop now. It might be a request asking you to calm down. This willbe apparent if someone places their dominant hand on top of a handshake. If they are leaning on their desk with their palms flat, this shows dominance.

If their palms face outward toward another person, they might be trying to fend them off or push them away. They might be saying "stop, don't come closer."

If they are pointing their finger or their entire hand, they might be telling someone to leave now.

Greeting

Our hands are used a lot to greet other people. The most common way is with a handshake. Opening up the palm shows they don't have any weapons. This gets used when saluting, waving, or greeting others.

During this time, we get to touch another person and it might send various signals.

Dominance

It can be shown by shaking hands and placing the other hand on top. How long and how strong they shake the hand will tell you that they are deciding on when to stop the handshake.

Affection

It could be shown with the duration and speed of the handshake, smiles, and touching with the other hand. The similarity between this one and the dominant one could lead to a situation when a dominant person will try to pretend they are just being friendly.

Submission

It gets shown by placing their palms up. Floppy handshakes that are clammy along with a quick withdrawal also show submission.

Most handshakes use vertical palms that will show equality. They will be firm but won't crush and for the right amount of time so both parties know when they should let go.

Waving is a great way to greet people and could be performed from a long distance.

Salutes are normally done by the military, where a certain style is prescribed.

Holding

A person who has cupped hands shows they can hold something gently. They show delicacy or holding something fragile. Hands that grip will show desire, possessiveness, or ownership. The tighter the fist, the stronger they are feeling a specific emotion.

If someone is holding their own hands, they are trying to comfort themselves. They could be trying to restrain themselves so they will let somebody else talk. It could be used if they are angry and it is stopping them from attacking. If they are wringing their hands, they are feeling extremely nervous.

Holding their hands behind their back will show they are confident because they are opening up their front. They may hide their hands to conceal their tension. If one hand is gripping the other arm, the tighter and higher the grip, the tenser they are.

Two hands might show various desires. If one hand is forming a fist but the other is holding it back, this might show that they would like to punch somebody.

If someone is lying, they will try to control their hands. If they are holding them still, you might want to be a bit suspicious. Remember that these are just indicators and you should look for other signals.

If someone looks like they are holding onto an object like a pen or cup, this shows they are trying to comfort themselves. If a person is holding a cup but they are holding it very close and it looks like they are "hugging" the cup, they are hugging themselves. Holding onto any item with both hands shows they have closed themselves off from others.

Items might be used as a distraction to release nervous energy like holding a pen, but they are clicking it off and on, doodling, or messing with it. If their hands are clenched together in front of them but they are relaxed, and their thumbs are resting on each other, it might be showing pleasure.

Chapter 3: Mind Control Techniques

It's interesting to see that manipulation has been around for a long time, and that is not a new or imaginary concept. Understanding what the art of persuasion is all about is vital to help you to deal with it.

Here, we briefly look at the psychology of manipulation. This allows us to see where it might occur in our lives. It will also help you in identifying those who might attempt to manipulate you. It is not only about people who like to dominate. If we don't know it is happening to us, might be encouraged to act in ways that are incongruous to our normal personality and behavior. Learn how commerce can persuade customers into buying their goods and services. Recognizing such methods will help in dealing with the power of persuasion.

We like to believe that we are individuals who make sensible choices. In our journey of life, we do not always have full control, and we don't always realize this. As children, we are influenced by our parents and have little control over how we are raised. Once in the education system, we are further manipulated. The teachers will tell us all about the social norms and what is expected of us in society. As adults, we are lured in by politicians trying to get their share of votes. Many are persuaded to vote for a party because of what they promise for the future, even if they don't necessarily believe in their policies. This gives such politicians power, and their decisions will affect our lives. Are we in full control of our lives, or are we merely influenced by those who know all the tricks of persuasion?

We will look at how to deal with various manipulative methods, even sometimes covert. First, you need to learn to recognize when you are being manipulated so you can counteract it.

Recognizing the Art of Manipulation

What then, in our everyday lives, do we need to be wary of?

Persuasive Language

The idiom that every picture tells a story is very true. Words can be so much more powerful as they inspire and encourage us, even to the point of manipulation. How many are the time you have been inspired by a good orator who's daring speech motives you into action? The art of words can be so influential in coercing us to believe something, even when our eyes tell us differently. Communication is a powerful tool, especially when it comes to making people do things.

Advertisers and salespeople use language to convince their goods are just what we are looking for. Using words, such as:

Affordable; Easy to use; Safe; Enjoyable; Time Saving; Guaranteed to last.

Note how all these words make us believe they are confident in their products.

Politicians will use language, such as:

- "We" to encompass you in their world.
- "Us" to make you feel a part of a team.

These are all communication tactics to make us feel included, therefore, important.

Bullies use language along with aggressive behavior to achieve their own selfish goals.

Criminal predators, such as psychopaths, sociopaths, and narcissists, are all people who learn the use of persuasive language. This is a means to get their way and gain control over another person.

Techniques Used in Mind Control

Present-day mind control is both innovative and mental. Tests demonstrate that basically by uncovering the techniques for mind control, the impacts can be diminished or disposed of, at any rate for mind control publicizing and promulgation. Increasingly hard to counter are the physical interruptions, which the military-mechanical complex keeps on creating and enhance.

1. Education — It has consistently been an eventual tyrant's definitive dream to "teach" normally receptive youngsters, subsequently, it has been a focal segment to Communist and Fascist oppressive regimes from the beginning of time. Nobody has been increasingly instrumental in uncovering the motivation of present-day instruction than Charlotte Thompson Iserbyt—one can start an investigation into this region by downloading her book as a free PDF, *The Deliberate Dumbing Down of America*, revealing the job of Globalist establishments in forming a future planned to deliver servile automatons reigned over by a completely taught, mindful exclusive class.

2. Promotions and Propaganda – Edward Bernays has been referred to as the creator of the consumerist culture that was planned principally to focus on individuals' mental self-portrait (or scarcity in that department) to transform a need into a need. This was at first imagined for items, for example, cigarettes, for instance. Nonetheless, Bernays additionally noted in his 1928 book, Propaganda, that "purposeful publicity is the official arm of the imperceptible government." This can be seen most unmistakably in the advanced police state and the developing native nark culture, enveloped with the pseudo-enthusiastic War on Terror. The expanding union of media has empowered the whole corporate structure to converge with the government, which currently uses the idea of promulgation arrangement. Media; print, motion pictures, TV, and link news would now be able to work flawlessly to incorporate a general message which appears to have the ring of truth since it originates from such a significant number of sources at the same time. When one moves toward becoming sensitive to recognizing the fundamental "message," one will see this engraving all over. What's more, this isn't even to specify subliminal informing.

3. Prescient Programming – Many still deny that prescient computer writing programs are genuine. Prescient programming has its causes in predominately elitist Hollywood, where the big screen can offer a major vision of where society is going. For a nitty-gritty breakdown of explicit models, Vigilant Citizen is an incredible asset that will most likely make you take a gander at "amusement" in a unique light.

4. Sports, Politics, Religion – Some may resent seeing religion, or even legislative issues, put together with sports as a technique for mind control. The focal topic is the equivalent all through: isolate and prevail. The systems are very straightforward: impede the common propensity of individuals to participate for their endurance and train them to frame groups bowed on control and winning. Sports have consistently had a job as a key diversion that corrals innate propensities into a non-significant occasion, which in present-day America has arrived at silly extents where challenges will break out over a game VIP leaving their city. Yet, basic human issues, for example, freedom are chuckled away as immaterial.

5. Food, Water, and Air – Additives, poisons, and other nourishment harms modify mind science to make mildness and indifference. Fluoride in drinking water has been demonstrated to bring down IQ; Aspartame and MSG are excitotoxins which energize synapses until they kick the bucket; and simple access to the inexpensive food that contains these toxins, by and large, has made a populace that needs center and inspiration for a functioning way of life. The vast majority of the cutting-edge world is flawlessly prepped for uninvolved responsiveness—and acknowledgment—of the authoritarian tip top.

6. Medications — We can equate this to any addictive substance; however, the mission of mind controllers is to be certain you are dependent on something. One noteworthy arm of the cutting edge mind control motivation is psychiatry, which expects to characterize all individuals by their issue, instead of their human potential. Today, it has been taken to considerably assist limits as a medicinal oppression has grabbed hold where about everybody has a type of confusion—especially the individuals who question authority. The utilization of nerve tranquilizers in the military has prompted record quantities of suicides. To top it all off, the cutting edge medication state currently has over 25% of U.S. youngsters on mind-desensitizing drugs.

7. Military Testing — There is a long history associated with the military as the proving ground for mind control.

8. Electromagnetic Range — An electromagnetic soup encompasses all of us, charged by present-day gadgets of comfort which have been appeared to affect mind work directly. In an implicit affirmation of what is conceivable, one scientist has been working with a "divine being head protector" to instigate dreams by adjusting the electromagnetic field of the mind. Our advanced soup has us latently washed by conceivably mind-changing waves. At the same time, a wide scope of potential outcomes, for example, phone towers is currently accessible to the eventual personality controller for more straightforward mediation.

Mind control is more common than most people think. It is not easy to detect because of its subtle nature. In many instances, it happens under what is perceived as normal circumstances like through education, religion, TV programs, advertisements and so much more. Cults and their leadership use mind control to influence their members and control whatever they do. It is not easy to detect mind control. However, when one realizes it, they can get out and start again.

Chapter 4: Stop the Manipulators

Many manipulators will do their best to make sure that the victim doesn't realize what's happening, but there are ways to use this to your advantage.

By creating stakes, the manipulator has control over you because they know that either way they win. During those stakes, it's important to recognize that they don't expect you to not play their game.

A manipulator knows how to use dark psychology to make the victim do what they ask. If they are constantly picking on you or taking note of every mistake you've ever made, the manipulator is planning to use this against you. Their reactions to the things that disappoint them are important too.

Pay attention to how they respond to you in the beginning because this will change as time passes. The manipulator will take note of how you react to things not going your way. If you are prone to fits of rage yourself when frustrated, the manipulator will know how to use that against you. If you get depressed or are deeply saddened by failure, the manipulator will use that against you. Dark psychology focuses on human reaction to situations and using that to influence a situation.

A manipulator will focus on every reaction, every moment of joy, sadness, or anger, and twist it to suit their needs. For example, Liam and Cierra are brother and sister. Liam wants Cierra to stay home from summer camp this year because he doesn't want her to ruin his summer. Liam knows that Cierra doesn't like Sarah D. from her grade and would do anything to avoid her. Liam tells Cierra that this year Sarah is going to be at the summer camp and she's going to be bunking in her cabin. Cierra not wanting to spend a whole summer sleeping in the same room as Sarah drops out of the summer camp, and now Liam gets to go alone as he wanted. Something as simple as knowing that his sister didn't like another student was all he needed to manipulate her into doing what he wanted.

It's easy to manipulate someone into doing what you ask when you know what grinds their gears. Using dark psychology could make it easier for a manipulator to take advantage, and the victim wouldn't know how they allowed them to use these weaknesses.

Narcissistically, they would believe they are smarter than their victim and pay close attention to how they react to even the manipulator themselves. Manipulators love over-sharers or people who don't care who knows about their lives. These people are easier to manipulate because they lay everything about them on the table.

For example, Tyra is always talking about her bad marriage to John, John's friend that wants to have sex with Tyra knows how bad his marriage to his wife is and knows how John acts. Hence, he portrays the exact opposite of that and manipulates Tyra into sleeping with him by complaining about his friendship with John.

A manipulator will always make things go their way by using keywords that may trigger a response out of the victim. They may berate them constantly for something small or make them feel guilty for having any reaction to what's happening around them at all. A manipulator's main tool to anything is pulling the wool over the victim's eyes. Dark persuasion is making the victim feel like they have no control over the situation or giving all the "power" to the victim. Prolonging events or constant empty promises may occur.

The manipulator will always show that they are in complete control, but it's up to the victim to say they aren't falling for it. They will find ways to make it feel like the victim has the power of choice, but the manipulator has carefully thought out every step from the moment they picked their victim.

Dark persuasion considers age, creed, upbringing, religion, and/or sexuality. The manipulator will take all these factors and create a trap for their victim. The victim would be completely unaware of what's happening, but they will feel like the events are correlated with their behavior or with what's happening as the situation transpires.

They won't be able to see how the manipulator has taken control of what's happening and leads them to do what they ask of them without much question. The manipulator is skilled at masking their true intentions of what they are doing, and the victim won't see they are being manipulated.

For example, Marie wants Donny to pay for her to go to Miami. She knows that Donny never got to travel because of his parents not being able to afford it, so she makes him feel bad that she can't afford it. Donny doesn't realize that she is doing this just to get her way and agrees to pay for the trip. Marie has known Donny for a few months and knew that from conversations they had together that something like that would work.

When unmasking the true intentions of another person, you must consider the person that you are dealing with. Sometimes you feel like they are manipulating the situation and when you feel that way, it's good to step up. However, if you can't identify the manipulation, one way is to focus on the person's choice of words.

If they are constantly repeating something or constantly return to one specific phrase in a spiral during a conflict, they are concentrating the focus on what they want. Look out for how they react to simple requests, something simple can become a chore for someone that is trying to manipulate a situation and they will use these repeated words or actions to get a rise of out the victim.

For example, Duncan doesn't want to do the dishes, so he complains to his sister about how he must do dishes all the time at work and that he gets cuts on his hands whenever he does them from the silverware and cutlery. Every time he doesn't want to do dishes, this is what Duncan will say and his sister will do it because she doesn't want her brother to suffer.

However, once she noticed that he only does this when he must do them, she eventually told him that she is no longer doing it. Once you recognize that you are being manipulated, it's easier to prevent it from continuing.

Manipulators may also get angry over very little things, to make themselves look and feel bigger. They will start fights over someone not listening to them or they will start a fight over the way a person looks at them.

A manipulator will shout, especially when they know they are in the wrong and don't want to admit it. As mentioned, if they feel cornered or don't know how to make themselves look like the victim, shouting is the next method. If someone for no reason just explodes, the fear they incite can make someone do what they want.

For example, Lorne wants Greg to stop asking him about why he came home late from work. Greg accuses him of cheating, Lorne tosses his coat down onto the floor and starts shouting at Greg for yelling at him when he's tired and has been working. Greg backs down because he is afraid of what would happen if he continued to yell at Lorne. And Lorne knew that Greg would if he yelled at him because Greg came from an abusive household. By knowing that piece and information and knowing his husband's reactions, Lorne can manipulate Greg and get what he wants.

It's these small interactions that manipulators need most, so pay close attention to how many questions they ask about your life. And pay attention to how much they share with you after they get the answers they want.

A manipulator would be hyper curious about your life or your friends or family. The victim would voluntarily share this with a boyfriend/girlfriend/partner, maybe even a close friend. If the manipulator seems to provide nothing to contribute to the stream of information they get, be careful with what is shared.

For example, Tammy knows everything about Veronika's life, but Veronika knows nothing about hers. Tammy would always ask her best friend to talk about her life, but Veronika would provide little to nothing in retort. It's important to pay close attention to that information as well.

It could be basic, easily relatable topics to avoid talking about their real life and intentions. Or they could even set up for manipulation in the future by planting false stories about their lives into the conversation.

Manipulators will make sure that the victim is dependent purely on them, constantly creating a situation where they would be the higher authority and not be able to lose the rank they have over the victim. Taking them out of their comfort zone would be the most important part.

They would never let them go to a place where the victim could be superior.

For example, Frank doesn't want to go with Amy to her favorite diner. Frank prefers his diner because he's the important one and they care more about him than they would his date. He also wants Amy to think he's better than what she believes he is. Frank talks up the diner and convinces Amy to go with him to the diner. Being in that diner, Amy hears stories about Frank's childhood and learns only about the parts of his life that Frank wants her to know. A manipulator will censor the content that is available to you and make it impossible for you to look past the manipulation.

Censoring what you know can also come in the form of overusing information. A manipulator will spend more time correcting you. They will question your intelligence and won't believe you if you claim to know any information. To the manipulator, the victim is always wrong and doesn't know anything.

They will do whatever they can to make sure the only information the victim ever receives comes from them. Pay attention to how much they correct the small things you do; watch the number of times this occurs and watch how they do it.

A manipulator might prevent them from going online or checking their phones or would get mad at them for trying to source check any information they come across during the relationship.

For example, Tom is with Jane. Tom doesn't want Jane to know anything about his past and gets angry with her every time she tries to look up anything. Tom deleted all photos on his social media accounts that had any inkling of him having any former partners as well as his old drug use. Tom doesn't want Jane to see anything before she started seeing him, and when she asks about his past, Tom tells Jane he was a good student and didn't get into any trouble.

Chapter 5: Persuasion and Influence

There are many times when the human mind is pretty easy to influence, but it does take a certain set of skills to get people to stop and listen to you. Not everyone is good with influence and persuasion, though. They can talk all day and would not be able to convince others to do what they want. On the other hand, some could persuade anyone to do what they want, even if they had just met this person for the first time. Knowing how to work with these skills will make it easier for you to recognize a manipulator and be better prepared to avoid them if needed.

The first thing that we need to look at is what persuasion is. Persuasion is simply the process or action taken by a person or a group of people when they want to cause something to change. This could be with another human being and something that changes in their inner mental systems or their external behavior patterns.

The act of persuasion, when it is done properly, can sometimes create something new within the person, or it can just modify something already present in their minds. Three different parts come with the process of persuasion including:

- The communicator or other source of the persuasion.
- The persuasive nature of the appeal.

- The audience or the target person of the appeal.

All three elements must be taken into consideration before you try to do any form of persuasion on your own. You can just look around at the people who are in your life, and you will probably be able to see some types of persuasion happening all over the place.

The above options are all positive ways that you can use persuasion to your advantage. Most people will be amenable to these happening. But on the other side, there are four negative tactics of persuasion that you can do as well. These would include options like manipulating, avoiding, intimidating, and threatening. These negative tactics will be easier for the target to recognize, which is why most manipulators will avoid using them if possible.

Now, you can use some of the tactics above. Still, according to psychologist Robert Cialdini, six major principles of persuasion can help you to get the results that you want without the target being able to notice what is going on. Let us take a look at these six weapons and how they can be effective.

The Six Weapons of Persuasion
Reciprocity

The first principle of persuasion that you can use is known as reciprocity. This is based on the idea that when you offer something to someone, they will feel a bit indebted to you and will want to reciprocate it back. Humans are wired to be this way to survive. For the manipulator to use this option, they will make sure that they are doing some kind of favor for their target. Whether that is paying them some compliments, giving them a ride to work, helping out with a big project, or getting them out of trouble. Once the favor is done, the target will feel like they owe a debt to the manipulator. The manipulator will then be able to ask for something, and it will be really hard for the target to say no.

Commitment and Consistency

It is like humans to settle for what is already tried and tested in the mind. Most of us have a mental image of who we are and how things should be. And most people are not going to be willing to experiment, so they will keep on acting the way that they did in the past. So, to get them to work with this principle and do what you want, you first need to get them to commit to something. The steps that you would need to follow to get your target to do what you want through commitment and consistency include:

- Start out with something small. You can ask the target to do something small, something that is easier to manage the change before they start to integrate it more into their personality and get hooked on the habit.
- You can get the target to accept something publicly so that they will feel more obligated to see it through.

- Reward the target when they can stick to the course. Rewards will be able to help strengthen the interest of the target in the course of action that you want them to do.

Social Proof

This is another one that will rely on the human tendency, and it relies on the fact that people place a lot of value and trust in other people and in their opinions on things that we have not tried yet. This can be truer if the information comes from a close friend or a person who is perceived as the expert. It is impossible to try out everything in life and having to rely on others can put us at a disadvantage. This means that we need to find a reliable source to help us get started. A manipulator may be able to get someone to do something by acting as a close friend or an expert. They can get the target to try out a course of action because they have positioned themselves as the one who knows the most about the situation or the action.

Influence is a powerful, but often a subtle tool. The ability to affect or change someone's opinion, or create a change in circumstances without forcing the change directly is an art form all its own. Creating changes or conditions as situations develop creates a lasting impact. It can make others sit up and take notice of you and your presence and often create a perception of you that may make others want to defer to you in the future. We will go over how to create influence, how to build your skills concerning influencing others, and how to utilize the influence you have built to achieve your goals.

Influence is based on basic, but key factors. Let's start with a room full of people whom you do not know. Your entrance into this room is vital. You may not know anyone, but not everyone present will know this. Presenting yourself in the most flattering way within the first few seconds will often dictate the way everyone in the room sees you. Smile as you enter the room, walking with your back and head in straight but relaxed alignment. Taking time not to rush or enter too slowly, imagine you are just walking into a room in your home. An often-effective trick to make you seem more approachable is to give a short wave as if you are acknowledging someone you know. This makes others assume that someone else in the room already knows you and that in and of itself makes you seem more likable or interesting.

When first meeting someone, making eye contact and firmly shaking their hand while smiling boosts your effective charisma with the other individual. Charisma is more about how you make the other person feel when they are in your presence. Charisma is not necessarily about being the life of the party. To work on your charisma; first, consider your own strengths. Are you humorous? Are you already outgoing and friendly? Do you tend to be shy and quieter? You can use any of your strengths to your advantage; it is all about understanding how to use them. If you are more of an introvert, pick one or two people off to the side of the crowd or room to engage with. When initiating communication, use your quieter presence to let others do more of the talking, and only steer the conversation in the direction you want it to go in when necessary. People love to talk about themselves! If you are outgoing, place yourself in a position of power, feel free to approach larger groupings of people, and greet them. Again, use your strengths to your advantage.

People that hold sway over others can attest, influence is all about give and take. When people feel a relationship is based on reciprocation, they trust the relationship easier and sooner and have fewer reservations. Try asking a small favor of someone, and then, in turn, offering them the same in return. An example would be offering to hold someone's place in line while they use the restroom, taking notes for them while they excuse themselves momentarily during a meeting or presentation, and then asking them to do the same for you upon their return. This 'give and take' lays a foundation of comradery, like you and the other party is already friendly. And people that feel like you like them, like you in return.

Building relationships overnight is not easy, but it can be easier by being friendly. Smiling and eye contact play a role in how you make other people feel. If you project that you are happy to see others that you are happy to be speaking with them, they will, in turn, feel happy to be communicating with you. Your body language speaks volumes, and others pick up on what you are conveying with yours, even if they aren't fully aware of it. When engaging with another, take note of how they are standing or sitting. If they are standing with their arms at their sides, you should mimic their stance. Mimicking someone's body language is another way of building an unspoken but solid foundation. If they are clearly exhibiting stress, mimic their stance. An example of this would be if their arms are crossed over the front of their body in a defensive pose. After a few minutes of conversation, move your arms to a more relaxed and natural position. In most instances, the person you are communicating with will subconsciously reposition their body language to mimic your own. This is an example of how you are already gaining influence and trust with someone you barely know.

When talking to individuals you want to gain influence over, another aspect to consider is your own attitude towards them. We know that our physical body language plays a role, and that reciprocating is important as well, but just as important is how you project yourself. Greeting another with a smile is great, but now that the conversation has started, maintains a neutral but relaxed facial expression. Staying involved and being attentive when others speak again makes them feel good speaking with you. Asking questions per the flow of conversation shows that you are listening to them, and everyone wants to be heard. Being respectful, calm, and diplomatic in your interactions makes you more friendly and approachable. Showing gratitude for their time and being appreciated will encourage others to appreciate your attention and time in return.

Chapter 6: Psychology and Dark NLP

One of the many fundamental lessons of the Enneagram is that psychological incorporation and spiritual recognition are not different steps. Away from our spirituality, recognize that psychology might not relieve us or direct us to the inmost realities about ourselves, and with no psychology, spirituality can head to grandiosity, misconception, and an effort to escape from real life.

The Enneagram is not dry psychology, neither fuzzy mysticism nor an instrument for improvement that employs the clearness and perceptiveness of psychology as a point of entry into a deep and common spirituality. Therefore, in an actual sense, the Enneagram is "the link between psychology and spirituality."

The foremost of this hallowed psychology is that our fundamental type discloses the psychological mechanisms by which we overlook our real nature—our divine essence—the ways in which we leave ourselves. Our personalities draw on the capabilities of our ingrained temperament to build resistance and compensations for where we've been harmed in early childhood. In an effort to endure no matter what difficulties, we all experienced during those times, we unknowingly figured out a limited collection of techniques, self-images, and habits that enabled us to deal with and thrive within our early environment.

Every person consequently has become an "expert" at a certain type of coping which, when used overly, also gets to become the core of the dysfunctional aspect of our personality. As the barriers and methods of our personality get more organized, they cause us a loss of nearness to our direct experience of ourselves, our essence.

The personality ends up becoming the origin of our identity instead of contact with our being. Our experience of ourselves depends more and more on internal images, thoughts, as well as practiced behaviors instead of on the natural expression of our real nature. This loss of nearness to our essence leads to deep stress and anxiety, using the model of one of the nine passions. Once established, these passions, which happen to be commonly unconscious as well as hidden to us, start to drive the personality. Knowing our personality type, as well as its dynamics, accordingly offers a specifically potent strategy to the unconscious, to your pains and compensations, and eventually, to our recovery and improvement.

The Enneagram lets us see where our personality most "trips us up." It stresses simultaneously what's feasible for us, and how self-defeating and needless a lot of our old responses and conduct are. This is precisely why, when we finally identify with the personality, we're settling on becoming far less than who we are. It's like we had been offered a mansion to reside in, with luxurious furniture and beautifully kept grounds, but have restricted our-self within a smaller dark closet within the basement. Nearly all of us have even ignored that the other parts of the mansion are obtainable, or that we're actually its possessor. As spiritual instructors from the centuries have remarked, we've fallen asleep to ourselves and also to our personal lives. Much of the time, we walk around obsessed with ideas, worries, uncertainties, as well as mental images. Hardly ever are we present to ourselves and also to our immediate experience.

While we continue to fix ourselves, conversely, we start to see that our focus has been exploited or "magnetized" by the preoccupations and attributes of our personality and that we are in fact sleepwalking through most of life. This particular view of things is as opposed to common sense and frequently feels insulting to the manner by which we see ourselves—as self-determining, mindful, and in command. Simultaneously, our personality is not "bad." Our personality is an integral part of our development and is particularly essential for the refinement of our fundamental nature.

The issue is that we end up being stuck in personality and don't understand how to continue to the next stage. This isn't the outcome of any inherent flaw in us; instead, it's arrested development, which happens simply because almost no one in our developmental years was conscious that a lot was possible. Our parents as well as instructors perhaps have had some glimmers of their real nature; but like us, they usually did not identify them, much less live as expressions of them.

Personality Does Not Go Away

The objective of the Enneagram is merely not to allow us to remove our personality. In case we could manage to, it won't be very useful. This is comforting to those individuals who worry that if we get rid of our personality, we'll lose our identity or perhaps become less competent or efficient. In fact, exactly the opposite is true. Once we make contact with our essence, we do not lose our personality. It becomes more transparent and flexible, something that helps us live rather than something that takes over our lives. We are most existing and alert—attributes of essence—while the manifestations of our personality oftentimes cause us to disregard issues, make a few mistakes, and make dilemmas of all sorts.

NLP, neuro-linguistic programming, is a fascinating approach to persuasion and communication that works. Invented by Bandler and Grinder in the 1970s, NLP has since developed into a multi-billion-dollar industry that many people turn to for guidance. The methods taught by NLP help people learn how to banish bad memories, improve their cognition and mood, and learn to cope with mental issues, and even seduce or communicate better with other people.

The great thing about dark NLP is that it is applicable to all areas of life. You can use it for seduction, persuasion, deception, or even making yourself more confident and powerful. You can use it in romance, friendship, career, or family. You are invincible in all areas of your life when you start to use dark NLP.

NLP is built on the premise that you create the world around you. The way that the world appears to you is created through information filtered through your five senses, your speech patterns, and thought patterns taught to you when you were little. Some of your behavior is very unhelpful, but you can use NLP techniques to change this behavior and develop healthier habits.

You can use visualization, meditation, and even hypnosis on yourself to correct your maladaptive behavior habits. You can basically get into your own head and change your basic thought habits. NLP allows you to restructure your thinking and erase bad memories using your senses, language, and self-talk.

But based on this logic, you can also use NLP to enter the minds of others and restructure their thinking. And this is exactly what dark NLP entails. Dark NLP takes helpful NLP practices and flips them on other people. Dark NLP can be used for good or evil. Either way, it gives you significant control over others by allowing you to rewire their brains and affect their thinking.

Using dark NLP, you break people's behavior down into simple parts. Then you affect change by showing people how to behave differently. You use subtle influence to make people think about their actions and approach situations differently. Dark NLP essentially provides a tunnel directly into someone's mind. You can access their mind with simple techniques like sensory stimulus, gestures, and phrasing words in certain ways. Encouraging people to envision things and to think in new ways also enables you to change their thinking effectively.

And the best part about NLP? It is performed through simply nuances in speech or sensory stimulus. Therefore, it is undetectable. You can gain control over someone and he will never guess that you are the reason he is changing.

What You Need to Know

You need to know a few things about a person before you can make him change. You need to learn what he likes about himself, what he hates about himself, what he wants, what he fears, and what he has doubts about. These are essentially the elements of his identity, but they are also weak points. When you target them, you can change them? You can hurt someone through his doubts, fears, and dislikes, or disable him by removing all the things that he likes about himself and hopes for. You can also persuade or seduce him by playing on what he wants or scare him into action by provoking his fears. Do you understand now why these five things are so important to using dark NLP?

Take some time to get to know your victim before you employ dark NLP. Pay attention to what he does and says. The things that he talks about provide dead giveaways into what he feels and who he is. He will avoid what he fears and get nervous about what he doubts. He will get excited and brag about his hopes and his sources of pride. You will find plenty of clues into his identity if you just open your ears and listen carefully.

You can also coax someone into sharing themselves with you by talking about yourself. Share your own hopes, fears, doubts, and self likes and dislikes. When you open up, you establish a trusting bond. You also make him want to reciprocate. Listen to how he responds to you and pay attention to what he chooses to share with you.

You can find out someone's insecurities and pride by complimenting him. He will preen himself if you mention something that he likes about him. He will get rather shy and even hesitant to thank you when you compliment something that he is insecure about. This information is crucial to owning your victim.

Play on Hope and Fear

Play on someone's hopes and fears using your word choices. When you want to influence someone to act a certain way, you want to show him how it might be related to his hopes and how it will benefit him. On the other hand, remind him of his fears about an action that you want him to avoid.

You can also frame his perspective based on his hopes and fears. Use positive, upbeat language that relates to what he hopes for, or wants. For instance, if you want someone to date your sister, you want to paint a visual of your sister that includes all the things that this person hopes for in a partner. "She's kind, she loves to give love and compliments." Then you can flip this and hint that his worst fears will come true if he dates someone else that you don't want him to see. "She tends to emasculate men."

Play with someone's hopes and fears by offering them what they want and then confronting them with what they fear. This emotional roller coaster is confusing and also makes people insecure. They don't know which way is up when they are forced to experience so many different emotions. Fear and hope are two very powerful emotions, so using them simultaneously will have an impact on people emotionally.

Insult Someone Subtly

An obvious insult will make someone hate you. But subtle insults allow you to shatter someone's self-esteem while appearing innocent. Find out what someone hates about himself. Then mention that every now and then in a subtle way. Don't ever make a direct or obvious insult. Disguise your insults as compliments, even.

Chapter 7: Thoughts and Actions

Link between Thoughts, Decisions, Actions, and Results

There exists a strong link between your thoughts, decisions, actions, and reality. They form a never-ending cycle of reactions as your ideas influence your decision-making skills. Your choices shape the actions you take, and actions impact reality influencing thought patterns. So, it is safe to say that your thoughts also influence your reality. You will learn more about this interdependent relationship here.

There might have been times in your life where you look at a situation and wonder how you got there. At times, it could be something as simple as eating ice cream when you promised yourself you wouldn't. Other times, it could be a major decision with significant consequences, like impulsively quitting your job with no safety net. To understand how your thoughts truly affect your life, you need to understand their connection.

Thoughts

All the information around you is absorbed by the brain, which is then processed to form your thoughts. Your mind is essentially the gatekeeper of all the information present around you. It decides the relevance of this information and thereby decides which thoughts must get your mental focus. Thoughts can easily transform themselves into beliefs that influence our feelings. This influence can be negative as well as positive. Let us take the example of bingeing on ice cream. Perhaps the thought was simply, "I had a rough day, and I deserve something nice," or "I'mstarving and this is my quickest option right now."

Feelings

Any emotional response to your thoughts or behaviors is known as a feeling. These act as indicators of your connection to a given situation. Feelings originate from past experiences as well as current perspectives. Things start getting a little tricky when you take a simple thought, "I am hungry," and add an emotional response to that thought. A lot of times we end up combining emotions from several other factors onto one specific thought, which really has nothing to do with that emotion. Thinking "I'm hungry," can have other connotations if linked to grief after receiving some bad news, stress from a hectic day, or anger from a fight.

Behaviors

The actions resulting from thoughts and feelings are known as behaviors. The way you behave is important because your thoughts are telling you that it is the best option at a given point. So, if you feel hungry, and feel stressed or sad, you might decide eating ice cream is the best way to deal with your emotions.

These three different aspects are interconnected, and one cannot exist without the other. So, when you start thinking about the impact your thoughts have, you will realize how much they affect your entire life. Thoughts not only trigger emotions but also guide your behavioral responses. Your perception of yourself and the world is altered by the way you feel. It, in turn, affects the way you respond to a given situation.

Your emotions and feelings guide your behavior, and your thoughts and beliefs guide your responses. You cannot act unless you have an idea on which you wish to initiate action and context as well. There's always a reason why we do the things that we do. Actions are never baseless, even if they seem completely random they are always caused by something even if you aren't aware of what. This something essentially relates to your feelings, emotions, thoughts, and beliefs. So, if you suddenly experience sadness, you might react in a specific way. If you feel angry or sad, your response will usually stem from your feelings at that moment. If you believe that someone should or should not do something, then your behavior might be triggered by your beliefs. For instance, if someone accidentally bumps into you, and you think they owe you an apology, and when they don't, your reaction if any will be triggered by your beliefs.

At times, you might be aware of any feelings or beliefs you have, and at times they are the result of underlying feelings you haven't processed yet. Feelings and beliefs don't appear out of thin air and have specific causes. They are generated from experience and starts from the moment you take your first breath until your last. Things will continue to happen, and we continue to come up with ideas about ourselves as well as the world around us. These experiences influence the way we feel about ourselves and the world.

For instance, a young child might be playing in the backyard, and after some time, decides to climb up a tree without success. Then, one day, he manages to scramble up the tree. He feels exuberant and triumphant in his success. He thinks it's the best time; he is having fun and feels safe. Then, suddenly, one of his parents comes out of the house and shouts at him for being in the tree. They tell him it's dangerous and he must never climb the tree again or will end up hurting himself. What is the child thinking at this moment? He is young, unsure, and doesn't fully understand the world around him so it could be any of the following:

- Having fun or feelings of fun are not safe.
- The world outside is dangerous.
- My parents don't want me to have fun.
- They are unhappy when I am having fun.
- I am not necessarily safe, even when I think I am.
- I will hurt myself if I have fun.
- It is dangerous to do things alone.
- It is not a good idea to try anything new.
- My parents don't think I can do anything.

As time passes, the child might forget the decisions he made or the belief that was formed because of it. Although he won't always recall that memory, it will be lodged in his subconscious in some way. Any other event or experience that reinforces this belief will slowly form his attitude towards life. So, there might be a time when the child is having fun with his friends and starts feeling uncomfortable about a good situation he is in. He starts to withdraw, and the previous belief he has formed about fun is preventing him from having it now. He might not even remember why he feels this way, but he knows he doesn't like it. As he grows up, he might think that he's not supposed to trust himself or the decisions he makes. And all this is because of a simple misunderstanding. This example, as mentioned earlier, is an instance of how beliefs are formed and the way they influence decision-making, actions, and results.

Once you understand the relationship between your thought process and actions, you give yourself a chance to choose your reactions. It, in turn, allows you to change because you know you have a choice. You can work on understanding your feelings, become more conscious about your decisions, and take action. There are three important things you must keep in mind while understanding this relationship.

The first thing you must do is validate your feelings. Regardless of what it is, never ignore the way things make you feel. If you wish to change something about yourself, the first step is to acknowledge and accept. If you feel sad or depressed, don't allow anyone to tell you otherwise. It is okay to feel sad or depressed. As soon as you accept your feelings, it becomes easier to work on changing them. When you understand what you feel and why you feel, you can take corrective action.

The second step is to guide your thinking. There's one thing you can always control, and that is the way you think. Your brain merely absorbs information, but it is a conscious decision to form thoughts. You can control your thoughts, and it must never be the other way around. If you allow your thoughts to control you, your life will become chaotic.

The third step is action. You cannot hold yourself accountable for the way you feel or the way you think. However, you can and will always be held responsible for the way you act. Your behavior, performance, actions, and the results are all dependent on you. If you get angry at someone and lash out physically, you will be held accountable for any altercation. Once you understand what it means to be accountable, it becomes easier to take corrective action. By merely changing the way you look at a problem, you can come up with a wide range of solutions.

Chapter 8: What is Emotional Manipulation?

You've likely experienced individuals who are emotionally manipulative and controlling.

They utilize these practices to get their direction or prevent you from saying or doing anything they don't care for.

Emotional manipulation can be unpretentious and misleading, leaving you befuddled and wobbly.

Or then again, it tends to be clear and requesting where fears, disgracing, and remorseful fits leave you shocked and immobilized.

In any case, emotional manipulation isn't worthy, and the more you enable it to proceed, the more force and certainty the manipulator gains in this uneven relationship.

Inevitably, any leftover of a sound association is pulverized, as the establishment of trust, closeness, regard, and security disintegrates under the sled of manipulation.

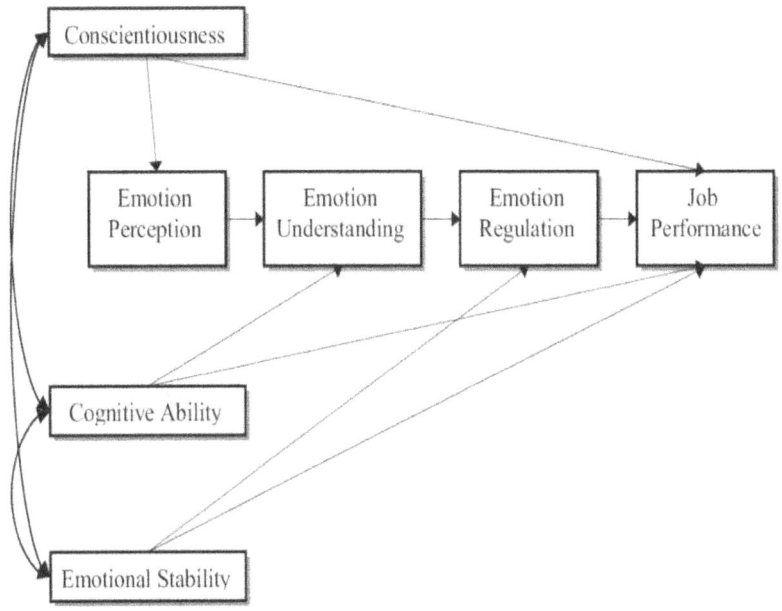

Specific Types of Emotional Manipulation

Within these major categories of emotional manipulation techniques, psychologists have also identified a wide range of more subtle variations that we all likely encounter daily.

These techniques include:

Lying

Dark Triad personalities, particularly psychopaths, are highly skilled at lying and cheating, so often we may not detect their intent until it is too late. Beware of those who have demonstrated a pattern of dishonesty.

Lying by Omission

Lying by omission is a little more subtle. The predator may not say anything untrue but may withhold information that is necessary for an effort to cause you to fail.

Denial

Often the damage from emotional manipulation is inflicted after the fact. When you confront someone with evidence of their dishonesty and abuse, their refusal to admit wrongdoing can cause even greater psychological harm.

Rationalization

The increase in popular news media has led to the growth of public relations and marketing firms who produce "spin" to deflect criticism in both political and corporate environments. A rationalization is a form of spin, in which a manipulator explains away his or her abuse.

Minimization

Like rationalization, a minimization is a form of denial in which the predator understates the seriousness of his or her offense.

Selective Attention and/or Inattention

Manipulators will pick and choose which parts of an argument or debate should be considered so that only their views are represented.

Diversion

Manipulators often resist giving straight answers to questions, particularly when they are confronted by their victims. Instead, they will divert the conversation to some other topic or change the subject altogether.

Evasion

More serious than a diversion, a manipulative person confronted with his or her own guilt will often completely evade responsibility by using long rambling responses filled with so-called "weasel words," like "most people would say," "according to my sources," or other phrases that falsely legitimize their excuses.

Covert Intimidation

Many manipulative people will make implied threats to discourage further inquiries or resolution.

Guilt-tripping

A true form of emotional manipulation, a manipulator will exploit the integrity and conscientiousness of the victim by accusing them of being too selfish, too irresponsible, or not caring enough.

Shaming

Although shaming can be used to bring about social change when large corporations or governments advance abusive or discriminatory policies, manipulators may attempt to intimidate their victims by using sharp criticism, sarcastic comments, or insults to make them feel bad.

Blaming the Victim

This tactic has become increasingly common. When a victim accuses a predator of abuse, the predator will attempt to turn it around by creating a scenario in which the victim alone is responsible for the harm that came to him.

Playing the Victim

Using the opposite tactic of blaming the victim, the predator will lure a conscientious person into a trap by pretending to have been grievously wounded and cultivating feelings of sympathy. The real plan, however, is to take advantage of the caring nature of the conscientious person by toying with their emotions.

Playing the Servant

This tactic is common in environments marked by a strict, well-established chain of command, like the military. Predators become skilled at manipulating this system by creating a persona of suffering and nobility, in which their bad actions are justified as a duty, obedience, and honor.

Seduction

This technique does not always have to involve sexual conquest or intimacy. Emotional predators may use flattery and charm to convince people to do their bidding, and they often look for people with low self-esteem.

Projection

This term is used in psychotherapy. Predators that use this technique will look for victims to use as scapegoats. When the manipulator does something wrong and is confronted, he or she will "project" his or her guilt onto the victim in an effort to make the victim look like the responsible party.

Feigning Innocence

This technique can be used as part of a strategy of denial. Under questioning, the manipulator will "play innocent" by pretending that any violation was unintentional, or that they were not the party who committed the violation.

Feigning Confusion

This technique can also be used as part of a strategy of denial. Under questioning, the manipulator will "play dumb" or pretend to be confused about the central point of the conflict or dispute. By creating confusion, the manipulator hopes to damage the confidence of his or her victim.

Peer Pressure

By using claims, whether true or not, that the victim's friends, associates, or "everyone else" is doing something, the manipulator will put pressure on his victim to change his or her behavior or attitude.

Signs That You're Being Manipulated

We are all potentially susceptible to emotional manipulation by people who show characteristic signs of dark psychology.

A very easy example can be Victimization: it can occur in our everyday relationships with co-workers, bosses and supervisors, family members, and significant others.

Emotional manipulation can also occur in professional relationships with people we may regard as normally trustworthy—such as sales representatives, government officials, and other representatives of institutions such as medical facilities, banks, businesses, schools, and law firms.

Emotional predators share one common trait: They look for people who are conscientious, dependable, loyal, honest, and reliable. People with these character traits are the easiest to manipulate because all the tricks in the manipulator's toolbox are designed specifically to take advantage of these emotional and psychological characteristics. More importantly, emotional predators lack empathy or morality. They do not regard their abuses as shocking or unacceptable; instead, they regard the overabundance of conscientious people as "job security" and a golden opportunity.

Emotional predators can be found in all walks of life. Throughout their lives, they have learned how to adapt, blend in, and even achieve high levels of professional and financial success in the "straight world."

Remember that having a valid and legitimate expectation that people will be honest in their dealings with you means that you are a conscientious person. Although you occupy the superior position, emotional predators are highly skilled at exploiting this expectation and avoiding detection and/or punishment.

As we have seen, emotionally manipulative people use a wide variety of techniques and methods to gain power in relationships. What's more, the people you are closest to and most familiar with—people whom you should be able to trust the most—are in the best position to use emotional manipulation to exploit and take advantage of your trust. In fact, establishing trust and familiarity is one of the most important aspects of a successful effort to exploit someone's emotional vulnerability, and then manipulate them either for personal gain or simply out of pure malice.

Of course, simply because this type of abuse has become common does not mean that you should automatically and necessarily regard all of your friends and trusted associates as predators and manipulators. Nor should you give in to the temptation to regard being conscientious, law-abiding, and honest as a problem. However, victims of emotional manipulation are often unaware that they are being exploited and abused, so it is important to learn how to recognize the signs of manipulation.

Specific Examples of Emotional Manipulation

- Insisting on meeting at certain locations: Manipulators may try to get the upper hand by insisting on a so-called "home-court advantage," thereby forcing you to function in a less familiar and less comfortable environment that diminishes your personal negotiating power. Examples:
    - If you have a dispute with a professional acquaintance or colleague, they may insist on always meeting in their office or at a café or restaurant that is more difficult for you to travel to.

- Premature intimacy or closeness: The manipulator will immediately shower you with affection and reveal all sorts of intimate secrets. Examples:
  - In a personal relationship, the manipulator may introduce themselves using phrases like, "No one has ever made me feel like this before. I know we were made for each other."
- Managing conversations by always requiring you to speak first: In professional relationships, this is commonly used as a sales and negotiation technique to mine you for your information to make a more lucrative sale. Examples:
  - A salesperson may say something like, "Rather than bore you with details about our products or services, why don't you tell me about yourself and how you think we can help you?"
- Distorting or twisting facts: Whether in personal or professional relationships, manipulators will use conversational techniques to distort facts in an effort to make you doubt yourself and back down. Example:
  - A manipulator may use a phrase like, "I understand how you feel. I'd be angry, too. But the truth is, I never made that comment. I don't think your memory of that conversation is accurate. I know what you really meant to say was that…"

- Intellectual bullying: An emotional manipulator may use an unnecessarily large volume of statistics, jargon, or other types of factual evidence to impose a sense of expertise.
- Bureaucratic bullying: This technique is similar to intellectual bullying. Unfortunately, this technique may indicate that someone is abusing their position of authority by insisting on placing as many obstacles, red tape, or other impediments in the way of what should be a straightforward resolution.

    Example:
    - Such a person may make a statement such as, "I understand your concerns, but I would encourage you not to pursue this any further. You have a legitimate complaint, but the expenses and time required will probably cost more than you will get in return.
- Passive aggression: There are many examples of passive-aggressive behavior in conversation in both personal and professional relationships to force you to back down to the predatory efforts of a manipulator.

    Example:
    - A manipulator may try to make you feel bad for voicing your concerns by saying something along the lines of, "I understand that you are voicing an important objection, but have ever stopped to consider what will happen to the rest of the team if you eventually get your way?"

- Insults and put-downs: Manipulators are good at following up rude or mean-spirited comments with sarcasm or some other attempt at humor to make it seem like they were joking.

  Example:
  - "I know you really worked hard on that presentation. It's too bad you wasted your time, though. But, hey, no worries. I'm sure it will be great preparation when you interview for your position."

Chapter 9: Dark Criminals among Us

Before a person orchestrates something malicious, they may have thought about everything for a prolonged period, for instance, in the case of a mass shooting. The perpetrator's main motive may be unknown; however, it is evident upon investigation that such people have usually engaged in negative behaviors that are harmful to others close to them.

Some researchers, such as James Alan Fox and Monica J. DeLateur in their paper Mass Shootings in America: Moving beyond Newtown (2013), have looked into the matter, and the difficulty of identifying a potential mass shooter in advance, especially at a tender age. Nevertheless, it is evident that there are some thinking patterns and behaviors that usually manifest with time, and educators also encounter them since they spend a considerable amount of time with pupils. The parents are also familiar with each of these patterns. The main hope is that the children who exhibit each of these traits can outgrow them, eventually. Some children do; however, some do not outgrowthese traits, and they can harm the people around them. When the patterns intensify, it is important to seek help, and we cannot wait for a seriously malicious action to occur.

When a person engages in crime at a tender age, it is a sign that there is some trouble ahead; not necessarily a mass shooting; however, the behaviors of such people may result in other people being financially, emotionally, and physically hurt.

People with Dark Triad traits may also engage in lying while also blaming other people for their misfortunes. The parents and teachers may not have the ability to control some of the choices that the children make; nevertheless, they may have noticed some warning signs.

Although Dark Triad traits manifest over time, children who simply exhibit some of these traits cannot be labeled as "criminals," since they have not done anything wrong. Since the children are still young, they may still be learning about the world, and they can develop more understanding and empathy as they grow. They can turn out as good, well-rounded people, so it is important to support and work with them, without labeling children negatively.

Children are delicate beings, and they should be molded accordingly. When a child is born, people strive to look into whether the child may have learning problems, physical disabilities, and emotional problems. We should also strive to ensure that we have identified other problems that the children may be suffering from so that they cannot injure their peers or because any harm to themselves, since they do not have any sense of responsibility at a young age, this comes with learning and maturity.

The mental health system should be improved. There should be some strict background checks, and gun laws should also be revised. We should also focus more on identifying some of the "errors" present in the thinking process. We all possess enough knowledge about how we can help children who show potentially harmful traits. The children can be mentored accordingly, and they can hopefully develop more positive traits in the future. Always embark on such a mission with sensitivity and compassion.

Criminal Mind vs. Cybercriminal Mind

The study is related to criminal anthropology, and it delves deep into what drives someone into becoming a criminal. Additionally, the study also looks into a person's reactions after committing a crime.

Criminal psychologists are frequently called up to the stand in court so that they may serve as witnesses since they have an in-depth understanding of the criminal mind. There are different types of psychiatry, and they also deal with some aspects of criminal behavior. It is, however, somewhat difficult to define the criminal mind.

The Role of Psychology in the Legal System

Psychologists and psychiatrists are normally professionals who are licensed, and they are tasked with assessing the physical and mental state of a person. There are also profilers, and they are tasked with looking for patterns in a person's behavior as they try to identify the person who took part in a certain crime. Some group efforts also focus more on attempting to answer different "common" psychological questions. If a sexual offender is about to commit a re-offending act after being put back into society, how can such an issue be handled? Other issues that arise include; is the sexual offender fit enough to take the stand in court? Was the offender sane when they were committing the offense?

A criminal psychologist may be required to undertake investigative tasks such as examining photographs that were taken at a crime scene. They can also be tasked with interviewing the victim and the suspect. At times, a criminal psychologist comes up with a hypothesis to assess what the offender might do after being released after they have completed their sentence.

The question about a person's competency to stand trial depends on the offender's state of mind as they engaged in the criminal act, and when they are about to take the stand in court. The criminal psychologist will have to assess the ability of the offender to understand the charges that have been placed against them and the possible outcomes that may arise after they are convicted. The offender should also have the ability to offer some assistance to their attorneys as they defend them in court.

The question of criminal responsibility is aimed at assessing the criminal's state of mind as they committed the crime. The main focus is on whether they understand the difference between what is right and wrong and anything that is against the law. The insanity defense is not commonly used, since it cannot be proved easily. If a person succeeds with the insanity defense, they will be sent to a secure hospital facility for a long period as compared to the period that they would have served in prison.

The Roles of a Criminal Psychologist

The roles of a legal psychologist are as follows:

Clinical

In such an instance, the psychologist is supposed to assess an individual so that they can issue a clinical judgment. The psychologist can make use of different assessment tools, psychometric tools, or they can take part in a normal interview with the offender. After that, they are supposed to make an informed decision depending on the outcome of the interview. The assessment comes in handy since it can help the police and other organizations to determine how the offender, in this case, will be processed. For instance, the clinical psychologist can find out whether the offender is sane so that they can stand a trial. They can also determine whether the offender has a mental illness, which relates to whether they are capable of understanding the court proceedings.

Experimental

In this instance, the psychologist is tasked with carrying out some research about the case. They can perform some experiments so that they can illustrate a certain point while also providing further information that will be presented as evidence in court. They may carry out eyewitness credibility and false memory assessments. For instance, they can try to assess whether an eyewitness can spot an object that is 100 meters away.

Advisory

A psychologist is supposed to advise the police about how they should proceed with the investigation. For instance, they can weigh into matters such as which is the best way to interview an eyewitness and the offender. They can also weigh into matters such as how an offender may act after committing a crime.

Actuarial

This is where the psychologist makes use of statistics so that they can inform a case. For instance, they can be tasked with providing the probability of an event taking place. The court may also consider the likelihood of a person engaging in certain acts such as defiling another person sexually after they have served their jail term or after they have been released if the evidence against them was not strong enough.

Profiling

Criminal profiling is also referred to as offender profiling. It is the process of linking the actions of an offender to the crime scene. The offender's characteristics will also ensure that the police can prioritize and narrow down all possibilities when considering all the possible suspects. Profiling is quite new concerning forensic psychology. The field of forensic psychology has grown in the past two decades. Initially, it was an art. Currently, it is a rigorous science. There are different sub-fields in forensic psychology, including investigative psychology. Criminal profiling currently entails carrying out some intensive research and also carrying out some rigorous methodological advances.

Criminals are usually classified based on factors such as sex, age, physical characteristics, geographic region, and education. When comparing some of the similar characteristics, you can easily understand a criminal's motivation when they decide to partake in criminal behavior.

Some national and international security organizations, including the FBI, usually refer to "criminal profiling" as "criminal investigative analysis." The analysts or profilers are normally trained. During the training process, they learn more about the behavioral aspects of different people and also learn more about the details of unsolved violent crime scenes, whereby there are some traces of psychopathy at the scene where the crime was committed.

The general appearance of the crime scene. It may be organized or disorganized.

The profiler can go ahead and interpret the behavior of the offender based on the crime scene. They can discuss everything further with their counterparts.

As a criminal psychologist, you may have to consider profiling from a racial perspective. Race plays a major role in the criminal justice system. In the past few years, the state and federal prisons have held more than 475,900 black inmates. The number of white inmates totaled 436,500. The difference is quite significant. Some of the black people are in prison because of negative stereotypes. Such stereotypes are ineffective, and some criminal psychologists can ascertain that the race of a person does not contribute to them being violent.

There are environmental, cultural, and traditional concepts that surround each race. Each of these concepts plays a key role in psychology. Some people may lack equal opportunities as a result of race or gender, for example, and that means that they have fewer chances to thrive.

Applied Criminal Psychology

For a criminal psychiatrist, the main question is, "Which offender will become a patient?" and "Which patient will become an offender?" Other questions that a psychiatrist should ask themselves are, "Which came first, the mental disorder or the crime?" Psychologists should take a look into the environmental factors and the genetics of a person while they carry out the profiling, to help determine whether the suspect committed the crime or not.

Some of the questions that criminal psychologists should ask themselves include:

- Is the mental disorder present at the moment? Did the person have a mental disorder when they were engaging in the criminal act?
- What is the level of responsibility of the person who committed the crime?
- Is treatment the best option when trying to reduce the risks of re-offending?
- Is there a possibility that the offender may engage in another crime, and what are the risk factors in this case?

Individual psychiatric evaluations normally come in handy since they help to measure an offender's personality traits through psychological testing. The results can also be presented in court.

Chapter 10: How the Mind Works When It IsManipulated

When it comes to working with dark manipulation, there are going to be a lot of different methods and techniques that we can use to get what you want. Remember, we are talking about some forms of manipulation that are going to help us to get what we want but may end up harming the other person in the process. This means that they may not be seen as the best options to work with, and youmay feel a bit uncomfortable with them if you have not worked in dark manipulation, or even with dark persuasion, in the past.

However, working with these techniques will help you to get the results that you want. They will ensure that the other person you are using as your target will be likely to do the actions or say the things that you would like them to, even though it may not be in their best interests to do so. With that said, let's take a look at some of the different dark manipulation tactics that you can use to get someone else to do what you want.

Using Isolation to Get What You Want

They like to spend some time talking with others, spending time out in public, having close friends, and family, and spending their time in more social situations. When we take this social aspect away from many individuals, it changes the way that they look at life.

Complete physical isolation can be the most powerful. This is when the subject is taken away from all contact with others, including email, social media, phone calls, and physical contact. This is something that has been seen in cults and with other groups. They will often take the person far away from others, and then the only human contact that the person can have is with the captors.

Now, this total physical isolation can be really hard to do, and it is usually only done in really intense situations. If you are just trying to use manipulation, you usually don't want to go through and completely isolate the target. But it is common for a manipulator will typically try to attempt their target mentally as much as possible.

There are several methods that the manipulator can use to get what they want with the help of manipulation. They could includesome seminars that last a week in the country and isolate the person from what they would usually do. They could be a lot of criticisms of the person's family and close friends so that the targetfeels bad and stops seeing them. It could be jealousy that keeps thetarget at home and limits the amount of influence that anyone outside the manipulator has on the person.

Once the manipulator is able to control the information that goes to the target, they can share information, withhold information, and do anything that they would like in order to continue influencing the target as much as they would like. The target is going to become reliant on the manipulator, and this is how the manipulator can work and get what they want from the target. There are no outside influences to tell the target that something is wrong, or that they should watch out, and this ensnares the target even more.

Criticism

The next option to work with when it comes to manipulation is the idea of using criticism. This one is sometimes used with isolated or on its own and it works well because it makes the target feel likethey are always doing something wrong, and that they are not ableto meet the high standards of the manipulator. The criticism can always show up on a variety of topics and could include how they look, who they hang out with, the clothes they wear, their beliefs, and anything that the manipulator thinks will work for this.

When a manipulator decides to use this tactic, they are going to be really good at hiding it behind one of their compliments to the other person. Or they will say something nice and add this little jab at the end of it. This allows them to say all the mean things thatthey want, and then they can say that the target misheard or misunderstood them and that they hadn't really meant any harm by it. This puts the target in a bad spot because they know the manipulator is being mean to them, but they are the ones who look paranoid and bad in this situation.

The criticism that the manipulator is going to use is often going to be small. They don't want to start out using really big criticisms that are obvious because the target doesn't want to be criticized. If the manipulator starts out with something big, the target is going to fight back and walk away. But when it starts out small with some little comments along the way, it starts to plant a bit of self-doubt, something that the target is going to notice, but they often are not going to fight back against.

They are going to start out with something that may seem like a compliment or like that is going to sound like they are being helpful, but in reality, they are trying to be hurtful in the process. They may say something like, "I didn't know that you liked the color blue. I think you should go with something else." This one is going to have the hidden meaning inside of it that you don't look good in what you are wearing, and your clothes don't look that well.

Or maybe you bring in your favorite outfit to a meeting to make yourself feel better. You are excited and you feel really good about the way that you look and feel in the outfit. But then they are going to say something about how they liked you in some other outfit better. It isn't necessarily mean, but it is said in a manner and at a time that it ends up hurting your feelings in the process.

As time goes on, the type of criticism that is going to be used against the target is going to get worse. And the criticism is going to become quite a bit more obvious as well to add in a bit more self-doubt here. This is going to make it so that the target starts to rely on the manipulator a bit more. This is because the target is going to feel like they have so many flaws that are hard to ignore, and that the only person who can like them and maybe even love them, through these flaws will be the manipulator. The fact that the manipulator is still around is a good sign that they care, and this causes the target to be more willing to do what the manipulator asks.

The manipulator is going to find that they are able to use this criticism more of us against them kind of idea if it works better as well. They could even choose to move their criticism to be against the outside world so that they can claim they are more superior.

When this happens, the manipulator is going to claim to their target that they are super lucky that the manipulator is even associating with them. The manipulator will ensure that they are important so that the target is more likely to stick around and do what they want. This alone is meant to be enough if it is done in the right manner so that the target feels lucky just because the manipulator is going to spend time with them.

Alienating the Target to Get What They Want

No one wants to be alienated. They want to feel like they are a part of the group. They want to feel accepted, as they belong, and more. This is never more apparent than when we see a newcomer. When someone is new to town, or to school, to work, or somewhere else, you will notice that they are trying to figure out how to join the group and get them to accept them. They are worried that they are going to be alienated and to avoid this, they will do everything in their powers to get others to like them and go along with them, and this is where the manipulator can come in and get what they want.

Newcomers who start to join a new manipulative group are usually going to receive a very warm welcome.

There are several reasons for this one. First, this gets the target to feel welcome and more indebted to the group and the manipulator. They are thankful that they have these deep connections, and it is usually easier to get a friend to go along with something that a stranger, so it works to the benefit of the manipulator as well. Add in that the target is scared to be alienated, then they are going to do what they can to keep the relationships going strong.

If any doubts end up arising, these relationships are going to become a powerful tool to ensure they stay with the group. Even if they aren't completely convinced, the target will start to remember their outside world, the world that they had before joining this group, and it is going to seem cold and lonely. They will instead choose to stay with the group, even if there is some manipulation going on.

Simply because we do not want to be taken away from the crowd and we don't want others to have anything to do with us, we are going to do what the manipulator wants us to. The fact that humans are very social creatures and like to be included in some kind of group all the time, it is likely that we are going to give in to these urges to do what the manipulator wants, even if we don't feel like it is the best thing for us.

Using Social Proof as a Form of Peer Pressure

We like it when we are able to be a part of the group. Sometimes we center this on wanting to fit in, and we will follow the rules and do what we can to make sure that we are liked and part of the group. And even when we are more introverted and don't want to be in the group all the time, we still want to find a group of people we can be around and fit in. The thing is that the manipulator is able to come in here and use the idea of wanting to fit in to help them work against you and get you to do things that you don't want to.

Chapter 11: The Role of Defense

To avoid falling victim to manipulators, you have to build your defenses so that you are prepared for any manipulative strategies that they may try to use on you. The best way to build your defenses is by taking steps to improve your self-esteem and your willpower. However, as a point of caution, you should be very careful about how you build your defenses because you don't want to create restrictions that will keep you from living a fulfilled life.

For example, as you try to guard against manipulation, you can't act out of fear. You can't hide from the world just to avoid scenarios where someone might want to take advantage of you. Remember that the world is full of people with dark personality traits who may harbor malicious intentions, so acting out of fear won't protect you from anyone. In fact, it will just make you more of a target. As you build your defenses, make sure that start on the premise that you are willing to confront manipulators head-on, and you will never run away or recoil. If you act out of fear, you lose by default.

The Steps to Raise Self-Esteem

To help you build your defenses, we will discuss the eight steps that you have to take to raise your self-esteem and to increase your willpower by extension.

Acceptance

Acceptance is about assenting to the reality of a given situation. It's about recognizing that a certain condition or process is what it is, even if it's characterized by high levels of discomfort and negativity. It's about consciously submitting to the fact that something cannot be changed, and that its reality is not subject to interpretation. It's about making peace with the situation that you are in.

Acceptance is the opposite of denial. Even the most rational among us tend to be in denial about lots of things in their lives, which are settled facts in the real sense. Denial can be a coping mechanism, one that can keep us from being overwhelmed by the reality of a given situation. However, denial does us more harm than good, because unless we can accept something, we can't change it, and we will be stuck looking for alternative interpretations and explanations for our prevailing circumstances.

Without acceptance, the door remains wide open for malicious people to exploit us. Take the example of a patient who is told that he/she is terminally ill. After seeking the opinions of several medical professionals and getting the same diagnosis, the patient is still left with the choice of either accepting or denying the situation. The one who accepts it will make peace and try to make the best out of what little time he has. The one who stays in denial will become susceptible to tricksters, who may offer "alternative cures," and he may end up losing all his savings paying such people so that in the end, he leaves his family with nothing. That is an extreme example, but it perfectly illustrates why acceptance is important in avoiding manipulation, even if the reality may seem too painful to accept.

The most crucial form of acceptance is self-acceptance. It refers to the state of being satisfied with yourself, the way you currently are. Most people have trouble accepting themselves as they are. We are all in a constant strive for self-improvement. We want to be more successful, to be wealthier, to be more attractive, or to be perceived more positively by others. Even the most accomplished among us have issues with self-acceptance.

In many ways, the desire to be a better version of yourself can be seen as a positive thing; it can help you study harder in school, work harder to earn a promotion at work or exercise more to get in shape. However, the problem is there is always room for improvement, so no matter how high you ascend, the dissatisfaction will always be there, and it will make you vulnerable to manipulation by people who want to take advantage of your desires.

To defend against manipulation, you have to accept your reality, and you have to accept yourself. People tend to think that if they accept themselves, they won't try to improve—that couldn't be further from the truth. Accepting yourself means owning up to your flaws, and that gives you control over your life. With self-acceptance, attempts at self-improvement would come from within, so when you decide to change, you will be doing it for yourself and not for anyone else.

Increase Awareness

Increasing your awareness means having a higher level of alertness when it comes to understanding what's going on in your environment. It means paying close attention to your surroundings, and to the way people behave around you. The higher your level of awareness, the better you will be when it comes to adapting to your surroundings and understanding the motivations of the people you interact with.

When you become more aware, you will be able to catch on quickly when people try to manipulate you. Many of us tend to be preoccupied with our own thoughts that we hardly ever notice the cues of the people we interact with. We tend to live life on autopilot, so when other people try to seize control over our lives, we only notice it when it's too late. If you increase your awareness, you will be equipped with the skills necessary to identify all the red flags, and you will be able to stop most manipulators on their tracks before they can do any real harm.

The first step towards increasing your awareness is to learn about the tendencies of manipulative people. You now know enough to be able to spot people with ill motives, but you should understand that the worst kinds of manipulators are very good at concealing their motives, so you have to keep working on increasing your awareness.

To be truly aware of manipulative people, you have to approach all interactions with some levels of skepticism. We are not telling you to turn into a paranoid person who doesn't let anyone in; we are just saying that you should take a deeper look at each person you interact with. Try to study their body language and their words, and try to see if they are trying to hide something.

Apart from increasing your awareness, you have to increase your self-awareness as well. Many people confuse those two things, but they are entirely different concepts. Self-awareness is about understanding yourself. It's about having a clear concept of your own personality. You have to examine yourself and figure out what your strengths and weaknesses are, what your values and motivations are, and what kind of thoughts and emotions you are likely to have in specific situations. Self-awareness helps you understand both who you are and how other people perceive you.

Self-awareness works as a defense against manipulation because when you know who you truly are, it becomes more difficult for someone to alter your thoughts and perceptions. If you have strong and well-articulated values, it becomes harder for a manipulator to get you to abandon those values. People who like self-awareness are more likely to be gaslighted or to be subjected to other forms of mind control.

If you end up in a relationship with a manipulative person, self-awareness can help you keep your identity. Manipulators will try to tell you what to think and how to behave, but if you are self-aware, you will experience cognitive dissonance, and your brain will push back against any attempts at manipulation.

Detach with Love

Detaching with love is a defense against manipulation that is most commonly used by people who have loved ones who suffer from substance abuse problems. Even though it was conceptualized to help people deal with addicts, it can also work when you are dealing with manipulators.

Detaching with love is about showing love and compassion for others without taking responsibility for their actions. For example, if you have a family member who is a drug addict, the way it works is that you try to support them and encourage them to get clean, but you let them make their own decisions, and you let them suffer the consequences of their actions. If the addict doesn't come home, you don't waste your time looking for them in the seedy parts of the city, you stay at home, and you do the things that benefit you and make you happy.

The point of detaching with love is to stop trying to control other people's lives, even if you are doing it for their own good. The idea is that you accept that people are different from you and that they have their own free will.

Detaching from love can defend you from manipulation in many ways. Some manipulators want to exploit you by making you responsible for them. They want you to give them all your attention; that is how they control you.

When you detach with love, you will learn to stop fixing everyone's problems. So, when the manipulator tries to play the victim to gain your sympathy, you will keep doing whatever is in your best interest, and you will tell him or her to take responsibility for his or her own actions.

Some manipulators may take up self-destructive habits because they want to dominate you by making you clean up after them. When they do this, you can detach with love by letting them follow the paths they have taken, no matter where they lead them. If they are causing you harm, you can get away from them, but leave your door open. If they find the right path in the future and regain control over their own lives, you can let them in again. You have to make it very clear, through your words and actions that you will let them direct their own lives, and you won't take any responsibility for them.

Detaching with love is about accepting others for who they are and respecting them enough to let them be in charge of changing their own lives. When you feel responsible for someone, and he makes a choice that harms you both, oftentimes, you will react with fear, anger, or anxiety. To detach with love, you have to learn to let go of those negative emotions.

Manipulators count on the fact that you will react in a predictable way to their machinations, but when you detach with love, you learn to calm yourself down and think about your role in the other person's life before you take any sort of action. This will keep you from falling into the traps that manipulators will set for you.

Detaching with love builds your self-esteem because it allows you to put your own needs ahead of those of the people that try to manipulate you.

Chapter 12: Toxic People

You can identify toxic persons by their behavior. Some relationships are also found to be toxic. Toxic people are suffering deep within, and they cannot take care of their problems. The person cannot meet their needs and feelings. They suffer from these ungratified needs and desires. To ease the suffering, they are experiencing the persons, behave in outrageous ways and their lives are one huge dramatic comedy. They cover up their wounded nature by portraying themselves as martyrs, perfectionists,bullies, and victims of circumstances. They also try these behaviors as they seek to satisfy their needs and heal from the wounds they sustained earlier in their lives.

These persons are dramatic, and they thrive in environments filled its drama. The person enjoys the attention they get from acting out. As a result, the person will magnify the insignificant issues and overreact causing others to turn heads. With little to show offfor in terms of personal achievements, the person feels irrelevant and invisible. Since the person wants to gain some recognition, they will seek drama in every situation to refocus others' attention.They are also needy, demanding attention all the time from everyone in their lives.

Toxic persons are also manipulative as they use other people to have their needs met. When you grow close to a toxic person, they will find ways to make you do things for them. They will fake illnesses to seek sympathy, which they use to benefit themselves. The person will act as a victim of his or her past. They will use their self-perceived wounds as an excuse for their outrageous behaviors and habits. The person is already aware of their weaknesses, and they do not want to lose your friendship along with its benefits, they will devise ways of manipulating you to stick close. They also enjoy controlling others to have them worshipping them and doing different tasks for them. Toxic people will enslave you by their demands and manipulative techniques, and if you are not aware of what is happening, you will lose yourself while trying to save them.

Toxic persons find faults in everything and everyone. They pass harsh judgment and criticism on themselves and others. The person cannot focus on positive things. They are also unable to expect positive outcomes. Even with such negative expectations, the person will not like the negative outcomes. They blame themselves and are too aware of their weaknesses. They will want to concentrate on their shortcomings and hardly see any significance in their strengths. The person fails to understand that no one is perfect, as we are all designed with weak points and strong points. When the person fails to recognize the strengths they hold, they are less likely to make an effort to discover their talents and unique abilities that are everyone's building blocks for success.

Toxic persons are also envious of others' achievements as they believe others are jealous of them too. They live in desperation, as they are always comparing themselves with others. The person lives in a moan-full mood as they compare other good fortunes with their misfortunes. It becomes difficult for such a person to see any beauty in their lives. The persons believe others are more advantaged, and they resent people who are doing better than them.

Toxic persons are more likely to hurt themselves because they do not find any value in their lives. The person has limited motivation, no goals, or plans for their future. These people also cause harm to others. They are at a higher risk of involving themselves in drugs. Such persons will hardly seek help as they don't view themselves as deserving of anyone's attention.

Toxic people are persistent in their demands, and however much you turn them down, they will persist. The person has no regard for the other person's values and personal principles. They are out to make others act out of their norm.

When having an interaction with a toxic person, your reaction to their words and behavior can lead to your acquiring toxicity. You need to watch your reactions and avoid losing your values to satisfy the person's demands. In such interactions don't lash out at the other person out of frustration, as it will result in drama in which you do not want to participate. You might also walk out on the other person once they start throwing negative remarks your way, which is an inferior way of facing challenges.

When in a relationship or friends with a toxic person, your life is chaotic in many ways:

You are in are always fixing the person's endless problems. Toxic people are attention seekers, and they will want to have others involved in sorting out their issues that seem to occur more often than normal. Some of the problems are of their creation as they attempt to have people around caring for them.

You are not comfortable with your own life and your progress in your goals. Friendship with toxic persons can ruin your life by diverting you from your personal purposes. The person demands all the attention they can get from you. If you are not cautious, you will set aside your goals and live to satisfy the person's demands. The negativity of the person can overcrowd your positivity, draining you out of your positive energy.

You feel exhausted following interaction with them. Toxic persons are tedious to deal with. Their constant demands will drain you physically and emotionally. You will listen to the person to complain about the least significant issues. Their views of others and life, in general, will haunt your intelligence.

Having them around fills you with anxiety. When you have a toxic person in your life; either family or close friend and you do not want to isolate from them, you have no choice but to tolerate them. You will experience anxiety when you are about to meet them because you would rather not. As you anticipate their behavior and attitude, you can't wait to get it over with.

You feel drained from their constant drama. Toxic people enjoy causing a scene as it draws others' attention. Whenever you are with the person; you are sure at some point they will over-react, causing others to focus their attention on you. If you are a nontoxic person, the experience will not be as thrilling. You will avoid interacting with the person, especially in a public setting because you do not want to be caught up in their drama.

When you are with the person, you feel as if you are getting out of touch with your being. You are either pushed around too much or reacting by controlling the toxic person. Toxic people have the habit of being too pushy. When you are driven to the edge by their persistence and demands you will result in acting too controlling to prevent them from pushing and dragging you around at their free will.

You also feel overly self-conscious and cautious. When in the company of toxic people, you can't predict what to expect from them. Their behaviors are rather shameful to an average person. You always feel like you are walking on glass.

How Negative and Toxic People Affect Your Life

Toxic and negative people are bound to infect you with their negative outlook on life. Their thoughts highly influence the behaviors of a person.

Interactions with others can also result in toxic relationships which are defined by the following;

Managing Negative Thoughts

Personal views and beliefs held by a person are a result of life-time experiences. Our beliefs are influenced by the environment we grew up in and other societal factors. Changing personal beliefs is a challenge because they make up our being. A person can't see any faults in their belief systems. Thought patterns are not easily notable either.

A person can manage negative thoughts in the following ways:

Start by consciously acknowledging the negative thoughts as they occur in your mind. When facing challenges, you will note your thought patterns shifting from solution seeking to self-defeating thoughts.

Once you have identified these negative thoughts, you can easily challenge them. Challenging our ideas involves trying to find enough evidence to support our conclusions. In challenging negative thoughts, we learn to introduce rational questioning in them. We look at the evidence in terms of the credibility of the source of this evidence; is the evidence we are basing our conclusion on credible? How trustworthy is the source of the information on which we are basing our conclusions? Are there facts supporting the evidence? Are these facts accurate? The answers to these questions will help us in passing judgment on the validity of our thoughts. Thoughts that are not substantiated enough should be discarded.

The following step involves replacing the negative thoughts with more positive ones. By embracing the positive thoughts and letting go of the negative, the person is effectively able to train the brain to focus on positivity. The challenging of negative thoughts might seem difficult to follow through, but over time it becomes natural for the person. People who have adopted the otherwise termed as Socrates questioning are always questioning the validity of their conclusions on decisions, and it helps them ineffective critical decision making.

Chapter 13: How to Fake Your Body Language

Regardless of being in the workplace or out with our partners, the non-verbal communication of the people around us says a lot. Peruse the full article to gain proficiency with every one of the eight regular non-verbal communication signals.

Concentrate on the Eyes - Eye Conduct Can Be Telling

Powerlessness to look can demonstrate fatigue, lack of engagement, or even misdirection—particularly when somebody turns away and to the side. If an individual looks down, then again, it regularly shows anxiety or accommodation. Students expand when subjective exertion increments, so if somebody is centered on a person or thing they like, their understudies will consequently widen.

Understudy enlargement can be hard to recognize; however, under the correct conditions, you ought to have the option to spotit. Now and again, the expanded flickering rate demonstrates lying—particularly when joined by contacting the face (especially the mouth and eyes). Looking at something can recommend a longing for that thing. For instance, if somebody looks at the entryway, this may demonstrate a craving to leave.

Looking at an individual can show a longing to converse with the person in question. Regarding eye conduct, it is likewise proposed that looking upwards and to one side during discussion shows an untruth has been told while looking upwards and to one side demonstrates the individual is coming clean. The purpose behind this is individuals turn upward and to one side when utilizing their creative mind to come up with a story, and gaze upward and to one side when they are reviewing a genuine memory.

Look at the Face - Body Language Touching Mouth or Smiling

Give specific consideration to the mouth when attempting to disentangle non-verbal conduct.

An authentic grin recommends that the individual is glad and getting a charge out of the organization of the individuals around the person in question.

You may likewise see a slight scowl that endures not exactly a second before somebody grins. Tight, pressed together lips likewise show disappointment, while a casual mouthdemonstrates a casual demeanor and positive temperament.

Covering the mouth or contacting the lips with the hands or fingers when talking might be a pointer of lying.

Focus on Vicinity

The vicinity is the separation between you and the other individual. Focus on how close somebody stands or sits alongside you to decide whether they see you positively. Standing or sitting in closeness to somebody is maybe probably the best marker of affinity. You can enlighten a great deal regarding the sort of relationship two individuals have simply by watching the closeness between them.

Check Whether the Other Individual Is Reflecting You

Reflecting includes mirroring the other individual's non-verbal communication. When interfacing with somebody, verify whether the individual mirrors your conduct. For instance, if you are sitting at a table with somebody and lay an elbow on the table, hold up 10 seconds to check whether the other individual does likewise. Another basic reflecting motion includes tasting a beverage simultaneously. If somebody copies your non-verbal communication, this is a generally excellent sign that the person is attempting to build up compatibility with you. Take a stab at changing your body stance and check whether the other individual changes theirs correspondingly. Watch the head development

The speed at which an individual gestures their head when you are talking demonstrates their understanding—or absence of. Slow gesturing demonstrates that the individual is keen on what you are stating and needs you to keep talking. Quick gesturing demonstrates the individual has heard enough and needs you to complete the process of talking or give that person ago to talk. Tilting the head sideways during the discussion can be an indication of enthusiasm for what the other individual is stating. Tilting the head in reverse can be an indication of doubt or vulnerability. Individuals likewise point with the head or face at individuals they are keen on or share a partiality with. In gatherings and gatherings, you can tell who the individuals with power depend on how regularly individuals take a gander at them. Then again, the less-critical individuals are taken a gander at less frequently.

Take a Quick Check at the Other Individual's Feet

A piece of the body where individuals regularly "release" significant non-verbal signals is the feet. The reason individuals unexpectedly convey non-verbal messages through their feet is that they are generally so centered around controlling their outward appearances and chest area, situating that significant pieces of information are uncovered using the feet. When standing or sitting, an individual will, for the most part, point their feet toward the path they need to go. So and when you see that somebody's feet are pointed toward you, this can be a decent sign that they have a positive assessment of you.

This applies to one-on-one collaboration and gathering association. You can enlighten a ton regarding bunch elements just by contemplating the non-verbal communication of individuals included, especially what direction their feet are pointing. What's more, and when somebody has all the earmarks of being occupied with discussion with you, yet their feet are pointing toward another person, it's presumable the person would prefer to converse with that individual (in any case if the chest area signals recommend something else).

Watch for Hand Signals

Like the feet, the hands release significant non-verbal signals when looking at non-verbal communication. This is a significant hint when perusing non-verbal communication, so give close consideration to this. Watch non-verbal communication turns in pockets when standing. Search for specific hand signals, for example, the other individual placing their hands in their pockets or hand on head. This can show anything from apprehension to inside and out duplicity. Oblivious pointing demonstrated by hand motions can likewise say a lot.

When making hand signals, an individual will point in the general heading of the individual they share a partiality with (this non-verbal prompt is particularly essential to look for during gatherings and when connecting in gatherings). Supporting the head with the hand by laying an elbow on the table can demonstrate that the individual is tuning in and is keeping the head still to center. Supporting the head with the two elbows on the table, then again, can show weariness.

At the point when an individual holds an article between the person in question and the individual they are associated with, this fills in as an obstruction that is intended to shut out the other individual. For instance, if two individuals are talking, and one individual holds a stack of paper before that person, this is viewed as a blocking demonstration in non-verbal correspondence.

Look at the Situation of the Arms

Think about an individual's arms as the entryway to the body and oneself. If an individual folds their arms while interfacing with you, it is generally observed as a protective, blocking motion. Crossed arms can likewise show nervousness, powerlessness, or a shut personality. Whenever crossed arms are joined by a veritable grin and by and large loosened up stance, at that point, it can demonstrate a sure, loosened up frame of mind. When somebody puts their hands on their hips, it is normally used to apply predominance and is utilized by men more regularly than ladies.

Is non-verbal communication a "learnable aptitude," and can it in this manner be faked? The appropriate response is yes and no. Most by far of the more common non-verbal communication can be scholarly. For instance, keeping your hands out of your pockets or utilizing the hands expressively to stay legitimate and open, or repelling the hands from the face to appear to be increasingly certain as effectively learned through cognizant idea and redundancy. In any case, another zone of study uncovers that there is an entirely different arrangement of signs that are significantly harder to control, if certainly feasible.

A Wrinkled Brow Can Occur in a Brief Instant and Uncover Negative Feelings

These are called micro-expressions or micro-signals. These signs can be utilized to disentangle liars from truth-tellers. Micro-expressions show up as wrinkles, grins, glares, grins, and wrinkles and can offer a precise, however short-lived, window into feelings. These micro-expressions are constrained by muscles, for example, the frontalis, corrugator, and risorius, and they are incited by hidden feelings that are difficult to control deliberately. One of these feelings is the phony grin to demonstrate submission instead of certifiable euphoria or joy. The phony grin is self-evident because the lips are pulled over the mouth, yet the muscles controlling the eyes have no influence.

With particular PC programming, specialists have had the option to identify these signs. PCs were utilized because the sign moves quickly over the face in divisions of seconds, making it difficult for people to lift the sign deliberately.

Hindering video on rapid camcorders and playing it back over and over to spectators can likewise be utilized to distinguish the articulations. So some portion of the story is that micro-expressions are hard to recognize and control, yet the remainder of the story discloses to us that if they exist (and they do), that we should at some level have advanced the capacity to peruse and distinguish them. Along these lines, we should be mindful about accepting that since they happen so quickly, that they can't be gotten and on the other hand that we can without much of a stretch phony our way through the non-verbal channel. It could be that the subliminal instinct is working diligently, giving us that intuition feeling that can't confide in somebody despite not exactly having the option to put it to words. The reason, it appears, is a blend of micro-expressions and our instinct.

A few scientists will disclose to us that the face is the most straightforward piece of our bodies to control, yet this isn't valid and is a sorry excuse for the full story. If our countenances were so effectively controlled, why have Botox medicines to stop up our appearances with low-level poisons to eradicate wrinkles? Why not simply quit utilizing the muscles out and out and, in this way, abstain from experiencing facial wrinkles during the maturing procedure? The straightforward answer is that it's not the basic.

While our countenances are in certainty under an enormous part under our influence, we can't generally be centered around it, in case we do not have the option to concentrate on whatever else. Not the least of which is controlling our discourse. Would you be able to envision what it resembles to build sentences freestyle while attempting to stay expressive and yet abstain from contracting "unseemly" facial muscles (whatever they may be)? When we talk or see, or do, our faces normally react to what is happening around us since they are firmly attached to our psyche and our feelings. It is circumstances and logical results relationship, or even a weapons contest, and it correctly because the face gives such an immense measure of data that we are so fixed on understanding it.

Different approaches to detect phony concerns incongruent non-verbal communication. That is, a language that is conflicting with either the words being communicated in and the non-verbal language that goes with it.

Chapter 14: Undetected Mind Control

Your mind is your sanctuary. No matter what else can be lost to others, the mind is yours and yours alone. Or so we think. People like to believe that they are the ones in control of their own actions and thoughts. Many times our minds can be susceptible to the influence of others, and this allows others to control our minds if we're not careful.

Think about a time when you watched a horror movie. Your mind and your emotions are already being led and influenced in the movie. All the decisions of the director, from the camera shot, the lighting, and the music can determine how you are going to feel and react. Even though you are in full awareness that you are just watching a movie, the brain is going to respond to the prompts when they are given. If our brain can be so influenced by something that we are aware of, how strong would the influence of a dark manipulator be?

Undetected mind control is often the most deadly type of mind control there is. If someone is already aware that their mind is being influenced, then they have the option to object, either physically, verbally, or mentally. For example, they can choose to avoid any contact with the person who controls them. A lot of people are going to run at the first sign they see a dangerous person trying to get inside the brain and take over. But if the mind controller is able to get into the brain of their victim without the victim detecting them, then the victim has no chance to put up their defenses before it's too late.

There are going to be two tactics that the manipulator can use to take over the mind of their victim without detection. This includes the use of media and interpersonal interactions. Traditionally, the media mind control was only possible for the larger company. Most individual mind controllers were left to deal with just the interpersonal interactions. But with the changes in technology now, this is no longer the case.

Smartphones and laptops have allowed even individual manipulators to have media mind control. This can make it a very powerful tool that the manipulator can use. While the undetected mind controller is going to be able to use all these methods, they are often going to be more deliberate and only take their actions after some careful consideration. They are sometimes seen as a big more coward compared to some other controllers, such as psychological manipulators, but they will take deliberate actions in order to find the right victim to do the attack on.

Undetected Mind Control Tactics

Now that we know a little bit more about undetected mind control, it is time to learn about some of the methods that are used by manipulators to control the mind of a victim in an undetected way. We are going to explore both the media and the interpersonal techniques that are in the toolkit of the manipulator. Let's take a look at some of the different undetected mind control tactics.

Finding Those Who Are in Need

The first principle that comes with undetected mind control is to find a victim who has a goal. It has been proven that a person who has a pressing desire or needs is someone who will be more susceptible to this type of mind control compared to someone that feels satisfied and at ease. This could range from a small physical goal, such as someone thirsty and looking for a drink. Or it can be a more psychological goal, such as someone who is craving affection and love.

A good example of this is the experiment that was conducted to look at a subliminal influence or undetected mind control. In this study, there were two sets of people who were shown a film, but this film had a hidden image of iced tea. One set of people in the study were thirsty, and the second group wasn't.

After the movie, when the participants were given the chance to purchase a specific drink from a selection, the ones who were thirsty would purchase the iced tea in greater numbers compared to those who weren't thirsty. This shows that, when the brain is desperate for something, they are gladly taking suggestions on what they should choose.

So, how would you be able to use this principle with an individual on more of an interpersonal level? If the mind controller is able to find a victim who is already craving something in their life, then the manipulator will find that it is easier to control that victim. One example is a victim who just got out of a long-term relationship. They may crave the company again and the mind controller would be able to influence their target into thinking that they are the savior for the victim. In reality, they are going to cause harm and even ruin for the victim, but the victim will crave attention so much that they will fall for the mind control that is put on them.

There are a lot of needs that a manipulator is going to seek to exploit their victim, including their need for company, their need to belong, and even monetary stability. These vulnerabilities are going to be exploited by someone who is more experienced for many purposes. They may want to financially or sexually exploit the victim. They may want to gain the victim's allegiance to form a cult or other extreme movement. Some manipulators just go through this process to toy with their chosen victim for their own pleasure.

Media Control with Images

Just like our five senses can be guides in our lives, they can also be our enemies. Our sense of sight is very powerful. This is why we can even dream visually, even when all the other senses are missing, and we can use our sight to see images of past memories.

This can make imagery as well as visual manipulation, a really powerful technique to use with media mind control.

Because of the changes in technology, impactful imagery techniques are in the hands of manipulators all over the place, and they can even take these techniques and tailor them to their specific victims. So, if their victim seems to have a fear or an aversion to something, the manipulator is able to use the feared images to help access and then warp the emotions of a person without the victim even realizing what's going on.

Let's look at how this type of mind control can work. We are in an age where there are lots of smartphones, videos, and more. Everything is shot in high definition clips and can be sent at fast speeds to someone else. This means that a high-tech manipulator can allude to the feared image. For example, if a manipulative boyfriend knows that his girlfriend has a big fear of insects, they could "accidentally" put a book with a picture of an insect on its cover in the background somewhere during that video chat. While the girlfriend may not consciously register that the book is there, on an emotional and subtle level, she is going to feel the impact.

Restricting Choice

Restricting choice is another form of undetected mind control. It can be a subtle form of this because it is going to provide the manipulator with a range of built-in "get out clauses" if the victim ever starts to get suspicious. The key to this type of mind control is to take away any real choices that the victim has in a specific circumstance, while still providing the illusion that the victim is the one who has the control.

Let's say that there is a woman who is being asked to go out on a date. A regular guy is going to spend some time to ask the question and then stammer out an open-ended question. They may say something like "Would you like to go out with me?" This question allows the woman to say yes or no based on their personal preferences. This is the way that people who aren't using manipulation will behave.

But someone who is trying to use mind control will approach all of this differently. They will confidently and smoothly work to charm the victim. They will get that person to laugh a bit and lower their guard. Then, with a lot of confidence and assurance, the manipulator will ask something like "So, am I taking you out on Thursday or Saturday?" This limits the choices that the victim can go with. The answer of no really isn't an option here, so the victim will pick one of the dates they are given. The victim can't really say that they weren't in control, but the manipulator had complete control the whole time.

Now, if the manipulator is caught, or the victim realizes that they are limited on the choices they are allowed to make, the manipulator can backtrack and still look innocent. They could say something to their victim like, "I can't believe you're analyzing my words so much. That really hurts me and makes me not want to open up to you." This can make the victim feel like they were being meant, and they will probably give in.

Media Mind Control with Sound

Sound is another method that the manipulator can use in order to do mind control. But personal experience and experiments can confirm this. Have you ever had a song that seems to get stuck in your head? How easy did you find it to get that song out of your head? The sound may have had a big influence on you, even though you knew it was there.

The power of audio manipulation is even greater when it is undetected. Experiments have shown that if customers are exposed to music that comes from a specific region, then they are more likely to order wine from that country. When they were questioned about it later, they had no idea that the sound around them was what influenced them for their decision making.

While there are examples of the media mind control with sound in the media and with the government, even individual manipulators are able to use this kind of mind control as well. One of the creepiest forms of this mind control is to influence the victim when they are asleep subliminally. A skilled mind controller can get their victim when that victim is at the most vulnerable, such as when they are sleeping, and then can implant the dark and devious commands in the ear of their victim. This allows the commands to sink into the lowest layers of the brain of that victim.

Another form of this auditory mind control is to mask the words with other words or noises that sound similar. Sounds that are outside the range of human perceptions can be this type of mind control.

Chapter 15: Effects of Narcissism in Relationships

You know you shouldn't fall in love with a narcissist, but somehow, you find yourself entangled in a toxic relationship with one. How did you end up here? After all, narcissists love no one else above themselves. You are looking for someone to love and cherish you as much as you love and cherish them, yet you end up with someone incapable of loving you or even recognizing you beyond a glance.

Why do we fall in love with narcissists? What is it about them, or ourselves, that makes this supposedly impossible connection possible? Someone who is too engrossed in their ideology of themselves should fundamentally be unattractive, yet here we are.

We live in a world where fantasy has been glorified, and everyone keeps chasing after something unreal at some point. At the back of your mind, you know what you seek, or what is before you is superficial a smokescreen, yet the allure of attaining the impossible is too strong, so you yield.

Take speed dating, for example. Many people have participated in one or more. How do you get to know someone by summarizing highlights of their life? Speed dating is one of the lamest things in as far as relationships are concerned, yet many people throng the venues in the hope that they can find someone to settle with.

In such a case, who is at fault? Is it the narcissist who presents their case as a well-to-do, accomplished, person of your dreams kind of partner, or the seeker who is impressed by, and accepts nothing short of what the narcissist says they are? However, speeddating is not our concern, but an attempt at highlighting how complicated relationships can be, especially in terms of needs assessment (Houser, Horan, & Furler, 2008).

Narcissists are desperate, not just for attention, but also for self-love. They need to convince themselves that they are good enough constantly. If they are good enough for themselves, they have to be good enough for you too. This is one of the reasons why rejection doesn't always work well for a narcissist. It is not easy for them to reconcile it in their minds that someone thinks and feels they are not good enough.

While narcissists are at fault for their grandiose perception of themselves, at times you have to look inwards to understand your role in some unfortunate events. For the record, this is not to blame the victim, but to help you see things from a different perspective. Narcissists might be held accountable for manipulating you into a relationship, but you can get out. You deserve to be happy, and you deserve a happy and healthy relationship. Earlier on we saw some of the defining characteristics and manipulative traits of narcissists. This helped us understand who they are, how to identify them, and why they behave the way they do. We will try to understand you, the victim, and how narcissism is perpetuated in your life.

Why Am I Attracting Narcissists?

Ever felt like you are a narcissist magnet? Somehow, you keep ending up in relationships with narcissists, and this is not just about personal relationships, but the whole spectrum, including professional relations. While you might worry about attracting narcissists, this is not the main problem. The real problem is that you are holding onto them.

Let's try an exercise. Answer the following questions about your interactions and relationships truthfully:

- Do you have defined boundaries about behavior and attitudes you can tolerate from your partner?
- Would you end a relationship because your partner is selfish and doesn't consider your needs?
- How do you handle an abusive relationship? Walk away or stay and hope your partner will change?
- Do you excuse ill behavior from your partner and make excuses for them?

These might seem like mundane things, but they form the platform upon which a narcissistic partner will get away with devaluing you and your opinion all the time.

Here are some reasons why you might find yourself in a relationship with a narcissist, an abusive relationship you struggle to get out of:

Caregiving Spirit

Caregiving is a good deed. You empathize with someone who lacks, and out of the kindness of your heart, you take care of them. Many high achievers in society are in relationships with narcissists, some without knowing it. As a high achiever, you know you can take care of yourself. As a result, you always turn down the chance for someone to take care of you. You offer to pay for meals and drinks all the time. There is nothing wrong with taking care of yourself. However, to compensate for this lack of vulnerability, it is easier for you to take care of others. In so doing, you end up attracting people who constantly need help.

You Fall for the Name-Dropping Charm

Everyone knows someone important. When it comes to celebrity stories, everyone has something that can light up a conversation. Whether it is true or another story, they heard from someone else; they tell their tales so vividly you can almost live in the moment through their words.

"Oh, you know Vettel too? He's such a nice person. He's friends with one of my buddies at work; we hang out from time to time."

If this kind of thing works for you, there is a good chance you will never see beyond a narcissist's name-dropping charm. Their stories and encounters are full of big names. It gets worse when they realize these appeals to you. They do this in a bid to conceal their insecurities about themselves and instead, lavish you with the idea of this glamorous life they live. Be warned, however, this charm is ingenuine. It is a ploy to seek and maintain attention. After all, who doesn't want to hear more about how to sneak into Buckingham Palace?

Flattery Is Your Undoing

Flattery can make you feel so good, but it doesn't last. At best, it can get you in a good mood. Narcissists crave attention. Nothing stands in their way when they want it. The use of flattery works for them because they can flatter you to get your attention, then immediately go on about them.

Flattery for a narcissist is not necessarily about needing compliments. In some cases, it is about paranoia, as the narcissist goes through their regular attention-seeking routine, and to boost their fragile ego.

Hovering for a Second Chance

If you are in a relationship with a narcissist and you break up with them, please let them go. Don't hold on, hoping that they might change and come back better. Narcissists love to hover around in the aftermath of a breakup. They had all your attention, which they don't enjoy anymore. This makes them feel helpless and abandoned, in which case the only alternative is to lure you back by any means necessary.

There are several tricks that they can use for this, including making a half-hearted apology, convincing you that they will not do what made you break up again, and so forth. Some will even send you photos of themselves looking sad. All this is to guilt you into taking them back.

Remember that you let them go because they disrespected you, and you felt that they cannot change. Such a person cannot changein a few days. They can, however, learn how to camouflage their real intent. Most people who take their narcissistic partners back usually suffer more pain and emotional trauma than they did earlier on.

You Sustain the Drama

Narcissists get bolder over time. They come at your boundaries, hoping you will cave and get softer with them. Your life with them is full of so much drama; you can't seem to catch a break. Netflix would be jealous of your life. Think about this for a moment: how peaceful is your life when your narcissist partner is out of town for work, or when they have traveled for some other reason?

When you are all alone, things are easy, smooth, peaceful, until they come back and all the upheaval starts. A narcissist will always leave you devoid of energy. All their demands will leave you worn, drained, and exhausted. All you ever do is provide for everything they need, from attention to affection. At the beginning of your relationship, this might feel okay, because perhaps you are trying to impress them or keep up with their energy. However, after a while, you realize you cannot keep up, and you are demoralized after an encounter with them.

You Are a Hopeless Empath

If there is one category that narcissists love and are surprisingly more drawn to it, it has to be empaths. Life can be very cruel and unfair. Why do such nice, loving, and caring people end up with partners who leave them more worn out than confidential documents having passed through a paper shredder?

The secret lies in your personality. As an empath, you are an understanding person. You believe that everyone deserves a chance. You see the good in everyone, even when you shouldn't. You believe that given time, you can turn a bad person into a good person. If you spend enough time with them, you can show them the goodness of their hearts, and make them change and embrace a new life (Stadler, 2017). This is where you go wrong, and open your life to toxicity.

Narcissists are wounded animals. As an empath, you want to take care of them. They know this better than you do. They know you are naturally inclined to try and fix them. When you meet, they will talk about how rough life has been for them in the past, perhaps in relationships, or their work, or anything else that draws your sympathy. While it is okay to be kind, you must be very careful about whom you show your kindness to.

Why Empaths Attract Narcissists

The attraction between an empath and a narcissist is one of those instinctive connections that just happen. You feel like you were meant to be together. You clicked the very first time you met, and it seems you have found the right person for you until you wake up from the bad dream that has been months or years of your life. What's unfortunate for most empaths is that they will often end up in another relationship with another narcissist.

Narcissist-empath relationships are very toxic. You are exposed to so much pain that people who were once close to you can barely recognize you. Narcissists and empaths share some attributes that are attractive to one another, which is one of the reasons why they always seem destined to meet one another.

For the empath, however, it is nothing but bad news. All your goodness will be misconstrued for weakness and exploited by a narcissistic partner. In order to understand why this relationship happens in the first place, here are some reasons why you are drawn together:

You Are a Natural Healer

A narcissist will always appeal to an empath because you have natural healer tendencies. There is something so nurturing about you. Everyone knows it and it shows. You are a natural healer because you are sensitive. You are sensitive to people's feelings and needs.

Chapter 16: Brainwashing

What Is Brainwashing?

In the early 1950s, Brainwashing was coined by journalist Edward Hunter, who wanted to describe the Chinese Communists' efforts to control the minds and to think processes of the Chinese people after their takeover in 1949. Brainwashing is a method of controlling or influencing the personal beliefs, thoughts, attitudes, or actions of people themselves to make them believe what they had previously considered to be false. The word "brainwashing" originated from its Nao, the Chinese term which means "washing the brain." Brainwashing is a method by which a person or group makes use of strict austerity measures to influence others to the will of the manipulator. But where does he stop honest persuasion and start brainwashing? Today, there are many forms of persuasion employed, especially in politics. For instance, a simple way to persuade a crowd to follow your instructions is first to state a few things that cause a' yes' response, then add items that are actual realities, and finally, recommend what you want them to do.

Methods

In psychology, the brainwashing study often referred to as the reform of thought, falls into the "social influence" sphere. Every minute of every day, social influence happens. It's the set of ways people can change the perceptions, values, and actions of other people. The enforcement approach, for example, attempts to bring about a change in a person's behavior and is not concerned about his ethics or values. It is the strategy of "Just do this."

Techniques That Are Used in Brainwashing

Isolation

Typically, the first tactic used in brainwashing is to isolate the victim away from his friends and family. They don't have to worry about any third party coming in and questioning what's happening.

Chanting and Singing

Chanting mantras is an essential feature of many religions, notably Buddhism and Hinduism, and nearly every church has some form of hymn-singing adoration. As each church member chants or sings the same words, their voices merge into one song, creating a strong sense of unity and collective identity. That, along with established singing effects such as lowered heart rate and relaxation, could cast the experience of community worship into a positive light. Increased suggestibility is a feature of such a state, and failure to maintain the trance is often followed by the punishment inflicted on cults, ensuring continuous enforcement of ultra-conformist behavior. They added that continuous lectures, singing, and chanting are used by most cults to alter consciousness.

Love Bombing

Cults want to reinforce the feeling that the outside world is threatening and gravely mistaken. In comparison, they also use "love bombing" to make themselves look accommodating. Love bombing means showering with lavish new or prospective hires and displaying attention and affection. The term has probably originated with either the Children of God or the Church of Unification, but can now be practiced in several different organizations. It is a phenomenon of social psychology that we feel strongly compelled to reciprocate other people's kind acts and kindness. It is, so the counterfeit affection, encouragement, and goodwill shown towards initiates by existing cult members are processed to create a growing sense of debt, obligation, and guilt. Margaret Singer called this an essential character of the cult, useful because it's precisely companionship and validation that many new cult recruits are searching for.

The psychologist Edgar Schein claims that people are triggered into a cult through a process of "unfreezing and refreezing. A new cult member starts to reject his old view of the world during the unfreezing stage and becomes open to the ideas of the cults. The cult solidifies this new perspective during refreezing. Schein mentions to love bombing as a critical point of refreezing—recruits who accept the philosophy of cults are rewarded with hugs and compliments but shunned when they ask too many skeptic questions.

Barratrous Abuse

Most cults hire attorneys to prosecute anyone who criticizes them publicly, no matter how trivial the criticism may be. Of course, the cult can usually afford to lose the lawsuits, while ex-cult members are often insolvent after giving the organization's life. Consequently, many ex-cultists are unable to mount an effective legal counterattack. Moreover, due to the ever-present threat of legal action, mainstream journalists are afraid to criticize cult or reference religious material.

Fatigue and Sleep Deprivation

Amway, a multi-level marketing company, has been charged with depriving its distributors of sleep during weekend-long events. It happened because they were including non-stop seminars lasting until the early morning hours, with only brief interludes during which musicians play loud music with lights flashing. A cultivation strategy that is sometimes used in combination with sleep deprivation includes advising participants to adopt special diets that contain low protein levels and other essential nutrients. As a result, the members of the cults will always feel tired, making them powerless to resist the dictates of religious doctrine.

Activity Pedagogy

How does a teacher motivate their students to follow ethical behavior and conformism? The solution is often to integrate some sort of physical exercise or sport into their teaching. Involved in jumping on the spot or running around, and consequently tired, children are less likely to argue or cause trouble. By acknowledging this phenomenon, several cults aimed to have members occupied as a means of control with an endless series of tiring activities. What distinguishes activity pedagogy from mere sports is that the increased mood and group identity experienced after physical activity will be used by a regime or cult to introduce ideological views that could otherwise be met with skepticism. Fatigue by exercise is yet another manner in which the barriers of people can be worn away as a means to enable them to embrace dubious ideas.

Lifton's Process

Robert Jay Lifton, the psychologist, studied former Korean War prisoners and Chinese war camps in the late 1950s. He determined that they would have undergone a multi-stage process that started with attacks on the sense of self of the prisoner and ended with what appeared to be a change of beliefs. Finally, Lifton defined a set of steps involved in the cases of brainwashing which he studied:

Assault on Identity

You're not who you think you believe you are. It is a deliberate assault on the sense of self of a target (also called its identity or ego) and its core system of beliefs. The agent hides everything that makes the target that he is: "You're not a soldier." "You're not a man." You're not protecting freedom. "For days, weeks, or months, the target is under constant attack to the point of becoming exhausted, confused, and disorientated. His convictions in this state appear less reliable.

Guilt

You are wrong. Whereas the existential crisis is setting in, the agent generates at the same time an intense sense of guilt within the target. He attacks the subject repeatedly and ruthlessly for any "sin" committed, big or small, by the target individual. For everything from the wrongness of his beliefs to the style he eats too slowly, he can criticize the target. The goal starts feeling a general sense of shame that all he does is wrong.

Self-Betrayal

Please agree with me you're awful. Once the subject becomes disoriented and submerged in shame, the agent pressures him to condemn his family members, friends, and peers who share the same "wrong" belief system that he maintains (either with the threat of physical damage or of continued mental attack). This abuse of his convictions and of those he feels responsible for heightening the guilt and lack of idea.

Leniency

I can help. The agent gives a small kindness or relief from the violence with the target in a state of crisis. He may offer a drink of water to the target, or take a moment to ask the target what he misses over the home.

Compulsion to Confession

You can help yourself. The target is faced with the comparison between the guilt and pain of identity assault. Then the sudden relief of leniency, for the first time in the brainwashing process, comes. The target may feel a desire to return the favor to the kindness that is shown to him, and then the agent may present the possibility of confession as a means of relieving guilt and suffering.

Challenging of Guilt

It is the reason because you are in pain. After some months of assault, confusion, breakdown, and leniency moments, the guilt of the target has lost all meaning—he's not sure what he's done is illegal, only knows he's wrong. It provides something of a blank slate that allows the agent to fill in the blanks: to whatever he wants, and he can add the remorse, that feeling of "wrongness." The agent attaches the guilt of the target to the creed system, which the agent attempts to replace. The goal comes to believe that the source of his guilt is his belief system.

That's not me; that's my attitude. The battled person is relieved to learn that there's an exogenous shock of his wrongness, that it's not himself who's intractably bad—that means he can escape his wrongness by running away from the corrupt system of beliefs. Then he can criticize the people and institutions associated with that system of ideas, and he will no longer be in pain. The goal can free itself from guilt by confessing to actions connected with its old policy of belief. The goal has completed its psychological rejection of its former identity with its full confessions. Now it is up to the agent to offer a new one for the target.

Self-Rebuilding
Progress and Harmony

The agent introduces a new belief system as the path to "good" if you want. At this stage, the agent stops the misuse, providing the target physical comfort and mental calm in combination with the new system of belief. The goal is made to feel it's he who has to choose between old and new, giving the goal the impression that his future is in his own hands. The goal has already abandoned his old belief system in reaction to leniency and abnormality. The choice is not a hard one: the new identity is safe and desirable because it is nothing like the one that has led to its breakdown.

Final Confession and Rebirth

I pick good. The target contrasts the agony of the old with the peace of the new. Then the target individual chooses a new identity, clinging to it as a preserver of life. He rejects his old system of beliefs and promises loyalty to the new one that will make his life better. There are frequent rituals or ceremonies at this final stage to induce the converted target into its new community. Some brainwashing victims have described this stage as a sensation of "rebirth."

Because Lifton and other psychologists have described variations in what seems to be a distinct series of steps leading to a deep state of suggestibility, an interesting question is why some people end up brainwashed, and others don't.

Chapter 17: Covert Hypnosis

This process is also called conversational hypnosis or sleight of mouth. This term is mostly used by advocates of neuro-linguistic programming (NLP). NLP is a pseudoscientific approach to communication and interaction.

The technique's prime objective is to change the person's behavior subconsciously in such a way that the target believes that he changed his mind using his own will. The success of this process lies significantly in the fact that the remains unaware that he was hypnotized or that anything unusual occurred. The focus and attention of the subject are imperative during the conduct of "Standard" hypnosis. This process is identical to salespeople talking to customers when they are tired. This is because critical thinking and questioning of statements require mental effort. The theme of "covert hypnosis" lies in approaching the subject when he is mentally and physically worn out. Covert hypnosis, irrespective of the fact, remains hypnosis. The element of fatigue is incorporated to make the critical thinking process more cumbersome.

Techniques

The notable trait of this process is that the hypnotized individual ultimately engages in hypnotic phenomena in an incognizant manner. There is a striking similarity between Covert hypnosis and "Ericksonian Hypnosis" in that both techniques work to reach deeper levels of consciousness operates by employing covert and subtle means. The surface structure of language then touchesthese more profound levels of consciousness. During covert hypnosis, the hypnotist controls another individual's behavior through establishing.

The subject feels a psychological connection with the hypnotist as he listens to him. The hypnotist, while displaying confidence and control, presents linguistic data in the form of metaphor:

However, it consequently helps in enabling a recovered deep structure of meaning that is directly relevant to the listener.

Put in another way, this process first builds unconscious states within the listener and then connects those states through covert conditioning. This is achieved, for instance, by shifting the use of time and use of identity in language.

An example:

The hypnotist may try to achieve a state of forgetfulness in the subject. This is done when the hypnotist talks with the subject of his feeling in that particular state in order to gain maximum knowledge about the subject. When the hypnotist discovers that this state is at its heightened peak, he can start talking about that state after this state has attained its maximum peak. That response will be contingent upon the fact that the suggestions were made to draw an immediate effect, and the reader was suggestible enough to be influenced in this way. The core objective of covert hypnosis is to shut down or at least minimize the analytical part of the subject's brain, lest he suspect something. All this may be achieved relatively quickly by an experienced practitioner.

Covert Hypnosis and Media

Real estate expert Glenn Twiddle in June 2010 appeared on the Australian television show A Current Affair. The segment reveals how he teaches real estate agents how to use these tactics on potential property buyers.

Covert Hypnosis in Fiction

Covert hypnosis has been portrayed in television series such as The Mentalist, although somewhat over-represented, the most prominent portrayal of covert hypnosis was in the "Russet Potatoes" episode in which a suspect uses covert hypnosis to manipulate characters in the episode and attempts to kill her boss. Another example of covert hypnosis was in the X-Files, where a man with a tumor in his brain is learning additional hypnosis abilities and using them to escape police captivity.

Learning Covert Hypnosis

If you want to learn covert hypnosis, first, you have to realize that it takes a long time to master properly, but if you practice every day, you will continually see positive results.

When learning how to do covert hypnosis, the difficulty for most people is not their inability to apply the methods, but rather their impatience and ignorance of how covert hypnosis is first and foremost.

There are extremely useful tips given below that will help you learn covert hypnosis.

Get into the Right Learning Mind Frame

It involves understanding how it takes dedication and persistence to master covert hypnosis. When you start learning covert hypnosis first, do not think it's going to be easy.

Covert hypnosis is all about knowing how the human mind functions and discovering how to interact effectively, mentally, and physically, with someone's mind in a subtle way.

While you can learn and apply such methods effectively within a very short space of time, you will not be able to do this effectively to different people without understanding the full processes leading up to that point.

Build Rapport

Many people make mistakes while establishing rapport. Relationship building involves creating a secure connection between the hypnotist and the subject of the hypnotist. The stronger the bond, the more powerful the technique of covert hypnosis is.

The partnership is more than what exists out there. It is an emotional and intense friendship, where people can be inside the minds of each other.

This hypnotic relationship bond is so strong that the subject will see the hypnotist as a figure of authority, and will be more than willing to do what the hypnotist wants them to do with little or no resistance.

Look for Trance Signals

Widening the social awareness networks by increasing the senses is of fundamental importance. It is construed as a critical step as it helps you to see the signs the subject gives as they enter a hypnotic trance.

Recognizing sure trance signs ensures you can move to the next stage of your technique of covert hypnosis.

Recognizing when someone is not hypnotically reacting to you is just as crucial because then you will realize that your manipulation is not working and that you have to find another process.

Understand Hypnotic Language

There is another name for Covert hypnosis, that is, conversational hypnosis, and you need to learn how to practice and sharpen your language skills to make it more hypnotic to influence a conversation.

Whenever you decide and manage to converse in a hypnotic language, it will cause the mind of the subject into a hypnotic state, which you can then influence to respond to in some hypnotic ways.

There is a range of primary and advanced methods in the hypnotic language, and you can do to achieve the hypnotic state of mind, from emotional triggers to manipulating someone's emotions to hypnotic storytelling.

What Hypnosis Is and Is Not

It is essential that you clear from the outset any doubts you have about hypnosis. Hypnosis is presented in the media as a means of total control over another person, and this enormous misconception has affected many people.

Any form of hypnosis won't give anybody complete control over the mind of another. This is just not possible.

Advantages of Covert or Conversational Hypnosis

You are directly influenced by the level of happiness and success of others. If you discover the fundamental secrets of ethical power, the world will be at your feet.

If you don't, you could end up living a quiet, lonely life, just like 95 percent of people who suffer from all kinds of problems needlessly.

Their suggestions and advice do not get much attention. They don't get their due respect. They lose clients and customers, and don't know why!

They are unable to communicate with confidence and have difficulty expressing their proposals to their colleagues. When they meet strangers, they lose their composure and make a poor initial impression.

They cannot get their children to listen and are usually discouraged because things don't seem to be going their way.

But it does get worse!

This is because no one tells you how to be as successful as you grow up. You've just picked up a few things here and there.

Covert Hypnosis Is a Simple Way to Convince People

Another big problem is conventional communications, and it doesn't work out by mere sales training.

You'll see people run away from you if they find you using such techniques.

There's a plethora of proof to suggest hypnosis might just be the answer you've been waiting for. The best part is the right kind of trance, which even works every day during routine interactions. That's okay. If you are talking to someone at a grocery store, at the post office, or elsewhere, you can successfully induce a trance in them. Conversational hypnosis is the technical term for this type of hypnosis.

It is the most potent way of influencing the human mind positively. Over the past 65 years, scientific research has shown that hypnosis can be used secretly. You can create ideas in the minds of people when communicating with them. They are not even going to know it's happening.

Neuro-scientific experiments suggest that all learning behavior and change unconsciously take place in the beginning. Afterward, the conscious mind catches up. So, if you want to be more successful, you've got to reach the people in their unconscious state. This is where the magic transpires.

Hypnosis offers the fastest way to tap into the unconscious mind! Research in the field shows the secret to persuasion is not to try to change people's minds, but to alter their attitudes first. For instance, you must first get somebody in the right mood. Only then can you change their perception and ability to agree with your point of view successfully.

Doctors, psychiatrists, and hypnotherapists have found that: hypnosis opens the mind to suggestion to the point that "normal" mechanisms in the brain can be overridden. At the unconscious level, it works profoundly to create near-instant shifts in hypnotic subjects.

The problem is that regular hypnosis is not possible. You can't walk around, holding a pocket watch, asking people to "look deep into my eyes." Traditional forms of hypnosis are best suited to clinical circumstances. However, you absolutely cannot apply any sort of hypnosis in everyday interactions. If you tried, at best, you will look foolish and outrage people at worst.

The conversational or implicit hypnosis is therefore suitable for typical situations. You can actually hypnotize someone who unintentionally asks for your assistance when chatting over a cup of coffee with them. Covert or conversational hypnosis:

- Is easy to learn, ethical to use, and enjoyable when you perform every interaction.

- Melts vital conscious mind resistance and makes way for easier and faster hypnosis.
- Participants simply don't know they're being hypnotized.
- Activates the suggestibility core of the brain so those thoughts sink into the unconscious mind and take root instantly.
- Creates an atmosphere for bringing someone else in.

Research-Based Evidence on Use and Utility

Since the early 1950s, the American Medical Association has allowed doctors to use hypnosis.

Covert Hypnosis Explained

Covert hypnosis can take many forms. It can be used as a pure and simple form of self-hypnosis, or it may be used to hypnotize another person or group of people.

Whether you choose to hypnotize yourself or another by using conversational hypnotism, the first step you'll want to take is to bring yourself in the desired state.

Getting Ready for Covert Hypnosis

You do not need to learn how to do hypnosis for yourself. Just relax by taking a few deep breaths in through your mouth and letting them out through your nose slowly and gently.

Chapter 18: How to Use Dark Psychology to Succeed at Work

The main reason many people want to learn about dark psychology is that they want to do better in their careers. They aren't content working the job they already have: they want to prove themselves to be capable of more.

But somewhere along the way, we figure out the truth: that getting ahead in our careers isn't necessarily a matter of skill, but of manipulation and persuasion. As you know, dark psychology is the best and most legitimate way to learn these skills, and now it's time to learn how to use them specifically in a work setting.

We have to think harder about how we interact with our co-workers. For instance, let's say we have a female early 20-something analyst in the midst of a post-graduation down-cycle who has encountered many challenges both professionally and personally since starting work a few years ago.

She frequently finds herself wanting to connect with people who are perceived to be more advanced in their careers or whose interests are different from her own. Being able to figure out why you are attracted to certain people is a valuable skill for early-career practitioners and likely contributes to her success as an analyst. If she wants to get ahead, she should follow along with all the directions in these pages, where we speak to dark psychology in the workplace directly.

Personality is an especially crucial subject for the context of the workplace because it is an environment where you have to interact with many different kinds of people, many of whom—you will soon find out—you don't actually know that well as people.

Dark psychology is broader than neurolinguistic programming, but NLP is where all of our tools and techniques of deep communication and manipulation come from. NLP is where the three big steps of manipulation and mind control originate from: establish your own state control and perceptual sharpness, imitate the unconscious cues of communication of your subject so that they incorporate you into their mind, and use one of the techniques.

People think constantly without even realizing it because most thought is unconscious. NLP is the way we take advantage of the unconscious nature of most thoughts to tell people's minds to change the structure before they even know it.

The topic of NLP is important for discussing personalities in the workplace because NLP has five main categories for the kinds of personalities people have. In the jargon of NLP, these "personalities" are actually called metaprograms. You would do well to identify the important people at your workplace within these metaprograms. Take advantage of your perceptual sharpness to ascertain this information.

As we have told you before, getting information about the subject is everything. But it is also true that our brains need to sort all the information we get into categories to understand the world better. These metaprograms do that job for you.

Metaprograms are more useful than personalities because they are more objective. They also focus on the motivations people have and the way they use logic, rather than on their mannerisms or less important patterns of behavior. Metaprograms do not simply describe how much you like attention or how nervous or relaxed you are—you may notice some aspects of each metaprogram that overlap with these traits, but metaprograms are much more specific than these less useful terms.

These NLP-styled personalities are not only a way for you to get more information about your co-workers. Remember the second step of NLP mind-reading and manipulation: you have to imitate the cues of communications the subject shows you. When you do this, you make them unconsciously see you as being like themselves. That means if you take on the traits of your co-worker's metaprogram, you make it easier for you to succeed in this step.

The last thing for you to know about metaprograms, in general, is that they are sorted in dichotomies. A dichotomy is a contrast between two items that are different. But while you should choose just one from each dichotomy in each metaprogram, you must remember that people are not as simple as being A or B. Any time we have a dichotomy—in any situation—picking one of the two is just a category you can use to simplify things and think of them differently. But you should not think of them as being always or exclusively one of the two. People are much more complex than this.

Our first metaprogram is between the dichotomy of options and procedures. People who are on the options metaprogram don't like being limited or being told what to do. They want as much freedom as possible, and they like to think about things from a general perspective rather than getting in the weeds. People on procedures, on the other hand, need to understand every small detail whenever they get into something new. Procedures people hate the feeling that there is something they are missing, and when detail is skipped, they fear they are missing something important.

The second metaprogram is external and internal. This metaprogram is concerned with people's incentives. External people want to be told by others when they do good work, and they want to be told when they do bad work, too. Internal people don't want to get outside opinions about their work, though. They feel they know when their work is good or not, and hearing what other people think is just a bother.

The third dichotomy in metaprograms is proactive and reactive. These metaprograms describe how someone deals with the future. Reactive people look at a calendar and are always thinking about how the work they are doing now fits into the picture of all of their work. This can be a hindrance because they think so much about planning ahead that they lose sight of what they are trying to do right now. Proactive people, on the other hand, hate thinking about the future or planning ahead. They only care about the here and now.

Our second-to-last is toward and away. This metaprogram is about goals and deterrents. All of us have things we look forward to in the future, but people are chiefly concerned about their goals, and they don't look behind them at all. Away people are the exact opposite of this. They can have issues looking ahead because they spend so much time thinking about what is behind them.

Finally, we have sameness and difference. Sameness people have a love for familiarity: they spend their time around things they already know. Things they don't know make them fearful, so these people avoid them at all costs. Difference people, on the other hand, are always craving new experiences to have, new people to meet, new foods to eat, and so on. If there is something they haven't experienced yet, different people want to experience it.

These are the five big dichotomies in metaprograms. Whoever the co-worker is who you want to use our dark psychology tricks on; you will want to sort them into these metaprograms. Now, when you use the Aristotelian technique of envisioning the future, you have a more objective stand-in for the person you will interact with.

You see, when we imagine someone in our heads, it isn't always accurate to how they really are. NLP's metaprograms are so useful because they make us think carefully about the kind of person our subject is.

Metaprograms are particularly good for the work environment because they force us to think about the people we work with more objectively. When you do Step 1 and prepare to get into the co-worker's mind with Step 2, you can use these metaprograms to paint a fuller picture of who you are going to use dark psychology on.

Since these are often just people we interact with exclusively in work environments, we can be surprised by how little we might know about them from a metaprogram standpoint. If you are being honest with yourself as you sort them into these dichotomies, you might realize you don't know very much about them at all. When this turns out to be the case, don't just go along with the dark psychology technique, anyway. There is no point in doing this when it won't work anyway—you can't adapt to the social cues of a person you don't even know yet.

That's why from here, you will have to do more intel-gathering on them first before you can even move on to Step 1. Step 1 can't successfully happen until you know the person and how they fit into all the metaprograms. Until you do that, you won't be able to properly imagine the interactions you have with them for Steps 2 and 3.

With that said, after you get to know the co-workers' metaprograms, let your senses do all the work in perceptual sharpness, use our exercises to prepare your state control, and imagine the interaction in your imagination, you are ready for Step 2.

For Steps 2 and 3, things go about the same when you are dealing with someone from your workplace. However, some techniques seem tailor-made for use in the work setting. We will go over these before moving onto our big lesson on neurolinguistic programming in psychology.

We will cover three big dark psychology techniques for the workplace before diving into the world of NLP. Social framing is a technique in which we paint a picture for the subject where adopting a certain behavior or idea will help them with social climbing.

Our social lives are one of the most important things to us as humans. That's why framing the truth about the subject's social environment is such a powerful tool for manipulating and mind-controlling people. As long as we make them believe they get a social reward for doing what we say, they will jump at the opportunity.

Executing this technique is simple. Assuming you have already mentally sorted them into the proper metaprograms, controlled your state, and are paying close attention to your senses.

Chapter 19: Knowing the Woman's Mind

Were you ever itching to get into the mind of a woman and ask what she is thinking exactly? But most people are motivated by the same fundamental motivations, as you are about to learn. When you know what they are, you can communicate with nearly every woman.

Also, if you haven't realized it, women are different from us. It's like they're from a whole other world sometimes, and they speak a different language. But it's not so difficult to understand people, and it's just different. Essentially, you need to understand the two primary ways women think differently from us.

How women get their way does not influence others in the same way that men do. We can't. They can't. We are less vulnerable than we are physically, and that is why most people (and some women) believe that they can easily overcome a woman through bullying. If a woman wants to get her way, she has to use other tools. The most common is the manipulation of the emotions of people.

She is a grown woman, and her emotions are controlled by her. However, men are real suckers for drama because they think they take responsibility for the emotional states of a woman.

When you think about it, it's hilarious. A woman can overwhelm a man with drama, literally. And who can blame them for this? For a very long time, it was their only choice. Not only physically are they weaker, but they have disadvantaged of authority for thousands of years and are compelled to use further creative ways to show men's strength. And of course, you've noticed that they've made it a science.

Let's clarify something before we go on: there is nothing wrong with the use of drama or manipulating people to do it. All of us use manipulation to obtain what we want. Some people refer to it as inspiration or influence. But we never force the person to respond to us, in any case.

In fact, men are more likely than drama to use bullying to get what they want. So it doesn't make sense to hate women to use the scene to get what they want. Instead, we will use this information to increase your choices for enhancing your relationships with women.

And that's just beginning to understand this: you will never find a woman who is "free of drama." People are emotional because it's a way to get what they want, what you have to do as a man is to learn how to handle the drama and prevent women from using it to dominate you. And believe it or not, this is precisely what women want of a man.

How Women Process Attraction

If this last statement puzzles you, it will clear the confusion to understand how women attract. This starts with understanding the one thing about women that most men have totally backward: what women want in a man. First, if you ask women for dating advice, that's right now because you'll just make yourself crazy. You might have worked this one out already.

Have you ever wondered why women don't seem to know what they want from a man's relationship? They say that they want a nice man who is good at treating a lady and who loves his wife. A sensitive man who opens the door to them asks them how beautiful they are and how wonderful a friend they are.

Instead; however, we are madly in love with people who are unrefined, crazy, cocky, a little childish, and who you just look at and wonder: "How the hell is this guy doing for him?" You are, in the meantime, the good-natured man who knows how to treat a lady and who loves his wife. A guy who is compassionate and caring and opens her door tells her how beautiful and kind she is.

And where do you get that? She slowly writes you out of her life as either a "great friend" or worse.

What's that all about in the world? You were the guy she said she needed. Why did you get to the place of your wife after watching her fall over her head for that "other jerk??" That's because what the women want is not what they think they want. And the sooner you recognize this, the sooner you will quit trapped in the 'Friends' Corridor.' Now you shouldn't be shocked. After all, almost everyone does not claim that they want things that are entirely different from what their behavior reflects?

How many (men and women) do you know who is healthy, but who is consuming sugar-filled sweets, unhealthy fats, salt, and preservatives? How many people do you know who are wealthy, but who spend their money carelessly and who can't wait to go home to see TV throughout the day? This is because, while people want to be wealthy and safe, they are motivated by deeper motivations that most people don't take time to comprehend.

Don't tell people to judge. Many people are quite naive about the real reasons behind their actions, so they genuinely believe themselves when they tell you what they want. Yet look at their actions, if you want to know the real story.

Don't listen to what she says, if you want to know what women find attractive to look at her actions. Believe it or not, there's something "jerk" that most women like a flame moth.

They're making women feel safe and exciting.

This is an enticing mix because security and anticipation are two of the primary emotional needs people are looking for in romantic relations. If a man meets those two emotional requirements of a woman, he ignites a powerful unconscious attraction that transcends the reasoning mind of a woman.

Sound difficult to believe? Only think of how men you know who have given up thinking because of a woman's physical appeal. Think of how many people give up their thought and eat food they consider to be bad because they taste good. Think of how many people know who is spending their money on things which they don't need and end up having broken and then buy lottery tickets as "they want to be rich." This is why "jerks" (we will call them Bad boys) spark unconscious causes of attraction that seem to contradict a woman's spoken desires.

How's that?

First, these "bad boys" are immune to drama control, making them unpredictable... which are exciting for women.

Think about that, how exciting is it to a woman when a man answers her with what he wants because he is afraid to make her feel sad, frustrated, jealous, angry, unsure, stupid, or some other dramatic emotional state?

It's pretty dull, as you can imagine. The more beautiful a woman is, the more acquainted she is with people who bow to her every time she uses drama to dominate them. And frankly, she's all right with most people because it gives her more power. She just doesn't date such men.

She dates the people who are able to take over and who are not frightened by the drama. And that's where security and security are needed.

Think of this: how comfortable does a woman feel when she has a partner she can present? Does that mean he is insecure, weak, and obedient or reliable and trustworthy? Obviously, many women would like to have a nice man who knows how to treat the lady and who loves his wife. A caring, responsible man who opens her door tells her how beautiful and a great friend she is.

But most men are either: the nice man they say women want or the unrefined bad boy. Exceptionally few people could be both, and as the bad boy sees her need for security and excitement, she selects him above the boring man of beauty.

Chapter 20: Characteristics of Manipulative People

The main traits that are associated with manipulators and how they are able to control people around them. Moreover, we have focused on the ways in which personality traits that lean toward manipulation tend to manifest themselves in an individual. That's why we have gone into great depth in analyzing how and why the average manipulator acts the way they do.

On the whole, there is a debate whether being a manipulator is a question of in-born traits or whether it is a question of upbringing. In other words, we're referring to a nature vs. nurture debate. The fact is that there is no conclusive evidence linking specific genetic predisposition to acting in one manner or another. While traits such as psychopathy can be linked to actual physiological conditions in which the individual's brain may differ significantly, the fact of the matter is it is almost entirely an issue associated with upbringing.

For most folks, manipulative traits, such as the dark triad, are fomented in early childhood and adolescence. When kids and teens are subjected to certain types of experiences, they generally develop coping mechanisms that grow into the personality traits that we associate with manipulation. For instance, narcissism is generally linked to abandonment issues, which typically translate into a need for control. Of course, this isn't an iron law. But it does show that there is a clear correlation between the experiences that a child and teenager may go through, and how that translates into certain behavioral patterns down the road.

Therefore, it's important to analyze all aspects of a person's life in order to determine where one set of traits may emerge. It can be rather foolish to dismiss the effects of the environment on a person's behavior. In fact, many folks make a rash judgment in saying that manipulators, or even psychopaths, are just "born that way." The fact of the matter is that while there may be a physiological component (mental illness has been found to be a hereditary issue), most of the time, manipulative traits are the result of a certain set of experiences that a person goes through from an early age.

How Manipulators Select Their Victims

One of the most important things to consider in this discussion is how manipulators select their victims. A victim, by definition, is the recipient of the manipulator's actions. Therefore, the victim suffers negative consequences from the behavioral patterns exhibited by the manipulator.

On the whole, victim selection is generally random. This means that manipulators will simply sniff around, looking for someone they can take advantage of. When there is a greater amount of premeditation in the selection of a victim, then we might be dealing with a psychopath. As such, these individuals might make more careful study as to the type of person they seek to attack.

Nevertheless, most manipulators will simply seek out those who are closest to them. This is why family tends to be the first target on a manipulator's radar.

Generally speaking, manipulators look for weak individuals whom they feel won't be able to put up a fight. This means that for one reason or another, the victim is powerless to stop them. When you think of physical violence, this is one of the main criteria that goes into the selection of a victim.

On a deeper, more emotional level, manipulators will seek out people who stand to lose quite a bit more than the manipulator.

Think about that for a moment.

Let's go back to the example pertaining to the workers who must deal with a manipulative boss. In the end, the workers need the job far more than the boss does. If anything, the boss manipulates the employees more for personal pleasure than a logical business reason. Consequently, the workers are faced with a dilemma: they either put up with the manipulation or find another job.

The ultimate objective of the manipulator is to subdue their victims to the point where they will offer resistance to the manipulator's tactics. This means that the victim eventually becomes complicit in the manipulator's behavior. Sure, there are instances where the victim is unable to extricate themselves from the abusive situation they are in. In such cases, the victim can only hope to endure the situation until a time comes when they are able to get out finally.

Highly skilled manipulators will take the time to scout for potential victims. This occurs when a manipulator is able to identify the choice traits they are looking to find in their victims. As such, they will scout their surroundings and places they perceive will have the highest number of vulnerable individuals. That is why it's always a good idea to be skeptical of someone you don't really know in a place that you often go to. You never know who you might be dealing with.

Signs of a Manipulative Partner

One of the objectives on the mind of a manipulator might be to find a partner they can manipulate. This may occur either as a conscious behavior or an instinctive one. In the event of instinctive behavior, you can assume that the manipulator is not acting out of malice, but rather out of their own sheer desire. When you consider a conscious choice on the part of the manipulator, then you might actually be dealing with an evil individual who has a hidden agenda. So, it is important to recognize the warning signs before it is too late.

On the whole, manipulators can be easily spotted in romantic relationships by the subtle hints and lapses they show. For example, they appear to be sweet and attentive, but suddenly change and appear to be disconnected. You can tell this by seeing the way they pay attention to your conversation. Also, they might be very polite and caring but suddenly react abruptly when something that they don't like happens.

These are very subtle signs that you are dealing with someone who might not be entirely forthcoming. But the red flags get worse when you're dealing with someone who is jealous and possessive. This can begin with incessant text messages and calls. It's a progressive matter; they start off by increasing the number of calls and texts until you find that they are controlling everything you do. Eventually, they expect a tally and report of all the things you do.

In addition, a manipulative partner will strive to find out things that are negative, embarrassing, or even traumatic about your past. Then they will use that every time they can. For instance, a manipulator may use their partner's weight as a means of shaming. They will use this to coax their partner to comply; after all, "no one will love you as much as I do." These types of statements are a clear indication that there is a manipulation attempt.

These red flags are important to keep in mind as they can quickly degenerate into an abusive relationship. Highly skilled manipulators will make the transition so subtle that the victim won't even notice the relationship is degrading to that level. In the end, all the victim can feel is the effects of the abuse.

How to Know You Are Being Targeted

It can be hard to know if you are being targeted by a manipulator. Perhaps the easiest way to go about this is to confront the manipulator. If you happen to run into someone who is overly friendly, then this ought to be a red flag for you. Also, if you happen to be surrounded by people who only remember you every time they need something from you, then you know you're definitely being targeted.

Unless you know a person well, it's always a good rule of thumb to keep an eye out on everyone. While this may seem like paranoid behavior, the fact of the matter is if you are able to be alert, the chances of being nabbed by manipulators are rather slim.

Here are some practical tips:

- Be wary of overly friendly strangers.
- Watch for offers and deals that are "too good to be true."
- Keep an eye out for sudden mood swings.
- Watch out for contradicting behavior and words.
- Pay attention to the moment in which people approach you.

- Avoid responding to unsolicited advice.

These situations are all indicative of a manipulator trying to "test" you. If they find that you are responsive, then they may feel compelled to continue their advances until you give in to what they want. In the end, it's usually best to just get away from these people. You may never have to engage them openly; all you may have to do is just move away from them.

How to Deal with a Manipulator

If you happen to find yourself dealing with a manipulator, here are three very important steps that you can take to help you better deal with this type of individual.

Try your best to get away from the situation. While there are circumstances in which getting away from a manipulator may be virtually impossible, it is the most recommended course of action to get away from them as far as possible. This will take away their opportunities to manipulate you. Moreover, if you can completely extricate yourself from a situation (such as finding a new job), then the entire better.

Find out what they are using to manipulate you and then take it away from them. If you can identify what they are using against you, then you will be able to take that weapon away from them. In fact, you may even be able to use it against them. That will be a clear indicator of the manipulator that they can't have their way with you any longer.

Know your rights. If you happen to be in an abusive relationship or situation, you have the right to seek help. This can be any form of help that may be available to you, but you must act on it. If you know you are being affected by a manipulative and even abusive person, but fail to say anything about it, you may never get the help you need. So, it's important to speak up.

Avoid the blame game. Do not think for a second that this situation is your fault. Also, there is no need to blame the manipulator, even though they are responsible for their actions. When you play the blame game, you are hurting yourself by making it seem that you are directly, or indirectly, responsible for what's happened. So, even if you are the victim, it's not your fault that this has happened to you. By the same token, the manipulator is not at fault for being a manipulator. However, they are responsible for their actions.

Know when to quit. If you choose to confront the manipulator, you need to know when you may need to get away from them. There is only so much energy you can spend on a person like this. Oftentimes, dealing with a manipulator becomes a war of attrition. So, your determination to win that war may leave you more spent, both physically and emotionally, than what you stand to gain.

Chapter 21: Victims

Just as manipulators frequently share all sorts of similar traits and behaviors, they also share similar taste in victims. Manipulators, like all predators, look for the easiest targets that pose the best chance of success. Just as the pack of wolves will pick off the weakest members of a herd, the manipulator will look for people who they deem are emotionally easy targets, using a sort of natural sense for whom to go after. Because they go for these specific traits, they are usually incredibly efficient in what they do. Manipulators have essentially mastered the art of picking up the perfect target. Take a look at some of the most commonly targetedtraits, as well as the signs someone around you may be being abused or manipulated.

Traits of a Victim

While some manipulators may go out of their way to target other types of people, the vast majority will go for ease of a target overlooking for a challenge. When they are going to manipulate others, they want to make sure they can get away with it, as well as to get away with any of the behaviors they wish to expose the other person too. Some manipulators never move beyond emotional exploitation, while others will go out of their way to work their ways up to physical or sexual abuse. Ultimately, these are some of the easily exploitable traits that manipulators everywhere look for:

Empathetic

The perfect manipulation victim is empathetic. When they are empathetic, they are far easier to manipulate. Think back to the reason's manipulators tend to manipulate—one is to get what they want. An empath is going to be quick to tune into whatever it is that the other person needs, and is much more likely to want to give whatever it is, whether it is attention, affection, or companionship. This makes the empath an ideal target.

Further, empaths, especially if they meet some of the other criteria on this list, are frequently quite forgiving. They will be quick to write off some bad behavior as a fluke or an unfortunate consequence of the circumstances, and they will be more likely to believe that the manipulator will not continue the behaviors. They are also more likely to fall for guilt trips, making manipulating them somewhat easier than others. What the empath offers most of all is the patience necessary to put up with the manipulator's antics.

Caregiver

People with caregiver personalities thrive upon taking care of others. They love to make sure those around them have their needs met. They naturally care about what others need and are often also quite empathetic. Because they feel fulfilled taking care of the needs of others, manipulators can typically twist things around to get whatever they want. The manipulator is quite skilled at convincing the caregiver that he needs something he does not, and the caregiver, wanting to make sure the manipulator is cared for, will do so.

Caregivers, in particular, tend to be quite patient—they are willing to put up with far more than necessary simply because they feel they can handle it. They are likely to forego ending a relationship they see as abusive or manipulative if they believe that the cause of that abuse or manipulation is old wounds within the manipulator that are causing the behaviors in the first place. Instead, the caregiver will put up with the manipulation while diligently attempting to fix the manipulator's problems.

Codependent

Codependency and caregiver personalities are incredibly similar—both the codependent and the caregiver will pour themselves into their relationship, hoping to fix the manipulator, but the codependent will wholly identify with the relationship. The codependent is more likely to put up with far worse manipulation and abuse simply because she feels she cannot move on from the manipulator. While she may recognize what is happening, she feels so intricately intertwined with the manipulator and that relationship that she feels there is no life without the manipulator.

Her very identity will be wrapped up in caring for the manipulator, catering to his every whim, even to her detriment. Even though it will hurt her, she continues to do so anyway to a fault. Her codependent nature becomes a point of contention for her as the relationship that she feels is all that she is also hurting her. She may not like the way she is being treated, but she will want to continue to pour herself into the relationship.

Grew Up in Dysfunction

Those who grew up in the throes of dysfunction oftentimes have skewed ideas of what normal is. They see the way they grew up as normal and will oftentimes revert back to what is familiar to them, even if familiar is harmful. For these people, they may see no red flags with the manipulator's behaviors, particularly if manipulation was one of the key features of their own dysfunctional upbringing.

Since they grew up around unhealthy relationships, their own tolerance for abuse is usually quite extreme. They may be annoyed, but see it as unworthy of ending a relationship or friendship. Even things like physical abuse may not be deal-breakers for those who grew up around it and had such abuse normalized for them. This makes them particularly easy targets because they will be so tolerant and already desensitized to too much of the abuse and manipulation that the manipulator will be utilizing.

Low Self-Esteem

Perhaps one of the most attractive of traits to a manipulator when looking for a victim is low self-esteem. You will learn that breaking someone's self-esteem is oftentimes a core theme in much of the manipulation you will be learning about. Manipulators need people with low self-esteem because they will not fight back or make things difficult—instead, they will put up with the abuse and accept whatever is being said simply because they do not have the self-esteem to trust themselves.

Because the first active step in much of the manipulation is usually breaking down self-esteem, manipulators love shortcuts. Just as how a wolf will go for the weakest in a herd, the manipulator will go for the easiest target, and frequently, those are the ones whose self-esteem is already so weak and shattered that they can do whatever they want with impunity.

Ultimately, the more of these traits that an individual has, the more attractive they are to the manipulator. With that in mind, if you feel like you see any of these signs in yourself, these are likely to be your weaknesses. If you know you have low self-esteem, for example, you should be aware of how that can work against you if you are not careful.

Signs of Abuse or Manipulation

Oftentimes, those who have been manipulated show very similar behavioral signs. After being victimized for so long, they pick up similar behavioral patterns in an attempt at self-preservation. Take a look at some of the most commonly exhibited signs and symptoms of manipulation.

Self-Sacrificing or Martyrdom

Those who have been manipulated enough oftentimes develop an attitude that they do not deserve to be taken care of. They see themselves as expendable, not worth the effort it would take to do things for themselves. Rather than focusing on bettering themselves, they focus on making sure the manipulator is cared for, just as the manipulator intended. They will oftentimes give up whatever they are asked to do, or volunteer to be the one missing out simply because they have been conditioned to do so.

Self-Sabotage

Oftentimes, the victim becomes so accustomed to not getting what he or she wants that they will begin to believe they are not deserving of having needs met. They are so used to being seen as expendable and with their needs as unimportant that they will begin to act as such as well. If they get something nice, they will believe that they do not deserve it, which can convince them that they should do something to sabotage what they have. For example, if someone has just gotten a new job that pays well, it is possible that he would decide that he does not deserve that job, and because he does not deserve that job, he would possibly perform poorly unconsciously, believing that he is not good enough anyway, so he has no point to bother trying.

Fiercely Protective of Abuser

People who are regularly exposed to abuse or manipulation frequently become fiercely defensive and protective of anyone they feel threatens them. Because the manipulator frequently convinces the victim that the victim is exceedingly lucky to have someone like the manipulator around, and intentionally manipulates the feelings of the other person in an attempt to trickthe other person into falling in love, the victim often feels conflicting emotions when the manipulator is talked poorly about.Oftentimes, the victim will vehemently defend the manipulator toanyone who says something they disagree with, feeling the need toprotect the manipulator.

Mental Health Issues

Through constant stress from the manipulator, it is not uncommon by any means for people to develop mental health issues. After extended periods of time being manipulated, belittled, and demeaned in order for the manipulator to gain a sense of control over the individual being manipulated, the victim is more prone to depressive and anxiety symptoms.

Being Distrustful

After time spent being demeaned and manipulated, people tend to grow to be quite distrustful. Especially once they have come to discover the truth and they understand that someone they had trusted actually was using them in some of the worst ways imaginable, they lose the capacity to trust easily and readily.

Fearful Behavior

Because people who are manipulated often find themselves getting to a point where they fear the reaction of the manipulator if they do not concede to whatever the manipulator wants, the victims tend to grow fearful in general. They are so used to someone taking advantage of the situation and making them feel bad about themselves when they are not living up to expectations that they often come to expect the worst from others as well. They grow timid and concerned with assuming that people around them have the worst intentions, and that leads to a fearful demeanor, especially when the victim perceives that he or she has failed in some way.

Paranoia

Typically, in a combination of becoming fearful and distrustful, those who are manipulated sometimes develop a paranoid view of the world. They worry that they are being taken advantage of, even when they are not, and they become inherently suspicious of those who do try to help, assuming there is some sort of ulterior motive at play when someone does offer help. For example, if a manipulation victim is asked if she wants help with studying for an upcoming exam, she may wonder what the other person wants in return, even if the other person is simply doing it out of kindness or a genuine interest in getting to know her better with no strings attached.

Chapter 22: Deception

Deception is going to refer to the act, whether it is kind or cruel or big or small, or causing someone to believe that something else is untrue. Even those who consider themselves pretty honest are going to practice some of this deception, and there are several studies out there that show how the average person, no matter how good-hearted they think they are, are going to lie several times in a day.

When it comes to these lies, some of them are going to be big lies that are meant to cause harm and hide the bad that the liar has done. But for the most part, the lies that we say are going to be small, usually white lies, that are used to spare the feelings of another person or get us out of a situation that is making us uncomfortable.

You will find that deception is not always going to be an act that is outward. It is also true that people are going to tell lies to them. There are a lot of reasons that they would do this, such as trying to maintain a healthy dose of self-esteem to some serious delusions that are sometimes beyond their control. While it is sometimes seen as harmful to lie even to yourself, some experts are likely to argue that certain types could also have a positive effect on your overall well-being as well.

Researchers have long searched for ways to find out when they can tell whether someone is lying or not. The polygraph test, which is something that a lot of us already know about, has long been controversial, and it has long been known that some people are easily able to lie to the test and get away with it. This is especially true if the individual has some psychiatric disorder.

With this, we need to take a look at why people lie. No one likes to feel deceived about anything, and when anyone, especially a public figure, ends up being caught in a lie, it can turn into a big headache for them. But while a lot of us are going to pride ourselves on our scrupulous honesty, and we try to stay as far away as possible from those who are fine with falsehoods, the truth is that all of us have lied at one point or another.

Experts find that having a small amount of deception can be important when it comes to maintaining a society that is healthy and can function well. The formal study of deception was once the domain of theologians and ethicists, but in recent years, more psychologists have turned over to look at the reasons why people are going to lie, as well as some of the conditions that make people more likely to lie.

The Types of Deception

Deception is going to include a lot of different things, but often, it is going to include a type of communication or omission that will serve to omit or change up the whole truth from another person. This is done in a manner that benefits the deceiver. If they hide the truth or change up the facts a little bit, then their victim will believe what the deceiver wants, and the deceiver will win. This can sometimes be a little white lie that helps to protect the feelings of the victim, but more often than not, it is going to be done at the expense of the victim.

Examples of this kind of deception are going to range from false statements to claims that are misleading, where relevant information is taken out. This is done so that the victim is going to be led to a false conclusion. In some cases, we may think that this oil is going to benefit the health of our brain more than some other foods we would eat.

However, the amount of omega-3 fatty acids that are found in sunflower oil is going to be low. And thanks to the other ingredients found in the oil, it is usually not seen as something that is all that good for the health of your brain. So, while sunflower oil does have some omega-3 fatty acids, and those are good for your brain, the information is going to lead the victim to infer false information about just how beneficial the sunflower oil is for them.

When it comes to deception, we have to look at the intent of the deceiver. If they got the information wrong on accident and shared it with the victim, then this is not deception. But if the deceiver wants to make sure that the victim is getting the wrong information on purpose, then it is going to be deception. The intent is going to be vital because it is going to show us thedifference between an honest mistake and deception.

A good thing to look at here is the Interpersonal Deception Theory. This theory is going to explore some of the interrelations that show up between the communicative context and the sender and receiver cognitions and the behaviors in the exchange.

Now, there are going to be a few different types of deception that can show up depending on the situation and what the deceiver is hoping to get out of the exchange. Some of the forms of deception that you can use or encounter in your life include:

Lies

This is when you will make up information or when the deceiver is going to give information that is opposite of the truth, or at least very different from the truth.

Equivocations

This is when the deceiver is going to make a contradictory, ambiguous, or indirect statement.

Concealments

This is when the deceiver is going to omit some important information or relevant to the given context, or they are going to engage in some behavior that will ensure that the relevant information is as hidden as possible.

Exaggerations

This is when there is a big overstatement, or the deceiver is going to stretch the truth as much as they can get away with.

Understatements

This one is going to head in the opposite direction. With this one, you are going to find that the deceiver is going to downplay the aspects of the truth as much as possible.

Untruthful

This is also going to be when the deceiver is going to try and misinterpret the truth a bit.

Many of us think that we are good at deception. However, this takes a lot of talent and work, and since most people are good at catching lies and deception, it is hard to pull off on someone.

Three main motives are focused often on when it comes to why people like to lie and deceive others. According to Buller and Burgoon (1996), there are three methods that you can use to distinguish deception based on that interpersonal deception theory from before. These include:

Identity

The deceiver may lie to save their self-image or to remain in the same position with others, or with that one person, as they did before.

Relational

This is the deception that is done to help maintain the bonds or the relationships that you have.

Instrumental

This is when the deceiver is going to lie because it helps them to protect their resources or avoid any punishment that they should receive.

Depending on who uses the deception, it can sometimes be easy to see. Many of us think that we are good at deceiving those around us when, in reality, we are not. We end up being caught, especially if we are close to the other person we are trying to deceive.

But some people are good at deceiving. They are so good at this that they can end up deceiving someone for many years or more, and the victim, as well as those around them sometimes, will never be any the wiser about it. This can be dangerous because often, we don't know what is being kept from us and what we should know about a particular situation.

Simulation

Simulation is going to be any time that the deceiver exhibits some false information. There are going to be three different techniques that can be used with this, including mimicry, fabrication, and distraction. Let's dive into each of these to see how they work.

The first method is mimicry. This is when you will copy another example or another model. For example, animals are going to use this to deceive their predators through auditory or visual means in most cases.

Then there is the idea of fabrication. This is when the other person is going to make up a brand-new lie or story that fits their needs. For the deceiver to make something appear to be something that it isn't, usually to encourage the other person to divert, endanger, or reveal the victim's resources, is going to be a fabrication. The deceiver wants to learn something from the other person, and they want to cause some harm to the victim. This means that they are going to tell a fabrication to completely throw the victim off guard and make it so that they aren't sure what to believe.

An excellent example of this would occur in World War II. During this time, it was common for the Allies to work with hollow tanks that they would make out of wood rather than the usual materials. This was done so that the German planes would think that a large unit of them was moving in on an area. In reality, the real tanks were hidden and were moving in the opposite direction towards their real target.

Distraction is the next simulation. This is when the manipulator is going to try and get someone's attention from the truth, usually with some bait, or something that they know will divert the attention away from whatever the deceiver is trying to hide. Bait and switch, as well as many of the fraud techniques that we hear about, are going to work with the idea of distraction as well.

How to Use Deception

Now that we have a better idea of what deception is all about, it is time to look at a few of the techniques that you can use to put deception to work for your own needs. It is often not considered ethical to use deception, even though most people are going to use it at one point or another to get what they want. Learning how to use deception properly can make it more likely that someone is going to do what you want.

Chapter 23: Distance in Communication

Focusing on the United States, there are four types of distances that people use to communicate on a face-to-face basis. These distances are intimate, personal distance, social distance, and public distance. Starting with the intimate distance, it is used for highly confidential exchanges as zero to two feet of space between two individuals marks this zone. An example of intimate distance includes two people hugging, standing side-by-side, or holding hands. Individuals with intimate distance share a unique level of comfort with one another. If one is not comfortable with someone approaching them in the intimate zone, he/she will experience a significant deal of social discomfort.

Firstly, personal distance is used for talking with family as well as close acquaintances. The personal distance can range from two to four feet. Akin to intimate distance, if a stranger walks into the personal zone, the one is likely to feel uneasy being in such proximity with the stranger.

Secondly, there is the social distance used in business exchanges or when meeting new people and interacting with groups of people. Compared to the other distances, social distance has a larger range in the range that it can incorporate. Its range is four to twelve feet, and it depends on the context. It is used among students, acquaintances, or co-workers. As expected, most participants in the social distance do not show physical contact with one another. Generally, people are likely to be very specific concerning the degree of social distance that is preferred, as some require more physical distance compared to others. In most cases, the individual will adjust backward or forward to get the appropriate social distance necessary for social interactions.

Thirdly, we have public distance, which is twelve or more feet between individuals. An example of public distance is where two people sit on a bench in a public park. In most cases, the two people on a bench in a public park will sit at the farthest ends of each other to preserve the public space. Each of the earlier types of proximity will significantly influence an individual's perception of what is the appropriate type of distance in specific contexts. One of the factors that contribute to individual perceptions of how proxemics should be used is culture. Individuals from different cultures show different viewpoints on what the appropriate persona; space should be.

Fourthly, there is the concept of territoriality, where individuals tend to feel like they own and should control their personal areas. We are inclined to defend our personal space. When someone invades this personal space, then the individual will react negatively as it is an invasion of territory without express permission. At one point, you asked a stranger to keep some distance from you because you felt uncomfortable with the person standing close to you. Sometimes standing next to a person may also denote that you are creepy and may be intending to harm the person.

If one is talking to someone, the person violates your personal space, and you allow it, then it signals that you are okay to intimate ideas. Intimate ideas in this context include highly personal issues that one can talk about with another person. For instance, if you walk and sit close and in contact with a woman watching television and she approves of your behavior, then it is indicative that she is likely to allow you to have a personal talk that may be intimate in nature. Such discussion may include your health challenges or mental health and not necessarily sexual issues. For this reason, one should carefully weigh the need to invade the personal distance.

Regarding children, violating personal distance will make them freeze due to feeling uncomfortable. If a teacher sits next to a student or stands next to a student, then the student is likely to feel uneasy and nervous. However, they are instances where the invasion of personal space is allowed and seen as necessary. For instance, during interviews or when being examined by a doctor, invasion of private space by the person with an advantage is allowed. The panel during an interview may move or ask you to move closer, which may violate your personal space. A doctor may also stand closer to you, invading your personal space, but this is necessary due to the professional demand for their service.

As such, when one avoids personal distance, and the individual is expected to be within this space, then the individual may be feeling less confident or feeling ashamed. For instance, if a child has done something embarrassing, he or she is likely to sit or stand far from the parent during a conversation. For this reason, it appears that one should feel confident, assured, and appreciated to approach and remain in personal space when needed.

Additionally, staying in personal space during intense emotions may portray one as resilient, understanding, and bold. Think of two lovers or sibling quarreling, but each remains in the established personal space. The message that is being communicated is that the individual is confident that he or she can handle the intense emotions from the other person. For most people, they only allow their lover to stay in their personal distance when feeling upset because they trust that the person can handle the known behavior of the affected person. Since being in personal space places a person within physical striking range, most people will only allow trusted and familiar individuals into their personal space.

Equally important is that invasion of personal space is justified because it is a part of professional demands. Think of a newteacher that is trying to help a student solve a mathematical equation. In this aspect, the teacher is a stranger because he or sheis new to the school. By sitting or standing close to the student, theteacher is invading the personal space, but the established norms in this context allow the student not to feel unease. For emphasis, this case is not unique as it aligns with stated expectations that people will welcome known or unfamiliar people in their personal space only if they trust them and, in this case, the student feels safe with any teacher. For this reason, the operationalization of distance in communication is mediated and moderated by established culture.

In most cases, one can start with public distance before allowing the interaction to happen in a personal or social space. For instance, as a student during tournaments, you could have initiated non-verbal communication with the student from the other college before suddenly feeling connected to the individual and allowing him or her to move into personal space as a potential girlfriend or boyfriend. At first, the target person saw you as a stranger but allowed you to make non-verbal communication within the public space. When the person felt the need to connect more with you and have given you the benefit of the doubt, the person allowed you to move through public distance and social distance to enter their personal space.

For instance, a lot can be learned from studying distance and space in communication. Being allowed into the social and personal distances implies that the person trusts that you will not harm them emotionally and physically. For the intimate distance, being allowed into this distance implies that the person trusts you so much and is confident that you can never harm them and that you share a lot. For instance, a mother holding her baby close enough to her signals that the baby is feeling assured of security and protection. When two lovers move closer until their faces are almost touching suggests trust and confidence that the other person feels safe and protected.

Relatedly, if arguing with your child or lover and the individual moves farther from you physically, then it suggests that the person no longer feels safe with you being within their personal distance. Issues that can cause someone to expand the distance between you and them include the risk of violence from you and emotional issues. If you occasionally act violently, then chances are, your lover or children will expand the personal distance to social distance because this is where they feel safe due to your personality and character. It then appears that your prior behaviorwill also affect the distance during communication.

Nevertheless, they are other issues that cause individuals to extend the distance of interaction, and these include having a medical condition or having hygiene issues. For instance, if you are sweaty, then chances are that the other person may prefer to extend the distance of communication between you and them. Having oral hygiene issues may also make the other person move far away from you because the smell turns them off. For this reason, interpreting the distance between communicators should also include hygiene and health-related issues that impact this distance.

For instance, some medical conditions can make people maintain some distance from you or be closer to you physically. For instance, some conditions may attract uneasiness, and this includes epilepsy. People with epilepsy get seizures, and this can make people feel unease being closer to them because they inadvertently fall. On the other hand, having hearing issues or sore throat may make people move closer to you physically to facilitate effective communication. However, these are exceptions when analyzing space and distance as forms of non-verbal communication, but they should be taken into account where necessary.

In some cases, it is welcome to invade personal distance merely by the circumstances. For instance, when attending a match in a full packed stadium or sitting to watch a movie in a movie theater, one will have his personal invaded due to the sitting arrangements. In this context, one may feel uneasy with this arrangement, but he or she has little control over the situation. While we value and seek to protect personal spaces, some situations make us allowing the invasion of this space because it is beyond control.

Chapter 24: When "No" Means "Yes"

Have you ever rented a car and been adamant that you didn't want insurance, but somehow walked out with it, anyway? Have you wondered how they got you to believe that you needed something that you didn't want in the first place? There is a sort of power and control within the resounding no. The rental agent already knows that you are going to walk in telling them what you want and don't want. Most people do not want the extra insurance because they have their own insurance and feel like paying extra for more insurance isn't worth it, especially when you probably aren't going to need it. The resounding "no" is so common that it is something salespeople don't even pay attention to anymore. It is an instant reaction that is driven by the fear of getting swindled into doing something that you do not want. So, you walk in already with your mind made up.

However, the rental agent found a way to get you to buy the product still. Think about it, before they even work on your contract, they go outside and walk you around the cars. During this time, they ask you questions about your trip, what you need it for, and then they start telling you about the amenities of the car—that they carry car seats, and they sell you the coverage based on what appeals to you through the conversation you had. You felt like you had a great conversation with the salesperson, but in reality, they were using the time to prey on you because they know what you will need on this trip you are taking and how what they have to offer will alleviate your stress and/or solve your problem.

When changing your audiences' answer from no to yes, it is about understanding how they make decisions, what appeals to them—by testing the waters—how they remember things, and how they look into the future. Most of the time, people remember important dramatic experiences that turn out badly. The rental agent might ask you if you have car insurance and you tell them that you have what the law requires because you own your car.

This is when they realize that they want to protect their car, but they also want to make you think that they are protecting you from having to pay tons of money out of your pocket. So, they will tell you that they have rental coverage that covers the car bumper to bumper. It is only $11–$14 a day depending on the car size, and there is no deductible. If anything happens to the car, it will be covered, and you will just walk away without paying a dime. This might sound appealing to the customer, but they still feel like they don't need it. So, they tell the rental agent "no" again.

This is when the agent moves to a story to sway the customer. The agent tells the customer they understand how they feel. Telling them that they buy the coverage doesn't help. They need to tell them a story that they will remember, a dramatic one that will sway them to their side. The agent brings up an encounter with a previous customer who felt the same way as the current one. The customer was adamant about not getting the coverage that covered the car and rented the car without it.

Another car ended up hitting them in the parking lot, and they walked back in asking if they could get the coverage. The rental agent had to end the rental contract and not give them the coverage because it is illegal to sell it after the rental agreement has been made and after an accident. The customer ended up paying for the damages out of their pocket, as well as the life of therental in the shop, which means they had to pay the amount of therental up to five days. All because they didn't want to pay an extra $30. Due to this story, the current customer ended up purchasing the coverage that covered the car.

When the agent was telling the story to the new customer, all they remembered was the outcome of the crash in the parking lot. They didn't remember anything else about the story, just that theydidn't want to go through what the previous customer went through.

Covert Persuasion can be used in different situations, especially when you are trying to win and bring them over to your side. In customer service, you want them to talk about your competitor and discuss their past experiences because if they were satisfied with that experience, they wouldn't be talking to you. One of the things that you have to do is make sure that you don't scare them away so that they do not want to purchase from you.

Have them tell you a story of a great purchase experience they had. This helps you from not scaring them off because you are having them remember a fun experience. For instance, if you are a stockbroker and the potential customer is someone who has lost money in the stock market, you will understand why they don't want to risk money again. But isn't that the risk with the stock market? You're not going to make money every time.

The broker has to be careful in this situation, and they cannot guarantee the potential customer or investor that they will not lose money again. That will be a lie, and that will break their trust right there. The broker has to point out that it is a possibility that they would lose money again. However, it is more likely that they will get typical returns with their investment.

Persuasion research is very clear, especially with covert persuasion. The speaker must show the audience both possible outcomes for them to be successful. If the speaker doesn't indicate that the investor might lose money in the stock market, they will continue to be afraid of it and choose not to invest with your brokerage firm.

When you show them that losing money is a possibility, you also show them what else could happen within reason. If you make it sound too good to be true, the possible investor will feel like they are being manipulated, and they will still choose not to go with your firm's offer. By keeping it realistic, there is a high chance that they will succumb to your persuasions.

Be clear with your message delivery. If the possible investor lost the first half of the game, they need to come in strong during the second half. Never let what happened in the past determine what they could possibly achieve in the future.

The whole idea of persuading people is to take away their fear of saying yes, which is normal. People tend to have a fear of the unknown and how their life will change. If you are trying to help someone quit smoking, the person will resist at first because the fear of deterring from their normal routine is too much for them. To help them overcome this fear, you will have to substitute their current fear with one that is far worse. Basically, you are scaring them beyond their worst fears. For instance, the speaker tells the person that if they continue to keep smoking every day that it is going to cause you to die. Can you imagine your kids and grandkids standing over your casket? They will remember you the way you looked in that casket. The idea of their family looking over their dead body scares them, especially when it is something that they could have prevented. This is when the speaker makes the fear less painful by helping them cut down. Tell them to start small by cutting down to half a pack a day this month, then only one every day next month and by the next month, you don't need them anymore. Wouldn't it be great to show your family that you don't need to smoke? Wouldn't it be great to show them how healthy you are?

The speaker used fear to persuade the person to stop smoking and then gave them a set of instructions that will help them with the new decision that they made. The person was able to see how changing their life and going with what you wanted wasn't hard if they worked at it. They weren't going to be worse off because of the decision, but better.

So, once the speaker can change or is persuaded to do what you want them to do, they should be happy that they listened to you and took your advice—whether it is to change their attitude or behavior or purchase what they are selling. This is not always the case, though.

There is a principle known as option attachment. Someone has a choice to purchase one of two puppies. Either puppy would be a good pet for her, but each one is different. They ponder which puppy they could see themselves keeping, and no matter which one they choose, even though they are not aware of it, they worry that the other puppy will be the better of the two because the person did not choose them.

Wouldn't they feel good about the choice they made? You would think that they would be happy, relieved, or even comfortable with their decision. Yet, they are miserable. They start to question the decision that they made.

When someone is left thinking about their options too long, they tend to think that whatever they choose; they are losing something by not choosing the other thing. The initial problem is the choice they are left with. The person feels a sense of disappointment and loss when they realize that they have to let the other option go.

Persuasion research indicates that it doesn't matter if the person has personally experienced both options set in front of them, or just imagining one. Whatever option they choose, the other one becomes more attractive because they cannot have it.

The second factor of option attachment is the feeling of loss. The person felt attached to the other option when they were deliberating.

There are two ways to help counteract option attachment:

1. Don't let the person feel any sort of attachment to both of the options. You don't want them to feel a sense of loss. So, make sure that they don't have a lot of time to make the decision. Tell them that the decision has to be fast.

2. If you have to give them more than one option, make the better option more attractive to them so that they do not spend a lot of time making a decision. Don't let them feel connected with

something they are never going to have. Give them info about the option and then make them understand why it is not feasible.

Chapter 25: Subliminal Persuasion

In our world, subliminal persuasion is everywhere. You can't watch television, read a magazine, or even go for a drive around town without encountering it. The definition of subliminal persuasion is the use of objects, photos, words, or another means of persuading someone into doing something or putting an idea in their head without them consciously knowing what you've done. A common example of this is advertising. When you see or hear the points made when someone is trying to sell you a product, your mind may think of the product as appealing. You usually won't know that the techniques used in the advertisement itself are the reason you feel like you need their product. Often you wouldn't have bought this item otherwise. Below is an example of how this advertising technique works.

Picture this:

A glass of soda is displayed in front of you, surrounded by warm colors. It is perfectly carbonated, as there is an emphasis on the infinite bubbles working their way to the top of the bottle. As it is being opened, the sound of carbon being released rushes from the bottle. It is a perfect day without a cloud in sight, and golden rays of the sun are shining overhead. The glare of the sun is shining on the pristine glasswork. The drink is so cold in contrast with the warm day that precipitation has formed into fat drops of water that are slowly sliding down the glass and following the way it's perfectly shaped to fit a hand.

As a model brings the drink to their lips, just a drop escapes and slides down her chin and it catches the golden light of the sun as it falls slowly out of the frame. The model's eyes slide closed slowly with pure bliss and satisfaction. The camera zeros in on the muscles of her neck contracting and stretching; and as she puts the drink down, a smile forms on her face.

You might not be in a warm area, nor may you particularly want a soda right now. However, that description was followed by your mind and you may feel thirstier than before you read it. This is because my words used subliminal persuasion to make you want the soda that was described. You've seen advertisements like this many times, and they might have worked. Never does a cold drink display so much precipitation as it does on the picture of an advertisement unless it has been sitting in water. However, because the body craves liquid when we are even a little dehydrated, the look will appeal to that natural desire. Even if what your body wants is water, this advertisement will appeal because of the unrealistic water droplets that have formed on the can or bottle.

When using this tactic in the form of manipulating another person, there are a few different ways to go about it. For instance, if you create a sense of "we" and equality in the request, it feels more inclusive. When sales clerks and advertisers work, they often create the idea that the product benefits both them and you as a consumer. They speak as if by buying their product, you not only get the benefit of having the product they think you need, but they will be happier for it.

If you word the request in a form that appeals to both you and the other person, you're more likely to achieve your goal. This form of persuasion can also combine well with cold reading techniques, as both involve the other person believing something without you outright offering the information to them.

Another form of persuasion is gathering favors. Debt is a constant in this world, and it doesn't always mean money. If you've done something for the other person recently, and have earned a form of gratitude, they're likely to feel indebted to you and therefore, more obligated to carry out your request. For example, if you save this person from an embarrassing situation, such as lending them a jacket when they've spilled a drink down their shirt, you may request a favor in return later on. Because you displayed kindness for no apparent reason that they can see, they'll feel the need to retaliate the kindness. Favors can be as large as saving someone's life, or even as small as some good advice. Every act doesn't need to be an all-out sacrifice. In fact, it shouldn't be. If someone catches a hint of deception or ulterior motives when someone is displaying such kindness, they will feel distrustful towards you, and you will lose the relationship that you've worked towards by now.

You can use this kind of persuasion technique yourself to get people to do as you wish, provided you do so subtly.

Cold Reading

Cold reading is known to be a con artist's best friend.

It provides the illusion of mind reading and magical abilities without the use of actual supernatural power. It is often used by those who make a living through fortune-telling and psychic acts. Many people have been completely sold on the act, as it is usually performed by someone who excels in reading others, has acquired enough general knowledge, and has practiced enough to deliver a very believable performance.

However, such an act is really only a form of psychology, and you could create this act yourself if you chose to.

You would do this by creating the illusion of knowing more than you really do through the power of observation. There are different names for different techniques. How many people are present decides how you should approach it. Shotgunning, for instance, is done in a large room packed with people. This is often the choice of mediums that are creating the illusion of connecting to a passed loved one because whatever they say, there is likely to be someone who can relate to the statement. When the medium speaks a few, usually vague, phrases, such as "I am connecting to an elderly man... the name John or Jack comes to mind. Does that speak to anyone?" he or she watches for anyone who expresses recognition. The names Jack and John are very common, and many people have lost a grandfather in their time. The medium will then choose one person and watch their face carefully. This is where true psychology steps in. Reading body language is essential to keeping up the ruse, as the medium will need to narrow down the descriptions of the audience members' loved ones.

If, for example, the medium says something about a white picket fence, yet no familiarity comes to this person's face, he or she will have to change their tactic carefully. He or she might explain that he never lived within a white picket fence, but wanted to, or that another relative was also present. If the audience member agrees or seems excited, this medium will know they are getting warmer. This act is continued and even peppered by what are known as "Rainbow Ruses." These are contradictory phrases such as "He was a gentle man; however, he would occasionally display a stern side". Most people have experienced these contradictory moments in their personality; however, the word choice feels so specific thatit seems as if it only applies to the supposed spirit the man or woman is referring to.

Another method of cold reading, which may be more suitable for a smaller population, is to use previous knowledge when observing someone's behavior. This method is often used in detective dramas, as the act is dramatic and exciting to watch, and the character appears intelligent and clever. It is, however, easier than it may appear, as it only takes keen observation skills. For example, if you meet a new person and notice there is graphite smudged along the side of their left hand, you will know that they are left-handed, as those who are left-hand dominant must drag their hand along the previously written words to continue writing.As a left-hander myself, I would know. This phenomenon, which has been jokingly called "The Silver Surfer Syndrome", is an unquestionable indication that this person is left-handed, and youmay say so with confidence as you shake their hand. The confidentstatement will shock this person, and they won't think to look for physical indicators. This can be used as a fun trick to amuse others,or as a shocking factor to carry into a persuasive technique, as those who have recently been surprised don't always think every factor of a decision through.

Cold reading, as any other manipulation tactic, can be used on anyone. And it is. Many people who are studied in the ways of cold reading have used it as a career, such as psychics, fortune-tellers, and any kind of con artist. Such a complicated set-up is not necessary to add this skill to your own toolbox, as you only need your own observation and shock factor. Another example is if you see someone you may already know is a student, you could confidently exclaim that they were studying late and fell asleep on their work as you note the imprint of math work on their left ear. These subtle observations build up over time, and you may gain a reputation with that person. The more you get to know someone, the more background information you will have stored away. For example, say you have a friend named Kyle. Kyle is a single father of an adorable six-year-old girl whom he spends every moment he can. To support her, he works at a grueling desk job where he files paperwork all day long and takes rude phone calls. You know that he likes light coffee with a lot of sweeteners and that he is right-handed.

Today, Kyle arrives with a large coffee in his left hand. You two always meet up every Tuesday at around ten in the morning. Today, it's almost eleven. In the back of his car is a pink hairbrush. When he gets close enough to greet you, you smell the strong aroma of black coffee rising from his cup, and you can see his clothes are wrinkled. Without asking him, what can you deduce from his situation?

I believe that his boss kept him very late and piled on the work the night prior.

He's gotten papercuts before, however even the light touch of his coffee seems to be too much pain this time, so he was working as quickly as he could. Even so, he got home late that night and overslept the next morning. Rushing to get her to school, Kyle likely tossed his daughter's hairbrush back for her to do her best with her hair on their way to school. Due to his exhaustion, he stopped to buy a coffee much stronger than he likes it before meeting with you. Of course, there are other indicators that weren't mentioned in the example. What situations you come to find yourselves observing will vary, as will the indicators that you notice.

Conclusion

The notion that dark psychology is prevalent and that it is part of our world can be a scary thought. The Dark Triad is a term in dark psychology that can be helpful when trying to pinpoint the beginning of criminal behavior.

Narcissism exhibits these traits: egotism, grandiosity, and lack of empathy.

Machiavellianism uses a form of manipulation to betray and exploit people. Those who practice this do not practice morality or ethics.

Psychopathy is a trick to those who put their trust in these types of people. They are often charming and friendly. Yet they are ruled by impulsivity, selfishness, lack of empathy, and remorselessness.

The fact that people can be used as pawns on a chessboard makes all of us want to understand dark psychology more and to figure out what it is, and how we can save ourselves from it.

There are many ailments that hypnosis can make better or even cure. And we are not just talking about mental ailments, but physical as well. Hypnosis can be used to help cure some of the side effects that are caused by chemo and radiation in cancer patients.

We all know that there has been a lot of skepticism for this alternative medicine due to the quacks that use it as a laughingstock. However, when used correctly, this type of medicine can do a lot better than harm because it wakes people's subconscious up to letting go of things that they are holding on to that might be causing a plethora of problems in their lives.

With this being said, all of these methods can be used for good; it is just based on their intentions and the overall outcome. Those who use manipulation tactics do not use them with the intention of helping anyone. Manipulating is changing someone's thoughts, actions, and behaviors to fit someone else's (the manipulator's agenda). There is no way to sugarcoat some of these techniques. And that is why they fall under the dark psychology umbrella, because they have been used by criminals to get what they want as well.

Because we all know that someone is going to try to make us a victim of one of these methods again, sometime in our lives, and I for one would want to be as ready as I could possibly be.

There are many examples of manipulation, mind control, and persuasion in history. Some of the most infamous examples are Charles Manson, Adolph Hitler, and Ted Bundy. When you look at Charles Manson, you are able to get a profile of someone who was able to use his words and "love" for his "family" to create a cult. He was able to take young adults and make them into murders. You need to remember that Charles Manson never actually killed anyone. He simply had the members of his "family" do this through manipulation, mind control, and persuasion.

Adolph Hitler was the same way. He started by getting people to like him through persuasion. People believed that he would be one of the greatest political leaders of all time. While he did go down in history, it is not because he was a great political leader.

www.ingramcontent.com/pod-product-compliance
Lightning Source LLC
Chambersburg PA
CBHW071801080526
44589CB00012B/635